Introduction

From Cruiser Tank to Main Battle Tank

By the end of the First World War in November 1918, the concept of the tank had been fully vindicated as an indispensable weapon of war. The tank was a British invention, and at the war's end Britain led the field in tank design and tactics, with France coming a very close second with innovative designs like the Renault FT.17, one of the best-selling tanks of the inter-war years.

The British Centurion tank – a magnificent fighting vehicle that finally proved that Britain's tank designers were capable of getting things right after years of producing tanks that were at best barely adequate and at worst disastrous – traced its lineage back to a change of armoured warfare doctrine that came about in the early 1930s, when the British Army, which had previously concentrated on developing dual-role medium tanks, took the decision to develop two separate types of armoured fighting vehicle, one an infantry tank to operate in support of ground forces and the other a 'cruiser' tank whose role was to break through enemy defences and then exploit the breakthrough by making surprise attacks on command and communications behind the forward battle area.

The British Army's armoured warfare doctrine was based on these two different types of tank. The first, the so-called 'cruiser tank', was fast and lightly armoured, its purpose being to break through enemy defences or bypass them. The second type, the so-called 'infantry tank', more heavily armoured and with a speed slow enough to enable dismounted infantry to keep up, would then exploit the success of the cruiser tanks, which by now would be roaming around the enemy's rear areas and causing as much disruption as possible. This doctrine, which was sound enough in principle, was refined in 1919 by a senior officer of the Royal Tank Corps, Colonel J. F. C. Fuller, who produced a plan that envisaged a large-scale armoured offensive designed to achieve multiple armoured penetrations of an enemy's forward defences and totally disrupt his command and control system in the rear. The plan was virtually ignored by the British War Office but enthusiastically adopted by a reborn German Army, whose tank commanders used it to excellent effect in the Blitzkrieg of 1940.

The revised doctrine was influenced by various considerations, some technical, others political. The main political consideration reflected the need to police the more remote parts of the British Empire in the Middle East and Northwest India, where the disintegration of other pre-war empires had resulted in a rise of nationalism and its accompanying unrest. To achieve this, armoured cars were ideal, often working in cooperation with aircraft, whereas tanks were useless in the terrain where most of the problems arose. In the 1920s the production of armoured cars assumed priority over the development of other armoured vehicles, and it was not until the rise of Nazi Germany and its emphasis on the development of a strong Panzer force that production of new types of tank in Britain was accelerated.

The technical considerations involved th choice of armour, armament and motiv power. One bold decision of the 1930s wa to provide the new generation of cruise tanks with a 40mm (2-pounder) mai gun in addition to a secondary armamen of one or more machine guns; the main gun, with armour-piercing shells, would be more than adequate to cope with the Panzer I and II tanks under development in Germany, armed respectively with machine guns (Panzer I) or a 20mm cannon (Panzer II). The problem here was a lack of foresight; British tanks were still using the 2-pounder gun well into the Second World War, by which time the Germans were deploying the Panzer III and IV armed with a main gun of up to 75mm calibre. One senior British officer, General Percy Hobart, Deputy Director of Staff Duties (Armoured Fighting Vehicles) persistently

Top: Vickers Mk I (A9) cruiser tanks pictured in the Western Desert, 1940.

Bottom: German soldiers examining a disabled Mk III (A13) cruiser tank in the desert, 1941.

called for British tanks to be armed with a 57mm 6-pounder gun in 1938, but no formal requirement for such a weapon was issued until after the fall of France in the summer of 1940.

Armour protection for the new generation of British cruiser tanks was also sacrificed to reduce weight, it was decided that vehicles would be powered by modified petrol engines of the type being produced for existing commercial vehicles.

Mk V Covenanter tanks on manoeuvres.

The Crusader Mk III, armed with a 6-pounder gun, was the most important British cruiser tank of the North African campaign.

A Crusader tank and infantry in action during the Battle of Alamein, October 1942.

The first cruiser tank, designed by Vickers in 1934, was the Mk I (A9), which entered production in 1937, albeit on a fairly limited scale. Its turret was power-traversed and the vehicle carried a six-man crew. Its main armament was a 40mm 2-pounder gun, supplemented by three machine guns, two of which were mounted in small subsidiary turrets. Production of the Mk I ended with the 125th vehicle, the early model seeing service in France and North Africa. It was followed by the Heavy Cruiser Tank Mk II, which had begun life as the A10 Infantry Tank based on the A9, but with thicker armour and other refinements, including the deletion of the subsidiary turrets.

The next cruiser tank design, the A13 Cruiser Tank Mk III, was the product of Nuffield Mechanizations Ltd and represented an important step forward in British tank development, as it used a suspension system based on that devised in the United States by J. Walter Christie. A prototype made its appearance in 1937 and proved to have an excellent performance, the Christie suspension making a huge difference. (The Christie system was also adopted by the Russian BT series of tanks, culminating in the excellent T-34.)

The Mk III's armament comprised one 40mm gun and a single machine gun, which made it possible to dispense with two crew members. Its big drawback was its inadequate armour, which led to substantial losses when it encountered German Panzer IIIs in France and the Western Desert, and this deficiency led to the development of the Cruiser Tank Mk IV (A13 Mk II) in which the thickness of the armour was increased to 20 or 30mm (0.79 or 1.18in). This was still not very substantial, and the vehicle was fast but very vulnerable. Nevertheless, it acquitted itself well against Italian AFVs in the Western Desert, where it saw considerable action. The next British cruiser tank in the series was the Cruiser Tank Mk V (A13 Mk III), which had a redesigned turret, better armour and a higher top speed. However, it was still armed with the puny 2-pounder gun, which had weaker armour penetration and could not fire high-explosive rounds. The Mk V was known as the Covenanter.

The next cruiser tank, also designed and built by Nuffield, was the A15 Mark VI Crusader, which played an important part in the desert war, despite being outclassed by its German opponents. The Crusader I entered service in 1941 and it was immediately apparent that its 40mm (2-pounder) main armament was inadequate, so plans were made to replace it with the new 57mm (2.24in) 6-pounder. It was this version, designated Crusader III that became the most important tank in the desert battles, first seeing action at the Second Battle of Alamein in October

A Cromwell cruiser tank on display in the Bovington Tank Museum, Dorset.

One of two Cromwell tanks on display at the Israeli Armoured Corps Museum, Latrun. The vehicles were used by the Israeli Defence Forces after being abandoned by the British Army in 1948.

The A27 Cromwell cruiser tank was a product of Nuffield Mechanizations Ltd.

1942. As more effective tanks such as the Churchill and the American M4 Sherman became available, the Crusader was gradually relegated to secondary duties and specialist roles. Yet even the Churchill – the most important British-designed tank of the Second World War – was plagued by many shortcomings in its early service, being underpowered and fitted with the same weak 2-pounder gun that had been fitted to the earlier cruiser tanks. The appearance of the Churchill Mk III, armed with a 6-pounder gun, finally resulted in an effective fighting vehicle that was to prove its worth in the last battles of the desert war in Tunisia, the invasion of Normandy and the advance across northwest Europe.

Meanwhile, the War Office persevered in its efforts to develop a British-designed cruiser tank that would be operationally acceptable and reliable. Vauxhall's offering was the A23, a scaled-down version of the A22 Churchill infantry tank with the same suspension. It would have frontal armour of 75mm (3in) thickness, be powered by a twelve-cylinder Bedford engine and carry a crew of five. Nuffield submitted the A24, heavily based on the Crusader design and powered by a version of the V-12 Liberty engine, a powerplant dating back to the latter days of the First World War and by now thoroughly outdated; its only advantage was that it could be put into production quickly, as it used many of the Crusader's components. The final entry was submitted by Leyland, whose design was similar to Nuffield's but with different suspension and tracks. All these designs were intended to mount the Quick-Firing (QF) 6-pounder gun.

The design competition was won by Nuffield's A24 in January 1941. It was expected to be in service by the end of 1942, but there was a snag. The War Office, at last recognizing the obsolescence of the Liberty engine, now insisted that the tank be re-engined with the Rolls-Royce Meteor, a version of the excellent Merlin Mk III. Refitting the A24 with the new engine was beyond the capacity of Nuffield, so the job was assigned to Leyland, working with the Birmingham Railway Carriage and Wagon

The Cavalier cruiser tank was originally known as the Cromwell I.

(BRC&W) company. The new tank would emerge as the A27M Cromwell. In fact, the name Cromwell had already been allocated to Nuffield's Liberty-engined A24; originally designated Cromwell I, it was later known as the Cavalier. The A27L Cromwell II was another variant to bear the name. Based on the Cavalier chassis, it was armed with a 95mm howitzer and, renamed Mk IV Centaur, was deployed in time to support the Allied landings in Normandy in June 1944.

The closing stages of the Second World War saw the emergence of the A34 Comet cruiser tank, a final attempt to rectify the deficiencies that had been revealed in the design of earlier cruiser tanks during combat in the Western Desert and Italy. The first attempt at redesign resulted in the Challenger, comprising a 17-pounder anti-tank gun mounted on a Cromwell chassis. The mounting of this larger gun carried its share of penalties, the biggest of which was that there had to be a reduction in armour protection, so ultimately the Challenger was not a success. In the Comet design, the gun was a 77mm version of the 17-pounder, with a lower muzzle velocity; the engine was uprated and the armour welded rather than riveted. The prototype Comet was rolled out in February 1944 and the first examples were delivered in September, in time to take part in the British XXX Corps' dash to the Rhine at Arnhem. The Comet went on to

Above: Wreck of a German Panzer V Panther in Normandy, 1944. The Centurion was designed to combat this and other new German tanks.

Right: Comet tanks of the 2nd Fife and Forfar Yeomanry, 11th Armoured Division, crossing the Weser at Petershagen, Germany, on 7 April 1945. The Comet remained in British service until 1958 and fought alongside the Centurion in Korea.

see action during the crossing of the Rhine at Wesel in March 1945. Production by the end of the war totalled 1,200 units, some of which were supplied to foreign armies.

The real solution to the British Army's tank design headaches, however, lay in a decision to combine the requirements of the infantry and cruiser tank and merge them into the design of a single vehicle, a so-called 'universal' tank. In 1943 the War Office, conscious of the vulnerability of existing cruiser tank designs to the formidable German 88mm anti-tank gun and a new generation of German tanks – in particular the heavy Tiger and the Panzer V Panther – instructed the Directorate of Tank Design led by Sir Claude Gibb to come up with a proposal for a new heavy cruiser tank under the General Staff designation A41. It would be known as the Centurion.

Top: The Centurion's design was partly influenced by the lessons of the campaign in Italy, where the nature of the terrain made tank operations very difficult. Here, American Sherman tanks are seen en route to Monte Cassino.

Right: The Panzerkampfwagen V Panther. Any possible encounter between this formidable tank and the Centurion was rendered impossible by the end of the war in Europe.

Development and Design

The original Outline Specification of the A41, issued in October 1943, called for a fighting vehicle weighing no more than forty tons, a weight limit imposed by existing tank transporters and the 80-foot Bailey bridges that the new vehicle would have to negotiate. This restriction was soon removed and the weight increased to forty-five tons to accommodate heavier armour and a wider turret. Although a high top speed was not considered important, the tank was to be as agile as the Comet and was to have a high reverse speed, a requirement dictated by the lessons of the fighting in southern Italy, where Allied tanks had often become trapped in narrow sunken roads.

The Directorate of Tank Design produced a larger hull by adding a sixth wheel to the Christie suspension used on the Comet, and extending the spacing between the second and third wheels. The Christie suspension, which featured vertical spring coils between the side armour plates, was replaced by a Horstmann suspension with three horizontally sprung, externally mounted, two-wheel bogies on each side. This did not offer as smooth a ride as the Christie system, but had the advantage that individual suspension and wheel units could be replaced fairy easily in the event of mine damage.

Taking a lesson from the German Panther and the Soviet T-34, the hull was designed with welded, sloped armour and featured a partially cast turret mounting a 76.2mm 17-pounder main gun and a 20mm Polsten cannon in an independent mounting on the left. (It was originally decided to mount the Polsten to engage enemy anti-tank guns, the 20mm shells being capable of penetrating their gun shields.)

The turret accommodated a crew of four: commander, gunner, loader and driver. Power was provided by a Rover-built

The Centurion's original specification imposed a forty-ton weight limit, enabling it to safely traverse a Bailey bridge like this one over the Taute river in France.

The Horstmann suspension system. The two wheels per bogie, two crank arms, springs between the cranks and single mounting point are all evident in this image.

The Rolls-Royce Meteor engine was efficient and reliable but had a high fuel consumption, limiting the Centurion's range to about fifty miles.

Rolls-Royce Meteor 650hp petrol engine, as used in the Comet and Cromwell, but with a Merrit-Brown gearbox with five forward and two reverse gears. As petrol engines were vulnerable and posed a significant fire hazard, measures were taken to reduce the risk; all the main ammunition, for example, was stowed beneath the turret ring. Prototypes of the original forty-ton design, the Centurion Mk I, had 76mm of armour on the front glacis, which was thinner than that of the Churchill infantry tank, but it provided effective protection thanks to the highly sloped glacis plate.

A design mock-up, built by AEC (Associated Equipment Company) Ltd, was ready for inspection in May 1944, and twenty development vehicles were subsequently ordered, these having different armament combinations: ten with the 17-pounder and 20mm Polsten gun, plus a Besa machine gun in the rear of the turret, five with the 17-pounder and a forward-firing Besa, and five with a 77mm QF gun and driver-operated Besa. The Polsten cannon was a Polish weapon, a simplified version of the 20mm Oerlikon. Development work had continued after the Polsten design team escaped to Britain following the German invasion of Poland in 1939. The Besa was a British version of the Czechoslovak ZB-53 air-cooled, belt-fed machine gun, a dependable and reliable weapon produced under licence by the Birmingham Small Arms Company.

Because of the priority given to the production of existing British tanks to make good the attrition suffered during the campaign in northwest Europe and Italy, it was April 1945 before the first development examples of the A41 were delivered to the Fighting Vehicles Proving Establishment at Chertsey in Surrey. The first six to be completed (three by the Royal Ordnance Factory Woolwich and three by the Royal Ordnance Factory Nottingham) were deployed to Europe via Southampton for operational trials with the 5th Royal Iniskilling Dragoon Guards and the 5th Royal Tank Regiment in an exercise codenamed Operation Sentry, but hostilities ceased before they could be tested in combat against German armour. Trials continued into July 1945 and various recommendations were made, one of which was to replace the 20mm Polsten cannon with a co-axial machine gun.

Comparative trials revealed that the A41 was highly mobile and easily outperformed the Comet in most respects. As the evaluation produced no significant problems, a production order was issued for 800 Centurion tanks, of which a hundred were to be Mk Is mounting a 17-pounder gun and a co-axial 7.92mm Besa machine gun and the remainder Mk IIs (A41As), all but a hundred of which would be armed with an 83.4mm 20-pounder gun then being developed by Royal Ordnance. Production of the Centurion began in November 1945 and the first examples were delivered to the 6th Royal Tank Regiment in February 1946.

Already, there were signs that the fragile alliance between east and west that had existed during the Second World War was becoming fractured. For once, the British Army would have a superb fighting vehicle to meet whatever threat might face it on land. The Centurion, designed as a cruiser tank, was now the progenitor of a new class of British armoured fighting vehicle: the main battle tank.

Centurion Specification (Mk II)

Armament: One 17pdr (76mm/3in) or 20pdr main gun, one coaxial 7.92mm (0.31in) Besa MG or one 20mm (0.79in) Polsten cannon
Armour: 17–127mm (0.75–4in)
Crew: 4
Dimensions: length 7.82m (24ft 6in), width 3.39m (11ft 2in), height 3.01m (9ft 11in)
Weight: 43,182kg (42.5 tons)
Powerplant: Rolls-Royce Meteor V-12 petrol, 484.7kW (650bhp)
Speed: 35kph (22mph)
Range: 80km (50 miles)

One major concern in the design of the Centurion was that it was powered by a petrol engine. The vulnerability of this type of powerplant had been demonstrated by losses of the Sherman tank that was so prone to catching fire that the Germans named it the 'Tommy Cooker'. Here, German paratroops pass a knocked-out Sherman in Normandy.

The 20mm Polsten gun had a variety of applications, including the anti-aircraft role. The weapon pictured here is in service with the Canadian Army.

All Centurion variants were powered by the Rolls-Royce Meteor Mk IV V12 petrol engine, produced by Rover. Five different variants of this engine – seen here with its associated transmission – were used, depending on the particular mark of tank.

A Centurion Mk II with 17-pounder main gun.

Had there been conflict in Europe during the immediate postwar years, the Centurion's main adversary would have been the Soviet T-34/85 medium tank, pictured here.

Centurion in Detail

The driving compartment

Access to the driver's compartment was by way of a hatch, fitted with two interlocking spring-assisted covers, located in the top of the forward hull plate, the hatches being positioned on either side of the driver's position. The right-hand hatch cover was fitted with a periscope to give the driver forward vision when the covers were closed. The driving controls were conventional, consisting of clutch, brake and accelerator positioned from left to right. The steering levers, controlling the direction of travel by altering the speed of the tracks, were on either side of the driver's seat, with a handbrake on the right-hand side. The gear stick was centrally mounted. The driver's instrument panel and engine controls were mounted on his right, and two CO_2 fire extinguishers were fitted on his left. Also on his left, protected by a longitudinal steel divider, were an ammunition storage bin and a ten-gallon freshwater tank. In later variants, the freshwater tank was moved to the fighting compartment.

The fighting compartment

The power-operated turret housed the other three members of the crew: commander, loader and gunner. The turret was of cast construction with the roof welded in place. An ammunition resupply hatch was mounted externally in the left-hand side of the turret, which featured stowage boxes on either side. The loader was seated on the left of the main armament, the commander on the right and to the rear, and the gunner was in front of and below the commander. In the Mk II and subsequent Centurion variants the commander had a vision cupola, enabling him to direct operations while having the benefit of armoured protection. The cupola was fitted with a 10x magnification periscope and could be manually traversed through 360 degrees. Additional periscopes to provide better all-round vision were added in later variants. The gunner had a periscopic sight etched with a ballistic-pattern graticule, while the loader also had a single observation periscope. The loader, who also doubled as the radio operator, was provided with twin hatch covers opening to the front and rear. He was also responsible for serving the co-axial Besa machine gun and the Mk II bombthrower, which was located in the turret roof next to his periscope and which could fire HE, white phosphorus and illuminating flares out to a range of about 300 yards. Its main function was to engage infantry anti-tank teams, which had caused such havoc among Allied tanks during the Second World War with their Panzerfaust and Panzerschreck weapons.

The engine compartment

The engine compartment at the rear was separated from the fighting compartment by a fireproof steel bulkhead. Air was drawn in through the engine deck louvres by two fans. Power was transmitted from the engine through the clutch to the transversely mounted transmission. This was a combined change-speed and steering mechanism and incorporated a differential. Drive from the output epicyclic gears at each end of the gearbox was transmitted through an internally toothed coupling ring and an externally toothed driving shaft to the final drive. The transmission gearbox was a Merrit-Brown Z51R with five forward and two reverse gears. The engine itself was a Rolls-Royce Meteor, which had already proved itself as the powerplant of the Comet and Cromwell cruiser tanks and which was basically a Rolls-Royce Merlin V12 27-litre engine stripped of its supercharger, reduction gear and other ancillary equipment. The pistons were cast, instead of forged, and output was reduced to 600 brake horsepower (bhp). Because of the demands for diesel fuel elsewhere the Meteor used petrol, although it was of a lower octane than the Merlin's aviation fuel and carried a significantly lesser fire risk.

Armament

The 17-pounder main armament and the Polsten 20mm cannon, which were features of the Centurion Mks I and II, were replaced in the Mk III and subsequent variants by the Royal Ordnance QF 20-pounder and Besa 0.303in (7.92mm) co-axial machine gun. The 20-pounder was a multi-purpose weapon, using high-velocity, armour-piercing rounds to engage armoured fighting vehicles and medium-velocity, high-explosive rounds to engage soft-skinned targets and fortifications. The 20-pounder's armour-piercing projectile had a muzzle velocity of 4,700 feet per second and could penetrate twelve inches of rolled, homogeneous armour, while the HE round had a muzzle velocity of 1,975 ft/sec. The gun also fired smoke shells and canister rounds (casings stuffed with metal balls) which effectively turned the weapon into a giant shotgun for repelling close-range infantry attacks. The gun was fitted with a very efficient stabilization system, permitting accurate fire while on the move. In 1959 the 105mm L7 gun was introduced and was used by all variants from the Mk V/2 onwards. The L7 was specifically designed to fit into the turret mountings of the 20-pounder, which enabled the Centurions to be upgunned with minimum modifications so that the fleet could be upgraded in a shorter time and at a lower cost. Trials of the L7 were undertaken with a Centurion Mk VII, and these proved the viability of uparmouring and upgunning the tank. The first tank to be equipped with the L7 was a single uparmoured Centurion MK VII which proved the viability of uparmouring and upgunning the vehicle. From 1959 onward existing Centurions were given upgrades with the L7 gun and armour and new builds incorporated the L7 at production.

A lineup of Centurion Mk III tanks with the 20-pounder main armament. The gun is not yet fitted with a fume extractor. Note the counterweight at the muzzle.

Armour

As with other fighting vehicles, the degree of armour protection incorporated in the Centurion varied throughout the tank's service, being constantly upgraded to cope with new threats. For example, the original 127mm armour thickness on the gun mantlet was increased to 152mm with the introduction of the Mk III. The turret roof had 29mm of armour, the turret sides and rear 89mm. The hull sides and rear had 51mm and 32mm respectively, while that of the glacis plate was increased from the 57mm of the original A41 Centurion to the 76mm of subsequent variants.

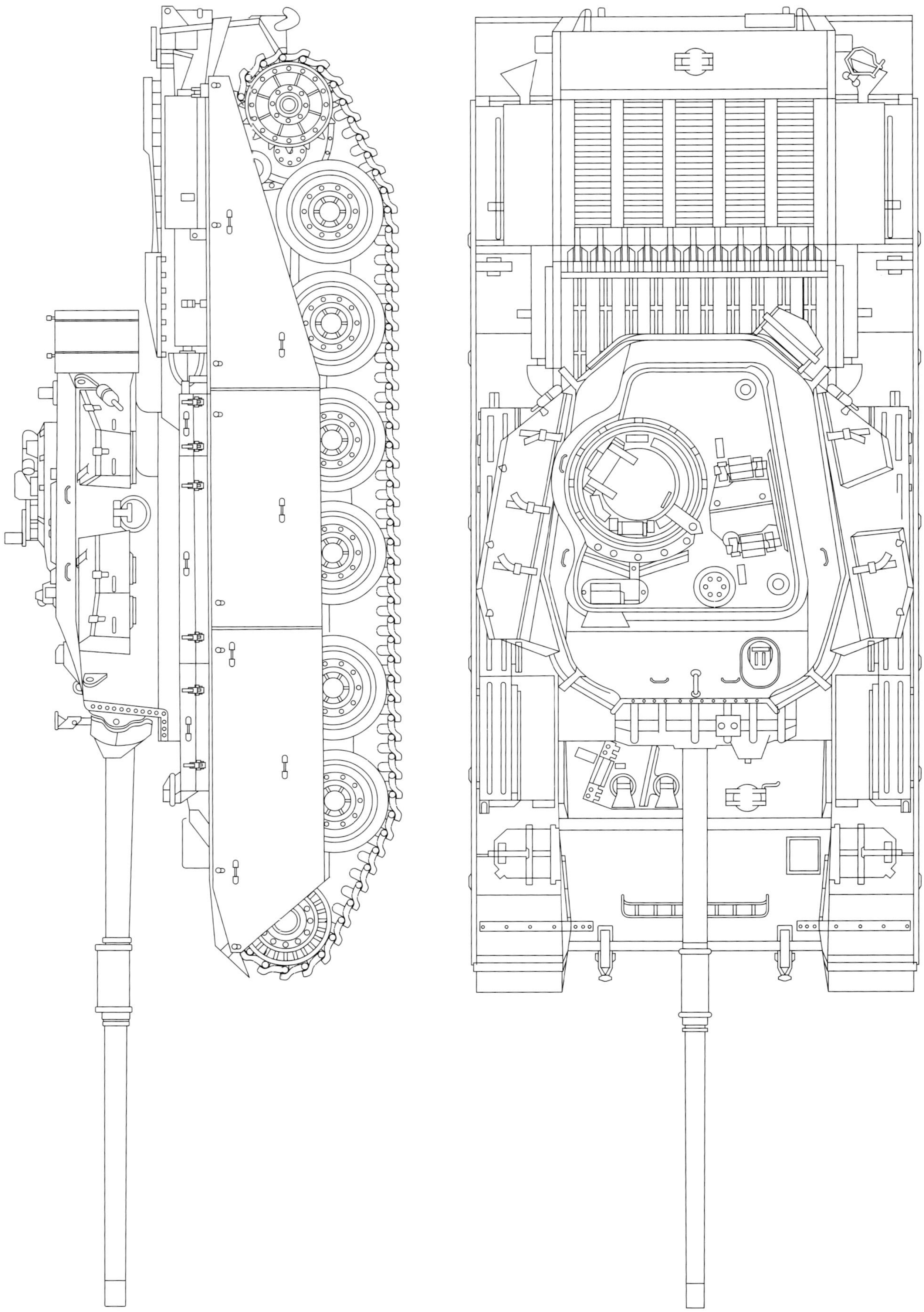

Side and top view of a Centurion Mk V 105mm Sho't IDF.

The turret details of the Olifant Mk IA main battle tank, the South African version of the British Centurion. Koninghippie, wikicommons

Photo shows details of the stowage box of the Olifant Mk IA. Koninghippie, wikicommons

Photo shows the loader's episcope of the Olifant Mk IA. Koninghippie, wikicommons

Photo shows turret details of the Olifant Mk IA. Koninghippie, wikicommons

Olifant Mk IA tank at the South African Armour Museum, Bloemfontein. Koninghippie, wikicommons

The Centurion Main Battle Tank Variants

- Centurion Mk I (A41): armed with 17-pounder (76.2mm) L/55 main gun and 20mm Polsten cannon, plus a linked (but not co-axial) 7.92mm Besa machine gun. Turret assembled from welded steel plates. 100 built.

- Centurion Mk II: armed with 17-pounder main gun and 20mm Polsten cannon, with provision for seventy-four rounds of 17-pounder ammunition. Fitted with a three-man, one-piece cast steel turret, with separate roof plate welded into place. Featured a co-axial 7.92mm machine gun. Periscope sight provided for the gunner. 250 built.
- Centurion Mk III: armed with 20-pounder (83.4mm) L/66.7 main gun and co-axial 7.92mm machine gun, with provision for sixty-five rounds of 20-pounder ammunition. Gun mantlet fitted with protective canvas cover. First British tank to be fitted with electric and gyroscopic gun-control equipment (developed by Metropolitan Vickers) permitting the tank to fire on the move. Powered by Meteor Mk IVB engine developing 630bhp at 2,400rpm. Most later brought up to Mk V standard. 2,833 built.
- Centurion Mk IV. Proposed close support vehicle armed with a 95mm mortar. Not placed in production; project cancelled in 1949.
- Centurion Mk V. Developed by Vickers Ltd at Elswick and armed with 20-pounder gun; Mk V/1 was an uparmoured version, and Mk V/2 was fitted with a 105mm L7 rifled main gun. Co-axial 7.92mm Besa machine gun replaced by 0.303in Browning. Late production Mk V gun barrels fitted with a fume extractor mounted midway along the barrel, its purpose being to prevent hot gases leaking into the fighting compartment. 221 built.
- Centurion Mk VI. An uparmoured version of the Mk V, with 105mm main

Top: Centurion Mk III on display outside the Redoubt Fortress, Eastbourne, East Sussex.

Above: The Centurion Mk VII/1 was an uparmoured version of the basic Mk VII. It bore the designation FV4012.

The Centurion Mk X was an uparmoured Mk VIII, upgunned with a 105mm gun and with an ammunition capacity of seventy rounds. Note the large searchlight.

A Centurion Mk XIII preserved and operated by the Norfolk Tank Museum. The museum offers visitors an exciting, hands-on experience of tanks, military vehicles and equipment. Visitors can climb aboard and even experience the confined inner workings of a tank, operating some of the controls.

gun and additional fuel capacity at rear of hull. The Mk VI/1 was a Mk VI with infrared night-vision equipment and stowage basket at rear of turret. Centurion Mk VI/2 was a Mk VI with 0.50in (12.7mm) ranging machine gun for the 105mm gun.

- Centurion Mk VII. Developed by Leyland, this variant was designated FV4007. It was armed with a 20-pounder gun fitted with a fume extractor and carried sixty-one rounds of 20-pounder ammunition. The Centurion Mk VII/1 was a Mk VII uparmoured and designated FV4012, while the Centurion Mk VII/2 was a Mk VII with a 105mm gun. 755 built.
- Centurion Mk VIII. This variant was developed from the Mk VII and had a resiliently mounted gun mantlet (mounted on trunnions) with no canvas cover and a contra-rotating commander's cupola. The commander could also raise his twin hatch covers in an umbrella fashion for improved visibility without revealing his position. Centurion Mk VIII/1 was a Mk VIII uparmoured, while the Centurion Mk VIII/2 was a Mk VIII with a 105mm gun. 108 built
- Centurion Mk IX. This was an uparmoured Mk VII, the latter's 20-pounder being replaced with a 105mm gun. The Centurion Mk IX/1 was a Mk IX with infrared night-vision equipment and stowage basket on the rear of the turret. Centurion Mk IX/2 was a Mk IX with 0.50in (12.7mm) ranging machine gun.
- Centurion Mk X. This was an uparmoured Mk VIII, upgunned with a 105mm gun and with an ammunition capacity of seventy rounds. The Centurion Mk X/1 was a Mk X with infrared night-vision equipment and stowage basket on rear of turret. Centurion Mk X/2 was a Mk X fitted with 12.7mm ranging machine gun. 155 built.

Centurion Mk XIII with searchlight. Note the large stowage basket at the rear of the turret.

- Centurion Mk XI. This was an upgraded Mk VI with ranging machine gun, infrared night-vision equipment and stowage basket on turret rear.
- Centurion Mk XII. This was an upgraded Mk IX with infrared night-vision equipment, 12.7mm ranging machine gun and stowage basket on turret rear.
- Centurion Mk XIII. The last of the long line of British Centurion MBT vehicles, this was a Mk X with 12.7mm ranging machine gun and infrared night-vision equipment.

Centurion in Foreign Service

Australia

The Centurion equipped the Australian Army's 1st Armoured Regiment from 1952, thirty-nine Mk IIIs replacing the regiment's Churchill tanks. The regiment itself had been raised on 7 July 1949, as part of the new Australian Army. Its nucleus was formed from personnel from the 1st Australian Armoured Car Squadron that had returned from Japan several months earlier after serving with the Allied Occupation Force. The Regiment was based at Puckapunyal, Victoria. Its Centurions would later see action in Vietnam. The Australian Army eventually acquired a total of 127 Centurions, including four bridgelayers and six Armoured Recovery Vehicles, all delivered by 1961.

Austria

Although the Austrian armed forces (Bundesheer) depended heavily on the U.S. and Sweden for equipment during the Cold War era, some 370 obsolete Centurion tanks were purchased from the Netherlands, their turrets and 105mm guns being mounted in fixed defensive positions situated in the northeast of the country for the purpose of meeting a Warsaw Pact invasion from Hungary and Czechoslovakia.

Canada

At the end of the Second World War, the Canadian Army had a considerable fleet of Sherman tanks, all of which – except for a number shipped back home for training – were left in the Netherlands at the close of hostilities. The plan was to replace them with a new generation of American medium tanks, but the experience of the early Korean War months revealed a need for better tanks than the U.S. Army had on its inventory at that time, and planned replacements were not yet available. The British Centurion, which had proved its worth in Korea, was the obvious choice, and Canada took delivery of 274 Mk III Centurions in 1952 and 1953.

The first twenty-one Centurions were issued to the Royal Canadian Dragoons in Germany in March 1952, serving under NATO command. The new tank was well liked, having a .50-calibre ranging gun in the turret to assist in determining the range to main gun targets. The sophisticated optics and ammunition types, however, provided a challenge to new gunners as each of the different ammunition types – sabot, High Explosive Squash Head (HESH), smoke and canister – had differing muzzle velocities. The .30- and .50-calibre guns

An Australian Centurion Mk III on display at the Seymour Tank Museum, home to the Royal Australian Armoured Corps Memorial and Army Tank Museum, central Victoria.

fired rounds on about the same trajectory as the HESH round; other rounds had to have the main gun adjusted according to muzzle velocity of the ammunition, as well as range, in order to ensure a hit on the target. The unsynchronized gearbox was also tricky for drivers to master, and faulty shifting could leave the 55-ton tanks rolling free in neutral on downward slopes, a condition nicknamed 'Mexican Overdrive'. In mid-1971 the Canadian Army still had 241 Mk V Centurions in service, together with six Mk V/2s, seventy-five Mk XIs, nineArmoured Recovery Vehicles and four Centurion bridgelayers. By 1975, the once-state-of-the-art tank was beginning to show its age, though as late as 1975 Canadian gunners could still outscore other tank types by considerable margins in exercises.

The Centurions continued in service, having undergone several life extension upgrades, until 2 June 1977, when the Royal Canadian Dragoons in Lahr, West Germany held a final parade with the vehicles. Some Centurions continued in service in Canada until 1979, until being replaced by the German Leopard.

Denmark

The Danish Army received the first of 216 Centurion Mk III tanks in 1953, under the terms of the U.S. Mutual Defense Aid Program. Many, having been progressively upgraded to Mk V standard, continued in service into the 1990s, alongside 120 German Leopard MBTs that began to enter service in 1976.

Egypt

Sixteen Centurions were ordered by Egypt, nine of which were delivered in late 1950. Further orders brought the total number of Centurions in service to thirty. Many were captured during the Arab-Israeli conflict of 1956, by which time the Egyptian armoured forces had mostly rearmed with Czech-supplied Soviet equipment.

India

The Indian Army was a major user of the Centurion, 186 (mostly Mk VIIs) being delivered in the early 1960s and serving alongside some 340 M4 Shermans.

Iraq

The Iraqi Army took delivery of fifty-five Centurion Mk III tanks in 1955/6. They remained in service until the late 1960s.

Israel

The story of the Centurion MBT in Israeli service began in 1958, when Israel purchased 250 Mk III and Mk V Centurions from Britain in a bid to upgrade its armoured forces and make good losses incurred during the war of 1956. Further acquisitions from other sources and vehicles captured during the war of 1956 (including thirty from Jordan) brought the eventual total to 390.

Austria made good use of Centurion turrets in bunkers at various points to defend against an attack from the Warsaw Pact.

A Canadian Army Centurion Mk XI, on exercise in Germany, passing an apparently unconcerned group of agricultural workers.

A Canadian Centurion on manoeuvres in Germany.

Centurion Mk III on display at the Borden Military Museum, Ontario, Canada.

An Indian Centurion preserved as a museum piece.

Jordan

Fifty Centurion tanks were purchased by Jordan between 1954 and 1956, and further deliveries brought the total to around ninety by 1967. After the 1967 Arab-Israeli war, the army was rearmed and more Centurion tanks were purchased. In 1970, the 40th Armoured Brigade, the Jordanian elite armoured formation, was re-equipped with Centurions. The brigade's Centurions were refitted with 105mm guns. Between 1982 and 1985, 293 surviving Centurions of the Jordanian Army were refitted with the diesel engine and transmission of the M60A1 tank in place of the original Meteor petrol engine, the Belgian SABCA computerized fire-control system that incorporated a laser range-finder and passive night sight for the gunner, a Cadillac Gage electro-hydraulic turret drive and stabilization system and a new Teledyne Continental hydropneumatic suspension in place of the Hortsman units. These upgraded vehicles were called the Tariq. After retirement from service with the arrival of ex-British Challenger tanks in the late 1990s, several Tariqs were converted into heavy APCs.

Kuwait

Kuwait received an initial batch of ten Centurion Mk III tanks, which were handed over to Somalia in the late 1970s.

Netherlands

The Netherlands initially received 435 Centurion Mk IIIs from 1953, purchased by the United States as part of the Mutual Defense Assistance Pact, the total increasing to 592 by 1956. These were soon upgraded to Mk V standard with 20-pounder gun and the British radio sets replaced by American types; one fuel mono-trailer was also available per tank. In 1959/60, seventy Mk VII tanks were delivered from the UK; these were all held in war reserve until 1969, when they were disposed of. Over the years 1960–72, (continued on page 49)

A Danish Army Centurion Mk III ploughs through sandy terrain on an exercise.

Centurion Mk III 'Arromanches' of 3 Squadron, 1st Royal Tank Regiment, Commonwealth Division, Korea 1953.

Centurion Mk III 'Caughoo' of C Squadron, 8th King's Royal Irish Hussars, commanded by Captain George Strachan MC, Yongdungpo, Korea, February 1951.

Canadian Army Centurion Mk V/2, Lord Strathcona's Horse (Royal Canadians, Soltau, Germany, September 1966.

Centurion Mk V, Israeli Defence Forces. This Centurion is shown in colours and markings of a vehicle knocked out inside Jordan during the Battle of Karameh on 21 March 1968.

Centurion Mk V 'Rattle', British Army, Suez campaign (Operation Musketeer), 1956. This is a vehicle of 6 RTR, as photographed in Port Said in November 1956. It is shown with the full set of markings worn by Centurions of this unit (insets), including the unit code, vehicle registration, and the tactical insignia of the 5th RTR.

Centurion Mk V 'Nasser's Nightmare', Suez 1956. This vehicle was also assigned to 6 RTR and was photographed in Port Said in December 1956, shortly before the British withdrawal. The black band around the turret is an identification marking and was applied by hand.

This is a vehicle of the 1st Armoured Division, Indian Army, deployed in north Punjab in September 1965. The name 'Ankush' is derived from that denoting a person or instrument used for guiding elephants. The tank also featured the tactical insignia of one of the regiments or brigades of the division (25 white on black square) on the front of its right fender, with unit insignia applied on the front of the left fender.

Centurion 'Sh'ot', of the IDF as deployed during the Lebanon War of 1982. Unit unknown, but the modified engine deck and all other extra fittings (including ERA blocks) are featured.

This Centurion Mk VII of the 40th Armoured Brigade of the Royal Jordanian Army was captured intact during the June 1967 war with Israel. It sported a camouflage pattern consisting of light earth and black-green. Unit insignia is shown in the insets.

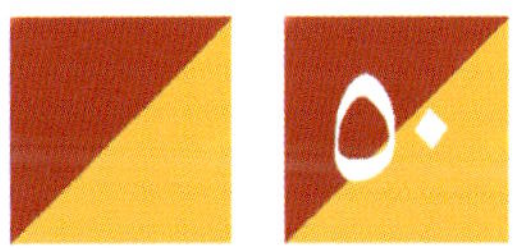

A Centurion Mk V, upgraded to Mk X standard, of the 1st Armoured Regiment Royal Australian Armoured Corps, deployed in the Phuoc Tuy Province, South Vietnam, in 1968. It is camouflaged bronze green overall, though carries a heavy dusting of reddish earth.

The Swedish Defence Ministry placed an order for eighty Centurion Mk III tanks at the end of 1952, the first being delivered in April 1953. A few years later, Sweden ordered a batch of 160 Centurion Mk Vs, followed by a batch of 110 Centurion Mk Xs around 1960.

A Swedish Army Centurion Mk III (Stridsvagn 81) tank. This vehicle, one of the first six to be supplied to Sweden, was subsequently fitted with a 105mm gun and upgraded to Mk V standard.

This is a vehicle of 1 or 5 RTR, deployed in the Aden Protectorate in 1964–1966. Camouflage was beige with glossy black (applied with very sharp borders).

This shows a tank from C Squadron, 16th/5th Lancers, Operation Armadillo's Delight, in the Wadi Msirah area, Radfan, Aden Protectorate, in 1965. This vehicle features much glossy black colour on its sides and the turret. Notable is the ID strip in white. The insets depict insignia applied on most of the vehicles of that unit (including its Saladins, Saracens, Fox/Ferrets etc.).

The Centurion Mk XIII was the last in the line of the Centurion gun tanks. It was essentially a Mk X fitted with infrared equipment and a ranging gun.

This was one of the Olifant 1Bs deployed by the SADF in Angola during the battle for Cuito Cuanavale, in the 1987–1988 period. Notable are the big 'grids' installed on the front of the turret and on sides of the fenders, for the purpose of keeping thick bush from hitting smoke candles and other equipment on the turret, or enmeshing into the treads. As a sign of their cooperation with Israel, the South Africans re-equipped their Centurions with US-made diesel engines, and with big baskets on the rear of the turret.

CENTURION

Mk V/1 Vietnam War

1/35 Scale
Brian Richardson

AFV Club's excellent kit has had some Mouse House Enterprise upgrades added with some jerry cans, ammo liners, boxes and boot scrapers fitted to the muffler heat shields. Mouse House decals were also used. A Firestorm mantlet cover and AFV Club ammunition conclude the after market additions. The hoochie was made from tissue and wire and this was fitted into pipe sockets 'welded' to the turret lifting eyes. Brass picture hanging wire replaced the kit tow ropes. ARN 169064 served in South Vietnam from May 1969 to December 1970 and still has the original sheet metal track guards and smoke grenade brackets in place. As the jungle took its toll on sheet metal fittings, the guards on many Centurions were replaced with stronger 1/4 inch steel fittings and US pattern steel pickets were cut up and welded between the stowage bin latches for added protection.

2A

2A

PHƯỚC MÉ

CENTURION

Mk VI West Germany, 1964

1/35 Scale
Jean-Vincent Roy

This is the Fort Garry Horse Troop Corporal's tank of 3rd Troop, C squadron from the 4th Canadian Infantry Brigade Group, West Germany, 1964. The base kit is AFV Club's Mk V/2 6 105mm gun (NATO). I also used a variety of the new TMD items: idler, wheel mount and adjuster, exhausts, replacement turret, tie-down cleats type 2 and 30-cal barrel. I used Firestorm Models replacement rubber tires. Unfortunately I made the decision to work with the kit's vinyl tracks. It doesn't look too bad but it was a tough fight. The base coat is a mix of Vallejo and Tamiya acrylics on Vallejo primer (which I don't recommend). Weathering was done using oils, pigments and washes.

CENTURION

ARV Mk II Vietnam War

1/35 Scale
Brian Richardson

This model started with Tamiya's Mk III hull that was altered to the correct length, AFV Club wheels, suspension and tracks were fitted and the superstructure was scratch built with plastic card. Academy 30cal MG's and ammo liners, various boxes, packs and tarps filled the bins. The M16 is from Tamiya and the FN SLR is a Mouse House Enterprises item. Tamiya acrylics, Humbrol enamels and oils took care of the paint and weathering. Decals were sourced from spare sheets. The number of days the driver had left to serve in country was chalked on the front bin.

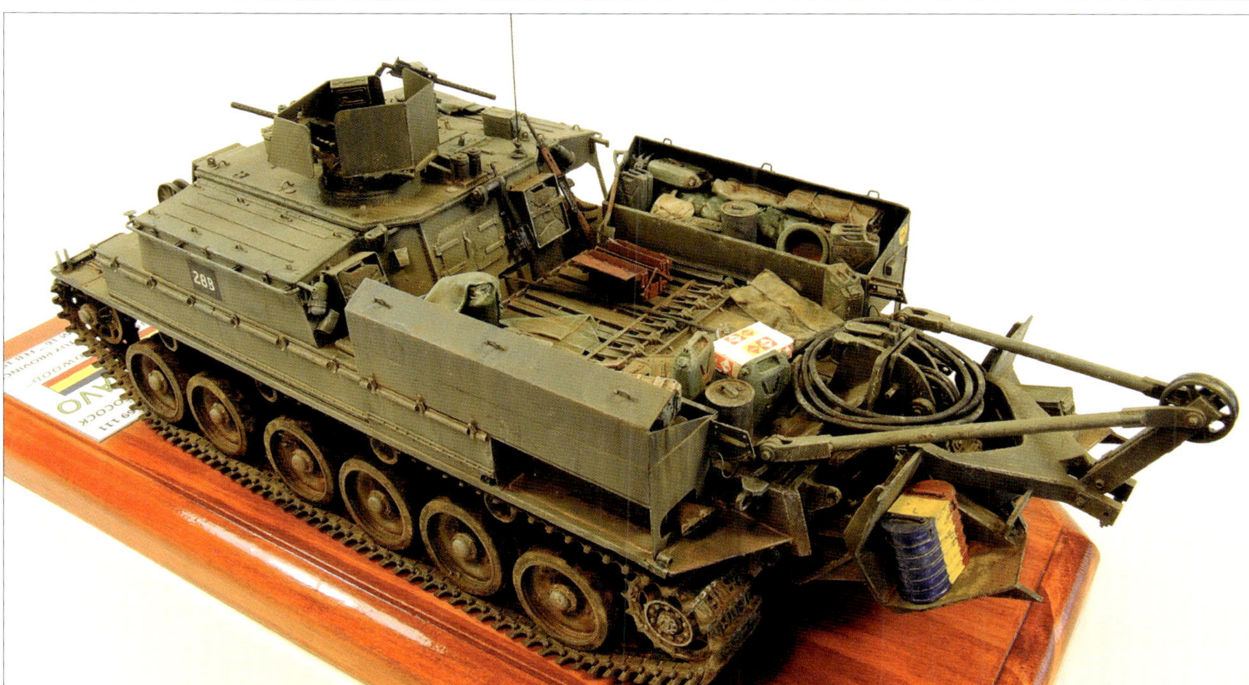

28B
169111

169111
28B

169111

CENTURION

Dozer Mk V/1 Vietnam War

1/35 Scale
Brian Richardson

The Dozer is another conversion this time AFV Club's 35106 kit. ARN 169071 'Contractor', a Vietnam vet that served from February 1970 to June 1971 in the Special Equipment Troop, C Squadron, 1st Armoured Regiment in Phuoc Tuy Province of South Vietnam during it's tour. It has all the changes including removal of the turret smoke launcher brackets, heavier track guards and bin reinforcements to mention a few.

CONTRACTOR

CONTRACTOR

92A
92A

92A

CENTURION

Mk III 'Caldera' Korea, 1951

1/35 Scale
Evgeny Grechanyy

This model represents the Centurion Mk III 'Caldera' of the 8th King's Royal Irish Hussars, Korea, 1951. This is the Tamiya edition 1971. It was built almost out of the box with slight modifications. There is an added Model Point metal barrel, a tarpaulin on the mask of the gun with a characteristic mount-strip with numerous bolt heads. On the turret I immitated a cast surface, made the wiring to the smoke grenade launchers. The machine gun is Academy and the fasteners for the cable of the tank-foil and added luggage are from different manufacturers, like the Alpine figure. The tracks are rubber from AFV Club – they are more detailed than the original one. It is painted with Tamiya acrylic and weathered with pigments and oils.

CALDERA

CALDERA

AFV Club's 1/35 plastic scale model kits are likely the most popular among Centurion modellers. It is easy to see why. AFV Club offers a variety of Israeli Defence Forces Sh'ot Kal versions: a Dalet with battering ram, a 1982 Gimel, a Mk V and V/1 and a Mk V 1973 variety, although at the time of writing the latter was unavailable. Separately, modellers can add to and upgrade their models with AFV Club's 20-pounder gun barrel, turret basket, with or without etching parts, a dozer and mantlet cover. It is felt that the latter should have been included in the kit and not be sold separately. Besides the Gimel and 1973 IDF Sh'ot Kal, AFV Club also do the Mk V in a RAAC (V/1) Vietnam version, a (V/2) NATO version with a 105mm gun and an IDF 1963 early type. New items for 2018, in conjunction with Hobby fan, includes a Korean War Mk III. The kits consist of many delicate parts and require a steady hand, but the quality of the kits with their finely detailed components – right down to the gooves on every track link – ensures a fine build.

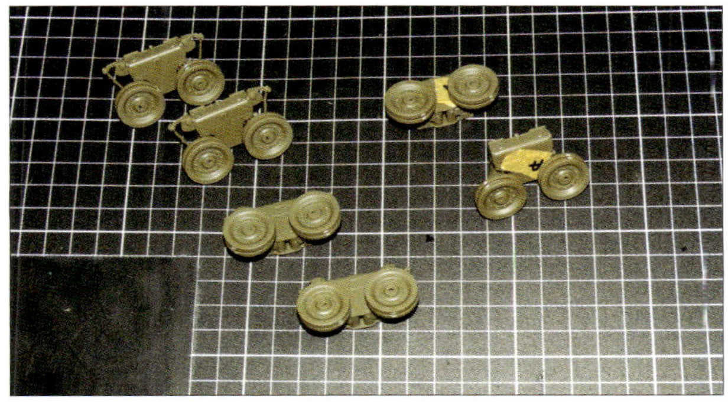

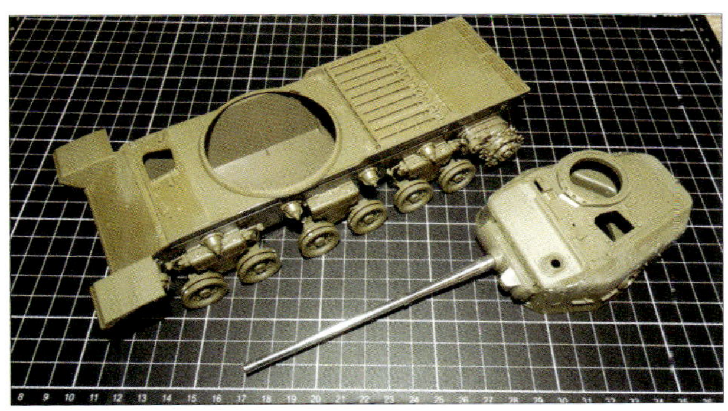

AFV Club kit images courtesy of Morgen Violet-Harris.

One kit is produced by **Academy**, a 1/35 scale Centurion Mk III. It is essentially the Tamiya kit in Academy colours.

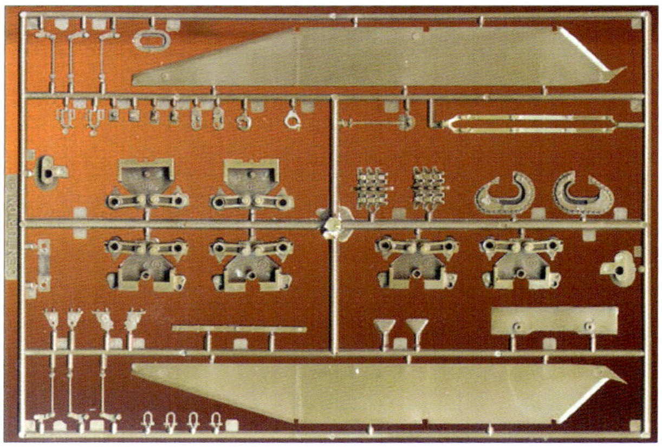

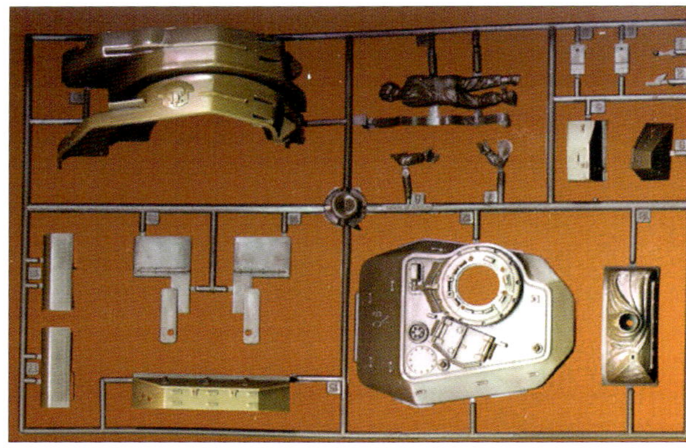

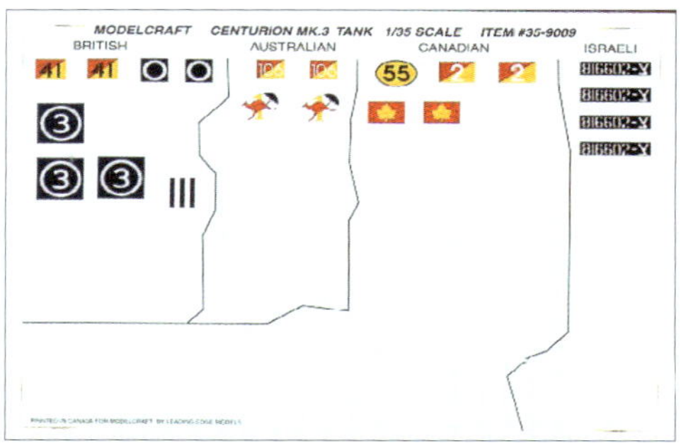

Images courtesy of Cybermodeler Online

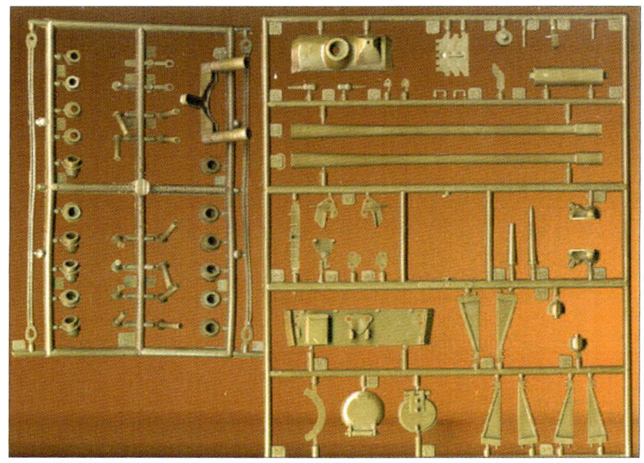

Accurate Armour has a wide range of 1/35 scale Centurions. It produces one of the few Centurion Mk Is with an ARV conversion option. Modellers can choose between short or long hull ARV Mk IIs or the Australian South Vietnam ARV Mk II. The Mk III conversion kits are also offered with either short or long hull. Finally a Gulf War ARVE is available that comes complete with cables, armour panels, etched detail sets, gulf stowage and MIMIC.

A Korean War Mk III is available from **ACE** in 1/72 scale as is a Mk V with Type A and Type B 20-pounder guns, and decals for the Berlin Brigade and the Suez Crisis. ACE's third product is a Long Range Mk V or V/1 with external fuel tanks. The Mk III is a very complete package, having both type A and B gun tubes on the sprues and a turret basket so many versions could be built from this kit.

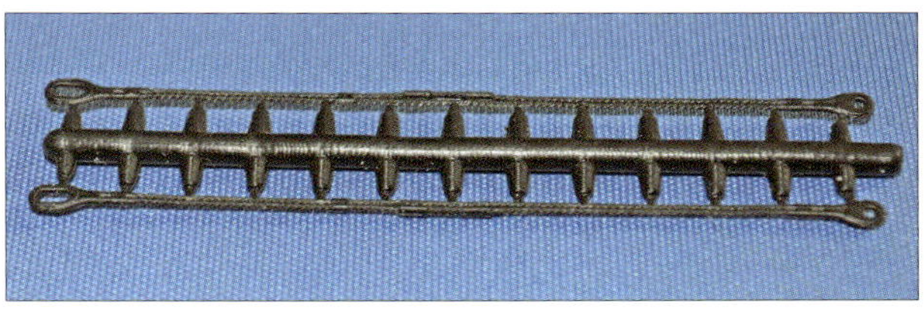

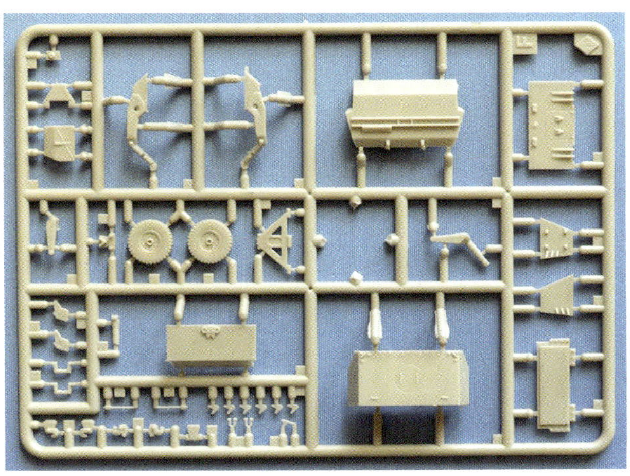

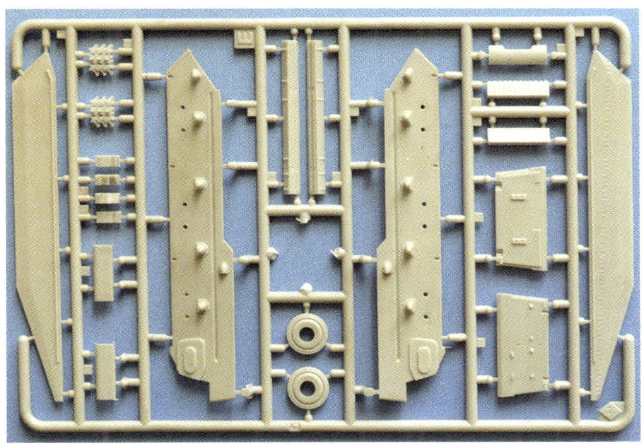

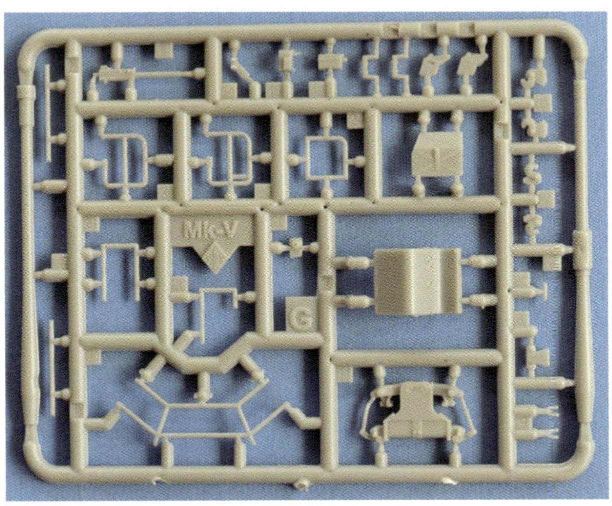

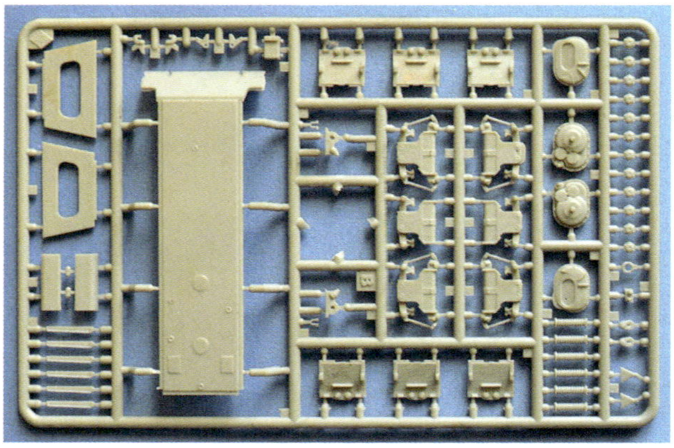

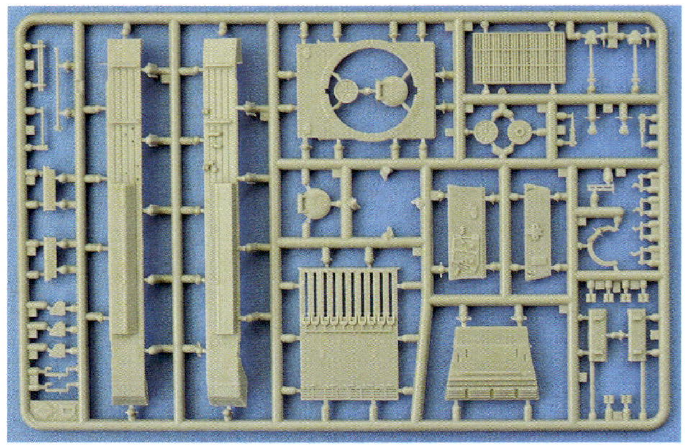

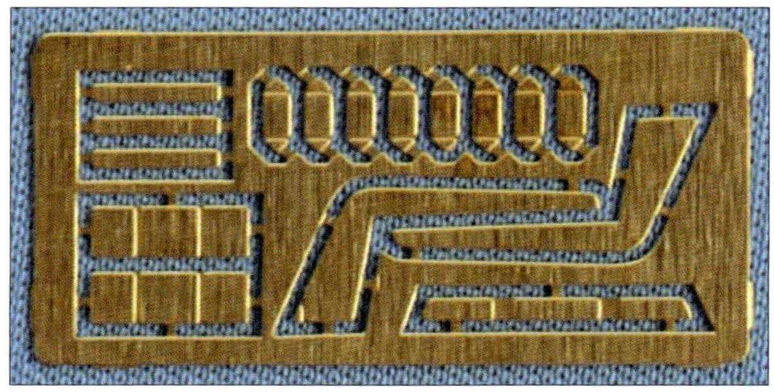

Tamiya is a first-rate scale model manufacturer and its 1/25 and 1/35 Mk IIIs are no different. This plastic model's form is well captured including the depictions of the turret and hull armour. A modeller can choose whether to include the waterproof cover for the mantlet – leaving it off enables better gun movement. The re-released kit includes three figures and there are a variety of British decal options with one IDF version. If you're looking to build a Centurion from the Korean War era then this would probably be your kit of choice, that is until the AFV Club Mk III is released and then one would have to reassess. These models are offered as remote control, motorozed or static models.

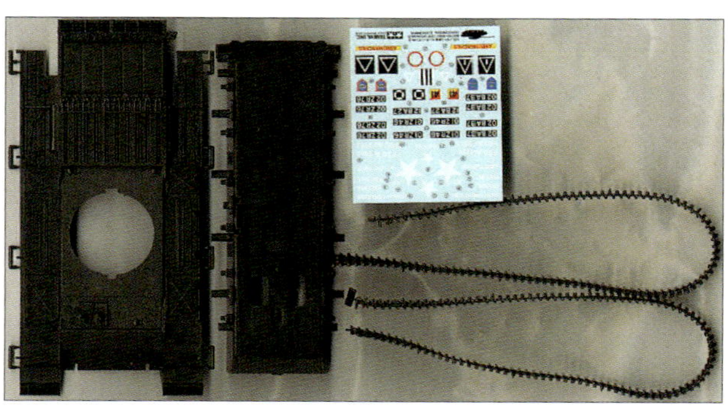

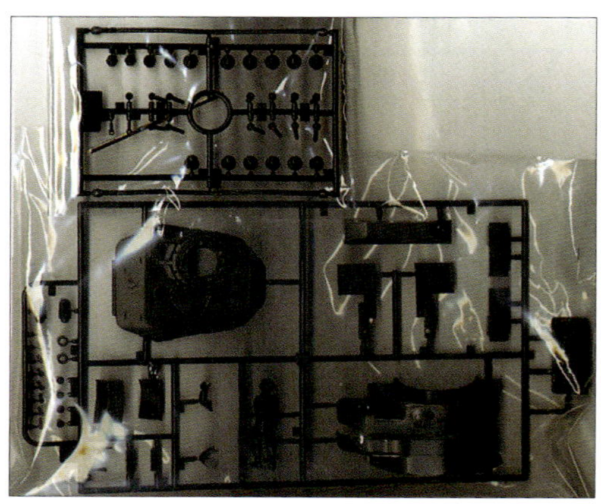

Models of Mk I Centurions are rare, besides Accurate Armour, **Matador Models** (previosly by Cromwell Models whose 1/76 range has been passed to Matador Models) do a 1/76 scale kit and **Atelier Infinite** offers a full Mk I kit too. It is resin cast and is in 1/144 scale. Japan's **Fairy Kikaku**, a small resin manufacturer that appears to be fairly unknown outside of Japan, produces a resin cast 1/144 Centurion Mk V, one vehicle in a set of three from the Indo-Pakistan wars, although markings are not included. **Modelcraft** offers a Mk III with four decal options: British, Australian, Canadian and Israeli. **Nichimo** plastic models offers the Mk X with 105mm gun. Modellers who prefer 1/48 scale would probably turn to Aurora or Tank Mania. **Aurora** produces an IDF Mk V and two, what it calls Second World War British Centurion kits, although neither of these were available at the time of writing and are possibly now only found through second-hand dealers or private sales. **Tank Mania** has a high quality Mk III resin kit available which includes photoetch and waterslide decals.

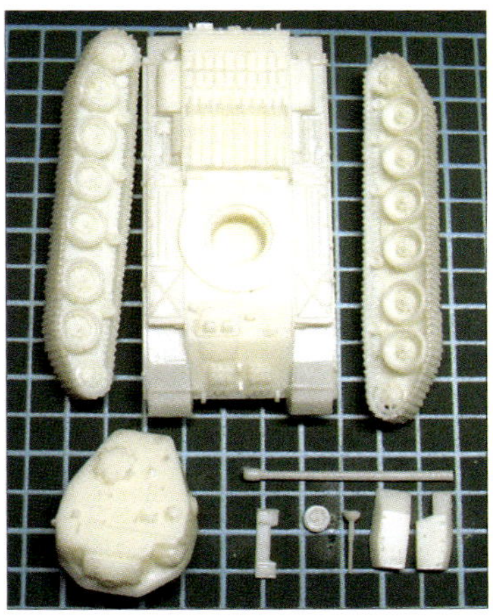

Atelier Infinite's resin Centuion Mk 1 in 1/144 scale.

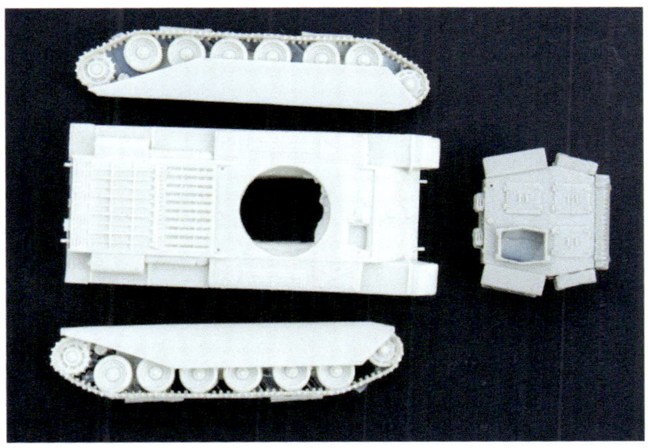

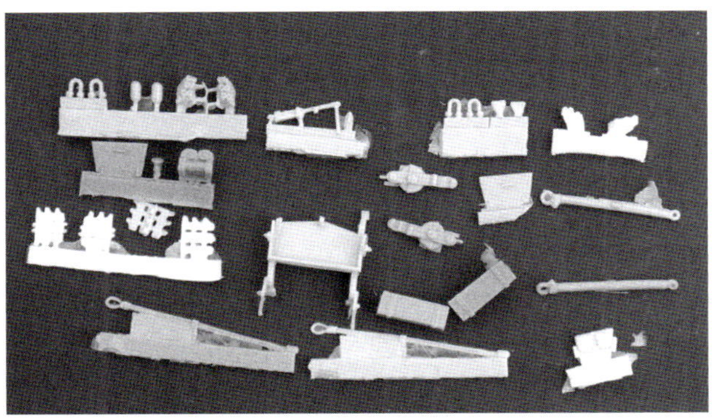

Matador Models' Centuion Mk 1 in 1/76 scale.

Tank Mania's 1.48 scale Centurion Mk 3. Images courtesy of Tank Mania.

(continued from page 16) 343 Mk V tanks were gradually upgunned with 105mm guns to Mk V/2 standard, as were nineteen Mk VIIs (to Mk VII/2) in 1966–68. All Centurions were replaced by Leopard 2 main battle tanks in the 1980s, after having been used alongside Leopard 1s in the 1970s. Many Mk V and all Mk VII tanks were returned to the United States (which had paid for them), which appears to have shipped most to Israel.

New Zealand
The New Zealand Army's first Centurion was a Mk III, shipped directly from England. Two more were delivered in 1953, followed by eight Mks III and V/1s supplied from British stocks in Hong Kong. All were withdrawn from service in 1968 and transferred to Australia.

Singapore
Sixty-three Centurion Mk III and Mk VIIs were bought from India in 1975 and more from Israel in 1993/4, all upgraded to Israeli standard with new main guns and diesel engines. Replaced by the Leopard 2SG.

South Africa
South Africa ordered 203 Centurions from the UK in 1953, these entering service between 1955 and 1958. South Africa's major strategic priorities at the time revolved around assisting the British armed forces and other Commonwealth nations in a conventional war in the Middle East and Africa, and the Centurions were procured specifically because they were compatible with Commonwealth tank tactics and British armoured formations.

Following South Africa's withdrawal from the Commonwealth in 1961, its priorities shifted toward internal security and diversifying national arms procurement outside traditional suppliers such as the United Kingdom. To that end, a hundred Centurion Mk IIIs and ten Centurion-based recovery vehicles were sold off to Switzerland in 1961. The remaining Centurions, together with others purchased from Jordan and India, were later refurbished and served with the South African Armoured Corps from 1985 as the Olifant Mk IA.

Sweden
The Swedish Defence Ministry placed an order for eighty Centurion Mk III tanks at the end of 1952, the first being delivered in April 1953. A few years later, Sweden ordered a batch of 160 Centurion Mk Vs,

Top: An Israeli Centurion.

Above: New Zealand Centurion Mk III, 3rd Armoured Division.

Olifant Mk II main battle tank on display during the 2017 SANDF Armed Forces Day.

A Centurion of the Royal Swedish Army.

A Swiss Panzer 57 (Centurion Mk VII) against the background of the Swiss Alps.

A Swiss Panzer 57 (Centurion Mk VII) on a tank transporter.

followed by a batch of 110 Centurion Mk Xs around 1960. The Centurions, together with the Stridsvagn 103 (the so-called S-tank), formed the backbone of the Swedish armoured brigades for several decades. The Mk IIIs and the Mk Vs were upgraded with a 105mm gun in the 1960s. Between 1983 and 1987, the Centurions had a midlife renovation and modification (REMO) done, which included among other things night-vision equipment, targeting systems, laser range-finders, improved gun stabilization, thermal sleeves on the barrel and exhaust pipes and reactive armour developed by the Swedish FFV Ordnance. The Swedish Army gradually phased out its Centurions and Strv 103 during the 1990s as a consequence of comparative tests of the T-72, Leclerc, M1A1 and Leopard 2. It was replaced by the Leopard 2 and the Stridsvagn 122, a Swedish variant of the German tank.

Switzerland

The Swiss Army acquired 312 Centurions in total, the first batch being ordered in 1955. These were delivered in 1956/7 and received the Swiss designation of Panzer 55. A second batch of Centurion tanks, this time comprising Mk VIIs, was delivered between 1958 and 1960. A third batch of Centurions was bought in 1960, comprising Mk Vs from South African surplus stocks. Some later modifications of these Centurions included fitting them with diesel engines.

Centurion Armoured Engineer Vehicles

Centurion Armoured Recovery Vehicles

The Centurion's hull lent itself well to conversion into a variety of engineer vehicles, the first, deployed in 1954, being a Mk I Armoured Recovery Vehicle (ARV) which was simply a hull minus the turret fitted with towing gear. This was replaced by the Centurion Mk II ARV (FV4006), which was essentially a Centurion MBT with its turret removed and replaced by an all-welded superstructure behind the driver's position. The commander's cupola could be traversed through 360° and was fitted with a 7.62mm (0.30in) machine gun. Mounted at the rear of the hull were spades which were used to stabilize the vehicle when the winch was being used. The winch's 31,000kg capacity could be increased with the aid of snatch blocks to a maximum of 90,000kg. The vehicle had a loaded weight of 50,295kg and a crew of four. All Centurion Mk II ARVs were built by Vickers Defence Systems at Newcastle-upon-Tyne, 345 being produced between 1954 and 1959.

Centurion Beach Armoured Recovery Vehicles (BARV)

The Centurion BARV was developed as a replacement for the Sherman BARV, which was no longer powerful enough to rescue a new generation of heavy armoured vehicles. A mild-steel prototype was followed in 1960 by twelve production vehicles. These were based on the hulls of Mk I, II and III Centurion tanks that by this time were redundant. Although initially assigned to the army, they were passed to the Royal Marines when the army's amphibious assault role was assigned to the Marines. The BARV was basically a Centurion body with built-up sides to accommodate wading in water up to eleven feet. The design was functional although somewhat crude, with sloped armour built above the tank hull. The tracks for the BARV were reversed so they had better grip biting in reverse gear. Centurion BARVs had a crew of four; two of the crew were members of the Royal Engineers, one of whom was a qualified

A Centurion ARV Mk II at the Borden Military Museum, Ontario, Canada.

British troops being ferried ashore by a Centurion BARV during the Falklands conflict.

A Centurion AVRE pictured on the foggy streets of Londonderry during Operation Motorman, 31 July 1972.

A Centurion AVRE. The short 165mm L9A1 gun was used to demolish structures such as pillboxes and gun emplacements.

diver. The Centurion BARVs were built to provide the essential role for the LPD's HMS *Fearless* and HMS *Intrepid* as part of the Beach Assault Squadrons. The Assault Squadron personnel were initially a mix of Royal Marines and army serving aboard the ships, but the responsibility was eventually assigned entirely to the Royal Marines.

Centurion Bridgelayer and Armoured Ramp Carrier (ARK)

Based on a Mk V chassis, the Centurion Bridgelayer carrying a No. 6 Tank Bridge that could span gaps of up to a width of 45 feet and support vehicles of up to 80 tons in weight. To negotiate gaps of up to 75 feet the Centurion ARK could be used, the tank itself acting as a central pier. The Bridgelayer/ARK entered service with the Royal Engineers in 1963.

Centurion Armoured Vehicle Royal Engineers (AVRE)

The FV4003 Centurion Mk V AVRE, armed with a short-barrelled L9A1 165mm demolition gun, entered service in 1963, replacing the Churchill AVRE. The vehicle was later renamed AVRE 165 relating to its primary armament.

The armament was capable of firing a 60lb (29kg) HESH round.

The vehicle added a dozer blade to the front, and frequently towed the Giant Viper for mine clearance or other trailers for stores. Large turret bins provided stowage. The dozer attachment was also provided on regular tanks as the FV4019 Centurion Mk V Bulldozer.

The FV4203 Centurion Mk XII AVRE, a modified artillery observation post vehicle, was armed with the conventional 105mm Royal Ordnance L7 rifled gun and provided with track-width, mine-clearance ploughs instead of the dozer blade on the Mk V. On 31 July 1972, several Centurion AVRE demolition vehicles were deployed in support of Operation Motorman, which was intended to break an increasing threat by the IRA in Northern Ireland. The tanks were transported to Northern Ireland aboard the amphibious landing ship HMS *Fearless* and were operated with their turrets traversed to the rear and their main guns covered by tarpaulins. The AVREs used their massive bulldozer blades to destroy twenty-nine barricades erected by the IRA in Londonderry.

Centurion Mk V Dozer

This was a standard Centurion Mk V fitted with a hydraulically operated bulldozer blade identical to that fitted to the AVRE. It entered service with the Royal Engineers in 1961.

In Service and In Action

When the Centurion entered service in 1946, the forces of the western allies had already embarked on a programme of rapid demobilization that would only be reversed in 1948, when the Russians – who still maintained substantial forces in their zone of occupation and elsewhere in eastern Europe – closed the access routes to Berlin and precipitated a massive air resupply operation that became known as the Berlin Airlift. During this period, the main Soviet medium tank was still the T-34/85, which had spearheaded the drive to the German capital in 1945. The Centurion would easily have been able to cope with the T-34, but another Soviet tank, the heavy IS-3, with its 122mm gun, would have presented an altogether more difficult problem. To counter it, the British developed the 65-ton Conqueror, armed with a 120mm gun, and the two served alongside one another for a decade from 1955 in the British Army of the Rhine (BAOR). The weight of the Conqueror, however, meant that it was slow, and in addition many river bridges in Germany were incapable of supporting it. Apart from its hitting power, it offered no advantage over the Centurion, and the last examples were withdrawn in 1966.

The Centurion served the British Army of the Rhine well during the most dangerous years of the Cold War. Led by a Ferret scout car, this Centurion is seen on parade in West Berlin.

By the mid-1950s, the majority of European armies assigned to NATO had rearmed with the Centurion under the auspices of the U.S. Mutual Defense Assistance Pact, and all were subjected to

The receiving end! 'Enemy' troops surrendering at gunpoint to a BAOR Centurion during an exercise in Germany.

ongoing upgrades following the deployment of a formidable new Soviet main battle tank, the T-54/55. Yet when the Centurion went into action, it was to be in regions far remote from the plains of Central Europe

A Centurion on exercise, with an umpire in a Ferret scout car keeping a watchful eye on proceedings.

A Centurion on exercise with the British Army of the Rhine. Constant operational practice with other NATO nations was the key to successful defence against the ongoing threat from the Warsaw Pact.

Built as a Mk XII, this Centurion entered service in 1955 and was converted to AVRE standard in 1981.

The Korean War

On 11 October 1950, three squadrons of the 8th King's Royal Irish Hussars, which then formed part of the Strategic Reserve at Tidworth with Centurion Mk III tanks, sailed from Southampton on the HMT *Empire Fowey* and deployed to Korea to support the 29th Commonwealth Brigade. They disembarked at the port of Pusan on 14 November and headed for the battlefront north of Pyongyang, but were forced to retreat, along with other United Nations forces, in the face of massive enemy attacks. They regrouped on the Han River, where, during the bitter winter of 1950/1, operating in sub-zero temperatures, they experienced the rigours of winter warfare: their tanks had to be parked on straw to prevent the steel tracks from freezing to the ground. Engines had to be started every half hour, with each gear being engaged in turn to prevent them from being frozen into place.

During this period it was decided to return A and B squadrons of the 8th Hussars to the UK, and until they were rushed back from Japan it was C Squadron that was left to bear the brunt of the fighting when, on the night of 22 April 1951, communist forces launched a massive offensive all along the front. The Chinese scored an early success when, striking hard at the weakest part of the Allied line, they cut the Republic of Korea (ROK) 6th Division to pieces, leaving a dangerous gap between the U.S. Marine Division on its right flank and the 24th Infantry on the left. It was now clear that the main Chinese objective was to isolate Seoul with an enveloping movement from the north and northeast. On 26 April the Chinese offensive was checked in the eastern sector by the 27th Commonwealth Brigade and the attention now switched to the west, where six Chinese armies were throwing everything they had into a bid to reach the South Korean capital. The main weight of the offensive here fell on the British 29th Brigade, which held a 12,000-yard front and defended the vital river crossings over the Imjin River. The epic stand of the 29th Brigade – and particularly that of the 1st Battalion the Gloucester Regiment on Hill 235 above the hamlet of Solma-ri – has gone down in history. The brigade held on for three days against overwhelming odds before a general withdrawal was ordered to new positions north of Seoul. This holding action not only saved the left flank of the Eighth Army's I Corps, making possible an orderly withdrawal down the road to Seoul, it also disrupted the entire timetable of the Chinese offensive, robbing it of its momentum. In addition, during three days of savage fighting, the 29th Brigade had destroyed an entire Chinese division.

None of this would have succeeded without the heroic action of the 8th Hussars, whose

Centurions engaged the attacking Chinese over a period of several days in order to prevent the enemy from capturing the high ground defended by the infantry, the tanks making several sorties into overrun positions to rescue infantrymen who had been cut off by the Chinese advance. One British tank commander, Richard Napier, in his book *From Horses to Chieftains*, recalled: "The Chinese had infiltrated behind them and were swarming around them, shooting at the infantrymen on the tank. The crew resorted to lobbing grenades out of the hatches at the mass of Chinese infantry. On one occasion, the Centurion tanks of the 8th were swamped by Chinese soldiers who were attempting to prise open the hatches to throw grenades inside. The response of the Irish Hussars was to turn the turrets of their tanks towards each other, and 'hose' the enemy off with their Besa machine guns."

In July 1951 the British Commonwealth forces in Korea, including the 8th Hussars, were banded together in a new formation designated the 1st Commonwealth Division, made up of fifty-eight per cent British forces, twenty-two per cent Canadian, fourteen per cent Australian, five per cent New Zealand and one per cent Indian. It formed an important component of the U.S. I Corps, which also included the U.S. 1st Cavalry Division, the U.S. 3rd and 25th Infantry divisions, and the ROK 1st Division. The division occupied the strategically important sector of front stretching from the Kimpo peninsula on the Yellow Sea coast to a point east of Kumhwa thirty miles from the South Korean capital, Seoul.

In December 1951 the 8th Hussars were relieved by the 5th Royal Inniskilling Dragoon Guards, and in November 1952 their Centurions, supporting the Black Watch, played a key part in driving Chinese forces from a position known as The Hook. In the following month the Inniskillings were in turn relieved by the 1st Royal Tank Regiment and redeployed to the Suez

The formidable IS-3 presented a new challenge to NATO armoured forces. It retained the 122mm gun of the earlier IS-2 but had a redesigned, more rounded turret resembling an upturned soup bowl. The IS tanks were the spearhead of the final assault on Berlin in April 1945, their power and protection enabling them to break through the enemy defensive barriers.

The Conqueror was developed in response to the threat posed by Soviet heavy armour like the IS-3, but apart from its firepower it offered no real advantage over the Centurion. The tank's size made negotiating narrow roads difficult, like this one passing through a German village.

A Conqueror firing its 120mm main gun.

The Soviet T-55 main battle tank, seen here in Czech markings, remained the Centurion's most formidable opponent throughout much of the British tank's operational life.

A heavily camouflaged Centurion of the 8th King's Royal Irish Hussars, Korea.

Centurion Mk III in Korea, showing commander's position and smoke launchers.

Canal Zone, just before its handover to the Egyptian government.

Suez 1956: Operation Musketeer

Operation Musketeer, the Anglo-French land, sea and air operation launched in October and November 1956, was in response to Egyptian President Nasser's seizure of British and French assets in the Suez Canal Zone earlier in the year. Much emphasis was laid on cooperation with tanks, as the plan called for the landing of an armoured regiment with the assault force. Since it was not thought likely that the Libya-based 10th Armoured Division could be used, it was decided early in August to raise a new armoured brigade as part of the 3rd Armoured Division in the United Kingdom, and one of its units – the 6th Royal Tank Regiment – was placed on the order of battle for invasion. The 1st RTR was also included, but could hardly be classed as combat ready. One of its squadrons had no armoured vehicles at all, its personnel working as mechanics with the Territorial Army; another was being used for training at the School of Infantry and the third was on garrison duty at Tidworth. The 6th RTR had recently completed a tour in Germany, and many personnel were still there; the rest were scattered throughout the United Kingdom, working with the territorials. The reorganization of both regiments was chaotic. Much of the equipment issued to them from storage depots up and down the country was outmoded and totally inadequate; some of it dated back to 1940. Many of the support vehicles lacked essential items of equipment such as wireless aerials and ammunition racks.

Transporting the armoured regiments to their UK embarkation ports proved a nightmare. The weight of the Centurion tanks made movement by rail out of the question, which meant that the journey from Tidworth to Southampton and Portland had to be made on road transporters. Since the army had only a handful of these vehicles, they had to call on the services of the civilian firm Pickfords, which used heavy transporters to move large industrial components. Pickfords' crews, however, were tied to union working hours, which meant that they took a week to complete a trip that could have been made by army crews in half the time. The result was that the move took four weeks, two of which might otherwise have been spent in valuable training. The 6th Royal Tanks, with forty-seven Centurions, finally sailed for Malta on 4 September. It would be nearly two months before 1RTR followed it. To complicate matters even further, out of the thirty-two tank landing ships available on paper to transport the regiments to the Mediterranean, only two were actually in service; the rest were in storage and had to be made seaworthy when their cocoons were removed. Only twelve more could be made ready in time. By the time the tanks of 6RTR reached the Canal Zone the main fighting was over, and their operations were restricted to escorting foot patrols until the United Nations ordered a withdrawal in December.

The Arab-Israeli Wars, 1967–73

At the start of the brief conflict known as the Six-Day War in June 1967 the Israeli Defence Forces had 293 operational Centurion tanks. Their armoured assets also included 250 upgraded M4 Shermans, although only 120 of these were operational, together with 250 M48A3 Patton tanks and about 400 French AMX-13s, the latter organized into three battalions. Although the AMX-13 was a light tank the Israelis used it in the role of main battle tank to which it was not suited, and it suffered heavy losses.

On the other hand, the Centurion – initially been unpopular with Israeli tank crews because of its relative complexity compared to earlier types of tank in Israeli service – soon proved its worth in action, notably on the West Bank, where the Centurion's 105mm L7 gun devastated the Jordanian Army's M48 Patton tanks, which lacked the upgrades of Israel's M48s. About a hundred Jordananian 170 M48s were captured by the Israelis during the conflict, many being pressed into service with the Israeli Armoured Corps.

The success of Israel's armoured brigades against very stiff Arab resistance during the Six-Day War was mainly due to the leadership and direction of General Israel Tal, who had assumed command of the Israeli Armoured Corps in 1964 and organized it into the leading element of the Israeli Defence Forces on land, formulating a doctrine based on high mobility and relentless assault. He retrained Israeli tank gunners to engage targets accurately at up to almost a mile, which was well within the capability of the Centurion's 105mm gun, instead of holding fire until their targets were much closer. This gave them a distinct advantage over their Arab opponents, whose tank crews normally waited until they were within 550 yards, and often much less, before opening fire with their Soviet-made tank guns.

Another major factor in the Israeli victory was air power. With the Arab air forces virtually wiped out in the first hours of the campaign, the Israeli Air Force was able to unleash its French-built Fouga Magister light attack aircraft against the enemy, their 68mm SNEB rockets with armour-piercing proving deadly. Operated by No. 147 Squadron, the Magisters, in action mainly on the Jordanian front and against Syrian armour on the Golan Heights, claimed 128 tanks destroyed during the war, the total including some fifty Jordanian Centurions supporting a thrust toward Jerusalem by the Jordanian Army. Six Magisters were shot down by ground fire and their pilots lost.

This Centurion Mk III fell victim to enemy artillery fire during the Battle of the Imjin River in April 1951. The damage is being assessed prior to recovery.

Centurion Mk III of the Inniskilling Dragoon Guards in Korea.

The War Office had to charter Pickfords low loaders, like the one pictured here, to transport the Centurions to their embarkation ports. The tank on the low loader is a Tortoise heavy assault gun, only six of which were built.

A British foot patrol in Port Said.

Only six years after the end of the 1967 conflict, war again erupted in the Middle East when Egypt and Syria launched an attack that threatened Israel's survival. The so-called Yom Kippur offensive took the Israelis by surprise, and this time they were confronted by an extremely well-equipped enemy armed with some of the latest Soviet military technology, including T-62 tanks and an arsenal of surface-to-air missiles and anti-tank weaponry.

By this time, Israel's Centurions had undergone a substantial upgrade. The Meteor petrol engine had been replaced by a Teledyne Continental AVD-S-1790-2A air-cooled diesel powerplant incorporating an Allison CD-850-6 automatic transmission, substantially reducing the driver's workload during long-distance travel. The engine was also fitted in the Israeli Armoured Corps' M48A2 Patton tanks, which were undergoing a parallel upgrade. All Centurions were now armed with the 105mm L7 main gun with stowage for seventy-two rounds. These, and other modifications, were introduced during a three-year programme that was completed in 1970. The tank was known officially as the Upgraded Centurion, but received the popular name of Sh'ot, which translates from the Hebrew as 'Whip' or 'Scourge'.

The Yom Kippur war began on 6 October 1973 with massive assaults on two fronts, the Syrians attacking the Golan Heights in the north and the Egyptians launching a two-pronged offensive with five divisions across the Suez Canal into Sinai. In planning the latter the Egyptian Army leaned heavily on the Soviet Army's river-crossing expertise, developed to a very high degree during the Second World War. During the

The British amphibious assault under way at Port Said, November 1956.

Sinai campaign, counterattacking Israeli armoured forces sustained punishing losses – as much as forty per cent – from Egyptian anti-tank weapons, ranging from man-portable RPG-7 rockets and RPG-43 grenades to AT-3 Sagger guided missiles. The latter knocked out 800 Israeli tanks during the conflict, many of them American M60s that had recently been delivered. It was the rapid delivery of more M60s, in fact, that enabled the Israelis to counterattack across the Suez Canal and engage Egyptian forces on their own territory.

A further factor in the eventual Israeli victory was the collapse of Syria's offensive on the northern front. Here, on the Golan Heights, the Israeli 7th Armoured and 188th 'Barak' brigades, with 177 Centurions, fought off an assault by some 1,200 Syrian tanks in a battle lasting fifty-one hours. When the Syrians eventually withdrew they left 500 disabled and destroyed tanks on the battlefield. This wholesale destruction of Syria's armour enabled the Israeli Defence Forces to launch a counterattack deep into Syrian territory, and at one point their tanks were within ten miles of Damascus, the Syrian capital.

Centurions vs the PLO, September 1970

In 1970, midway between the two principal Arab-Israeli wars, the Royal Jordanian Army's Centurion Mk VII tanks were used to crush Palestine Liberation Organization factions in Jordan, which were attempting to seize control of the country with the help of incursions by T-55 tanks of the Syrian Army. Elements of the Jordanian 40th Armoured Brigade, supported by the Royal Jordanian Air Force, broke up an attack by

One of Israel's Centurions seen in typical desert colour scheme.

General Israel Tal, a hard-bitten and resourceful commander, led Israel's armoured forces to success in the Six-Day War of 1967.

Israeli Centurions advancing in the Negev desert.

Israeli Air Force Fouga Magister trainer/light attack aircraft, armed with 68mm SNEB rockets, inflicted considerable damage on Jordanian and Syrian armour.

Israeli Centurions preparing for action just before the outbreak of hostilities in June 1967.

Centurion and Shot tanks in Israeli service. Benjamín Núñez González wikicommons

Centurions on the march: Israeli main battle tanks en route to the Golan Heights in the Yom Kippur War.

This Centurion was left in place on the Golan Heights as a memorial to the tank crews of the Yom Kippur war.

Israeli Centurions in the Sinai desert.

the Syrian 5th Division near Ar-Rathma, inflicting heavy losses on the enemy.

The Indo-Pakistan wars, 1965 and 1971

India's Centurion tanks participated in both Indo-Pakistan conflicts. On 10 September 1965, an attack by the Pakistani 1st Armoured Division was blunted at the Battle of Asal Uttar by three Indian armoured regiments, one of which, 3 Cavalry, was armed with forty-five Centurion Mk VIIs. The majority of the 135 Pakistani tanks engaged were Shermans which were totally outclassed by the Centurions; only twenty-four were more modern M47 and M48 Pattons. Intense fighting continued over the next two days before the Pakistani forces conducted a tactical retreat toward Chawinda, at which point India claimed to have destroyed sixty-seven Pakistani tanks. Indian losses were six Centurions. A United Nations ceasefire was concluded on 22 September.

In 1971, in the Sialkot area, two Pakistani armoured regiments engaged the Centurions of the Indian I Armoured Corps in a renewed outbreak of hostilities following Bangladesh's declaration of independence from Pakistan.

The Yom Kippur War cost Israel many of its Centurions, like this one caught in the battle for the Suez Canal.

The speedy delivery of arms from the U.S., including M60 tanks seen here passing a wrecked Syrian T-55, helped the Israelis to secure victory.

The wreckage of a Pakistani M48 Patton, victim of a gun duel with an Indian Centurion in the Indo-Pakistan War of 1965.

Vietnam

In February 1968, Centurions of C Squadron, 1st Armoured Regiment, Australian Army, deployed to Vietnam as part of the 1st Australian Task Force, and were based at Nui Dat in Phuoc Tuy province. The squadron initially comprised two troops, each of four tanks, and two tanks of the squadron headquarters, as well as two dozer tanks and two bridgelayer tanks. A third troop was created by placing the two headquarters' tanks together with the two dozer tanks. This number constituted only half of the squadron and it was not until August that the rest of the squadron arrived from Australia. This brought the squadron up to its full strength of twenty tanks, with another six in reserve.

Prior to their deployment to Vietnam, the Centurions underwent a number of modifications. These included the installation of a large external fuel tank on the back of each tank, although this was later deleted because of the increased fire hazard. The main gun system was upgraded, a ranging machine gun was fitted and an infrared illumination system was also installed for improved night vision. The tanks side skirts were removed to avoid a potential buildup of mud and debris around the tracks in jungle warfare conditions, and were replaced with heavy-gauge steel plate. Storage racks were welded to the rear of the turret for the carriage of ammunition and other equipment, and an additional radio was installed to permit communication between the tank crew and infantry. In February 1969 C Squadron was relieved by B Squadron, the latter remaining in Vietnam for the rest of the year. The Centurions provided fire support for infantry operations, were used to directly attack enemy positions, and helped defend the Fire Support Bases.

By late 1970 Australia was beginning to reduce its commitment to the war and the size of 1ATF was reduced from three infantry battalions to two. The tanks, however, continued to be engaged in operations in 1971, providing decisive armoured firepower in many actions which often involved very fierce fighting.

The 1st Armoured Regiment's tanks worked closely with the Australian infantry and the APCs of 3rd Cavalry Regiment on operations throughout Phuoc Tuy and neighbouring provinces. During 1971 troops were progressively withdrawn from Vietnam, as the government reduced Australia's commitment to the war. In June and July the tanks of C Squadron were progressively phased out of operations and the squadron returned home in September.

An Indian Centurion entering the town of Philora during the Indo-Pakistan War of 1965.

South Africa

The South African Army deployed a single squadron of thirteen Olifant Mk IA tanks to the Angolan border in 1985, where they were attached to the 61st Mechanized Battalion Group. They were withdrawn after a ceasefire between South Africa and Angola was concluded, but reactivated when this broke down, and on 9 November 1987 they destroyed two Angolan T-55s during a nine-minute skirmish. During operations in Angola, South African forces typically dispersed into an arrowhead formation, with Olifants in the lead, Ratel-90 armoured cars on the flanks, and the remainder of the mechanized infantry to the rear and centre. Three Olifants were abandoned in a minefield and subsequently captured by the People's Armed Forces for the Liberation of Angola (FAPLA), while another two were damaged beyond immediate repair by mines but successfully recovered. A number of others suffered

An Australian Centurion Mk V/1 'Diabolical' used in Vietnam, with a UH-1 'Huey' helicopter hovering nearby.

Australian Centurion tankmen being briefed prior to an operation in Vietnam. Despite many misgivings, the Centurion performed well in the Vietnamese jungle.

varying degrees of track and suspension damage due to mines or Angolan tank fire, but were able to keep moving after field repairs.

The South African Olifant main battle tank. (61 Mech)

A South African Olifant Mk II tank carrying out a demonstration, with Westland Lynx helicopters hovering in the background.

A patrol passes an abandoned FAPLA artillery piece deep in the Angolan bush. The Olifants have had their track skirts removed because of the build-up of broken vegetation behind them. (61 Mech)

One of the Olifant battle tanks on the firing range at Omuthiya. At this time the Olifants, as yet untested in operations, still mounted the Centurion's trademark armoured side skirts, but during later deployments in Angola they were removed because they proved to be excellent bush-catchers. (61 Mech)

Olifant Mk IA tank at the South African Armour Museum, Bloemfontein.

ARDUINO PROJECTS

Paul and David Bradt

FIRECROWN

ACKNOWLEDGMENTS

This book has truly been a collaboration. The talents of Dennis Drury and his friends provided a great deal of material related to actual signaling systems being modeled on several different layouts. Steve Spence and Tom Ward have provided insight and encouragement over the years, and some of the projects listed in this book trace their roots to projects they completed. We want to thank all of them for sharing their expertise, developments, projects, and solutions to problems.

— *Paul and David Bradt*

On the cover: Main photo: A Rio Grande freight waits at a red-over-red signal as a passenger train rolls by on the main line on Jim Petro's HO layout. Chapter 6 includes a description of his Centralized Traffic Control signaling system. *Jim Petro* **Top photo:** An Arduino Uno provides a lot of microprocessing power in a small device.

Back cover, top: An IOX board allows adding additional inputs/outputs to an Arduino. *Model Railroad Control Systems*
Bottom: A work train approaches CTC signals at the end of the siding at Rifle on Jim Petro's layout. *Jim Petro*

All photos by the authors unless otherwise credited

Firecrown
605 Chestnut Street, Suite 800
Chattanooga, TN 37450

Shop.Trains.com

Published in 2025
29 28 27 26 25 1 2 3 4 5

Manufactured in China

ISBN: 979-8-89491-017-8
EISBN: 979-8-89491-018-5

Editor: Jeff Wilson
Book Design: Lisa Schroeder

CONTENTS

INTRODUCTION
Unlocking the Power of Animation 4

CHAPTER 1
Arduino basics 6

CHAPTER 2
Stand-alone Arduino projects 16

CHAPTER 3
Welding shop with lighting and sound 30

CHAPTER 4
Integrated Arduino layout projects 42

CHAPTER 5
Basic detection with Arduinos and JMRI 54

CHAPTER 6
CTC system with Raspberry Pi and JMRI 65

INTRODUCTION

UNLOCKING THE POWER OF ANIMATION

Model railroaders spend a lot of time and money creating well-detailed, prototypical locomotives and rolling stock. However, in many cases these wonderfully accurate mobile items roll through a still-life layout. The Arduino microcontroller and its cousin, the Raspberry Pi, provide powerful tools for us to help change that and bring layouts to life.

Arduino and Raspberry Pi microcontrollers have been revolutionary in their ability to pack a lot of computing power into a small, inexpensive device. A large general hobby following has developed around these devices, including a subgroup of many model railroaders who are looking for better, more economical, and easier ways of animating models and controlling signals and lighting. Learning to program and control an Arduino or Raspberry Pi requires some time and effort — and there's definitely a learning curve — but many projects are well within the abilities of most model railroaders. And as with many high-tech devices, the more you work with (and experiment with) them, the more your comfort level will increase and the more your knowledge will grow.

We have spent considerable time adding Arduino-based projects to model railroads of various sizes from dioramas to large empires. Each type of project has its own unique opportunities and challenges. Our focus in writing this book is to provide information and ideas that teach the basics of how Arduinos (and their programming) works, and to help you become confident in not only building the projects shown, but adapting those ideas to projects of your own.

The chapters start with an overview of basics for Arduinos and related key components. We then proceed to some basic stand-alone projects that provide animation aspects and can be added at any point to a model railroad. The next chapters describe more extensive projects that entail connection of the Arduino to other devices or control systems, often through Java Model Railroad Interface (JMRI) and Computer Model Railroad Interface (C/MRI). This, combined with detectors, allows advanced block signaling as well as signal and train control with Centralized Traffic Control (CTC).

As we have developed and built Arduino-based projects, we've often faced coding challenges or issues with wiring or other mechanical features. Building experimental and breadboard systems helped resolve many of these problems in early planning stages. Doing this helped us learn more about these systems, and we encourage you to do the same. The chapters include notes about how we overcame many of these challenges, as we hope to help you avoid some of these pitfalls.

These Arduino projects have given us a lot of satisfaction, and we've seen how they give layouts a new level of realism. We hope that these concepts inspire you to develop your own Arduino systems. Let's get started!

The operating fast-time clock, driven by an Arduino, adds a bit of animation to this N scale Denver Union Station scene. Chapter 2 provides details on the project.

CONTACTING THE AUTHORS

We have done our best to explain the steps involved in all of these projects. If you're looking for clarification, or if something isn't working for you, feel free to email authors Paul and David Bradt at contact@pdanalytic.com; you can also contact Dennis Drury, who developed many of these projects, at cowrr1984@gmail.com.

DIGITAL (PWM~)
ARDUINO
UNO R4
WIFI
TX
RX
POWER
ANALOG IN
IOREF
RESET
3.3V
5V
GND
VIN
A0 A1 A2 A3 A4 A5

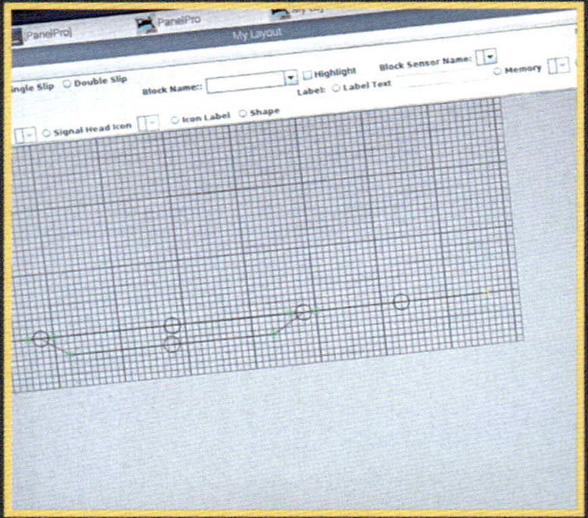
PanelPro
My Layout
Double Slip
Block Name:
Highlight
Block Sensor Name:
Memory
Label:
Label Text
Signal Head Icon
Icon Label
Shape

© Raspberry Pi 2018
CE

Before trying out some of the unique Arduinos that are utilized in this book, we recommend starting out with an Arduino Uno. The Uno is a robust device that works well and is good for developing consistent, reliable projects. After you've developed basic skills with the Uno, you'll be ready to try other Arduino versions. We have run across a few styles of Arduinos that don't work well or exhibit quirks. When using these unique Arduino versions, in many cases the codes can be verified on an Arduino Uno.

Brief history and description

The Arduino board was first developed around 2004 or 2005 as a tool to help students learn programming. It is an open-source tool, with examples of code available online for use or modification to meet a large variety of user or developer requirements. Arduino users have developed a large base of helpful online websites and user groups. It represents a breakthrough as an easy-to-use (and relatively inexpensive) programmable interface between a computer and various devices. This code development tool, or Integrated Development Environment (IDE), can be downloaded for free from the Arduino website. The Arduino site (www.arduino.cc) is a good place to start and has a lot of useful information. Other good sources of information include YouTube videos, maker fairs, and other user group sites.

Arduinos come in several versions and sizes, **1, 2**, and we'll use several versions of Arduinos throughout this book. The Uno is the standard version; a larger version of the Arduino board is the Mega, which has 54 digital input and output ports and 16 analog pins which can be used as input or output. The Nano is a small version of the Arduino used in the common-cathode signal system in Chapter 4 and the arc welder simulation project in Chapter 3. The Pro Mini is an even smaller version of the Arduino.

One of these other styles might be the perfect choice if size is a factor or if you need a lot of inputs/outputs.

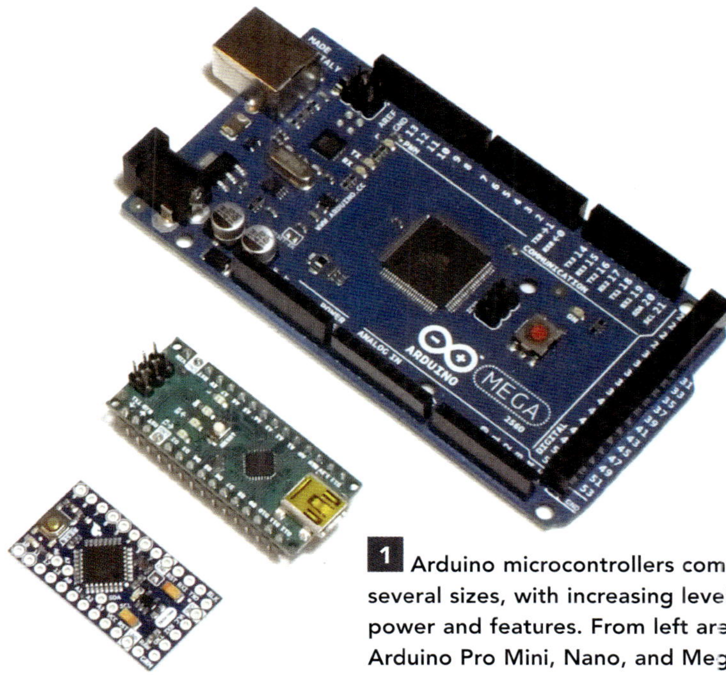

1 Arduino microcontrollers come in several sizes, with increasing levels of power and features. From left are an Arduino Pro Mini, Nano, and Mega.

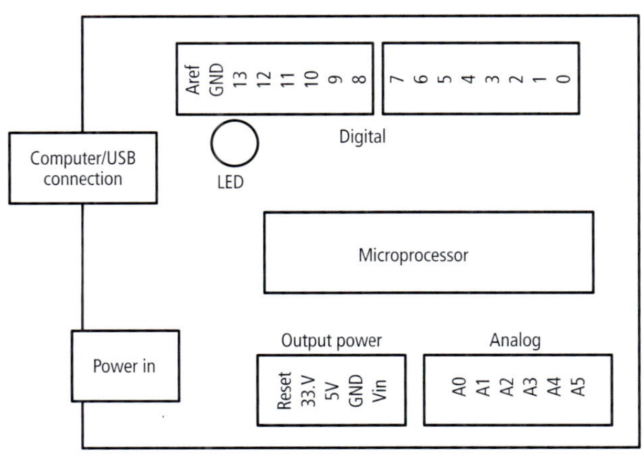

2 This view shows the typical component layout of an Arduino Uno. The digital pins (upper right) and analog pins (lower right) are clearly labeled, as are other connection points.

3

An Arduino Uno is connected to a computer via a USB cable. It's running Blink, a good program for testing the functionality of the microcontroller.

The same IDE tool is used to program these devices, but it does require selection of the correct Arduino to work properly.

The Arduino connections and components all have specific names. Here's a list of what they are and what they do:

Output power port: These are plug connections that provide 3.3V and 5V DC power for sensors, LEDs, or other devices. The amount of current provided is limited. There is also a reset button and an input voltage connection.

Analog device ports: These provide connections for analog inputs or outputs from other devices.

Digital device ports: These are digital inputs and outputs that are often used to turn a device on or accept a high or low input from a sensor or other device.

SCL and SDA ports: Next to the digital ports are the SCL (clock line) and SDA (data line), which are used to communicate with other devices. The clock line sends pulses to aid in timing, while the SDA port sends or receives data from another device. They are used as part of an I2C two-wire protocol.

Effector: This device operates and effects movement or another result.

Sketch/IDE: The Integrated Development Environment (IDE) is the programming tool that runs on a computer for writing code. The code is called a "sketch," which in the Arduino world is a coded process or procedure. Once the code is developed in the IDE, it is uploaded to the Arduino. The IDE tool must be downloaded from the Arduino website.

The version primarily used in this book is 1.8.57. As with other software, it is constantly being upgraded. The newest version as of 2024 is 2.2.1, and although it looks a bit different it works in the same way as described in this book.

Shields and breakout boards: These are add-on boards used to provide various functions. Shields are boards that plug directly into Arduino ports. Breakout boards are connected by wires and sit beside or near the Arduino.

Libraries: These are packages of software that are called upon repeatedly when code is running. The Arduino allows the use of libraries in the same way each time, despite having several other components in the software that could change from program to program. These libraries are updated from time to time and the Arduino IDE helps manage those changes to libraries.

If necessary, check both document > arduino > libraries and %arduino installation path% > libraries locations to ensure the libraries are correct.

We have in the past encountered a problem with out-of-date Arduino libraries. We had a program and board that both worked flawlessly on a fresh installation of Arduino IDE, but on another laptop the Arduino IDE had older library editions which resulted in complex errors. Multiple libraries contributed to the errors. Our solution was to clean out the older libraries (in multiple folder locations). To avoid these issues, keep all libraries in the library folder inside the Documents/ Arduino folder. (This may not make sense to you at the moment, but it will once you gain experience with a few Arduino projects.)

Computer port: This is the primary port connected directly to the computer. This port uploads the sketches or programs to the Arduino. It is also the serial data port that allows the Arduino to send data to the computer.

Power: This port allows unplugging an Arduino from a computer and using battery power or a 9-12V DC power supply to operate the Arduino.

Ports and interfaces

The simple schematic and image in **2** identifies the relative location of Arduino Uno major components and in particular, the board's main connection ports. The Arduino is connected to a computer via a USB port, **3**. The Arduino in the photo is running a code called Blink, which flashes the onboard LED.

One new product recently released is the official Arduino Uno R4 minima and Wi-Fi versions, **4**. These have the same form factor of shape and ports as the Uno R3, but they have some interesting features compared to the R3, and the more powerful chip on the Arduino R4 minima provides better performance compared to the R3.

The Arduino Uno R4 Wi-Fi has a nice LED matrix built into it. It is based on a powerful Wi-Fi/Bluetooth-enabled system-on-chip device (the ESP32) that lets the programmer set up a Wi-Fi connected Internet Of Things (IOT) system. There are several aspects to setting up one of these IOT systems, and they are outside the scope of this book.

However, in many ways the new Arduino 4 will behave and run code the same way as the old Arduino 3. It has been noted online that there may be some differences and potential issues with libraries using the R4. Some Uno R3 libraries are set up to use the AVR architecture chip configuration and are not compatible with the architecture of the R4 Wi-Fi ESP32 Chip. There may be new libraries created for the UNO R4, however there are libraries that have already been ported.

We recommend that anyone new to the Arduino world start with the UNO

4

This Arduino R4 Wi-Fi includes a small LED matrix. It's connected to a computer via USB.

Basic Arduino coding information

By Paul Bradt

The Arduino is a microcontroller. That means it is a small electronic printed-circuit board that has ports for inputs and outputs, and it uses a simplified set of code or logic that causes it to operate in a certain way given key inputs.

The basic Arduino coding structure has two main parts: the setup section and the loop section. The setup section identifies and configures everything that is needed in the loop section.

Setup section: This is needed to establish what will be used and how it is going to be used. For example, if a switch is connected to the digital port, then it will need to be called out as an input. Once this input is set up, then it can be used by a different part of the code.

Loop section: This section of code continuously loops, exercising any commands within the time established or a set parameter is reached.

There are some common attributes that require setup:

Inputs/outputs: Need to be defined.

Serial port communication rate: This is set up based on the board; for most Arduinos this is 9600 baud.

Include libraries: The libraries called up will be defined in the setup section of the code. Constants and variables definitions that are used in the code need to be defined.

Once the items needed by the code are set up, you can then move to the loop section of the code. The loop section part of the code is the set of instructions that the Arduino will follow. It normally starts with a code line: void loop() {

One other important aspect about Arduino code is that each command sequence starts with an open bracket, {, and ends with a closed bracket, }. Keep an eye on these: We've experienced issues caused by mismatched brackets, as the code will not compile or run and it indicates something like unmatched brackets.

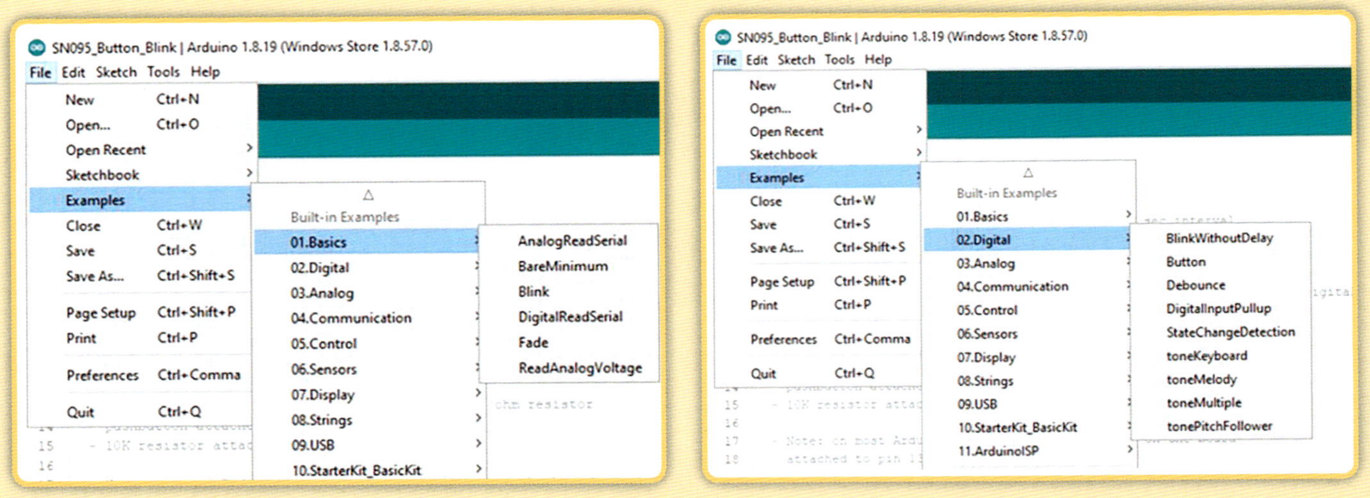

5 Blink (left) and Button (right) codes can be found under the Examples tab under Files.

R3, because most of the examples in this book and on the internet are geared toward and work well on this version.

Setting up Blink with switch input

Blink is a very good test program to ensure an Arduino is working. It can be used to adjust the flashing rate of the onboard LED. It's a good tool to ensure that you are communicating with and can program the Arduino. We adjust the blink rate in the code, upload it to ensure an Arduino is working, and see that the serial cable works to program the Arduino.

For this example, we'll modify Blink with a code called Button. Both of these example codes are included in the Arduino IDE examples section. Button sets up a pushbutton to tell the Arduino to do something.

This code uses a pushbutton to start the onboard LED blinking. When the button is released, the LED stops blinking.

See **5** to locate Blink, which is in the Basics tab of the Arduino website, and Button, which is in the Digital tab. When you click on the link it opens a new a window with that code ready to be modified.

The accompanying code (see page 11) is a combination of Button and Blink. The board is wired as in **6**, with the pushbutton wired between digital pin No. 2 and ground. When the

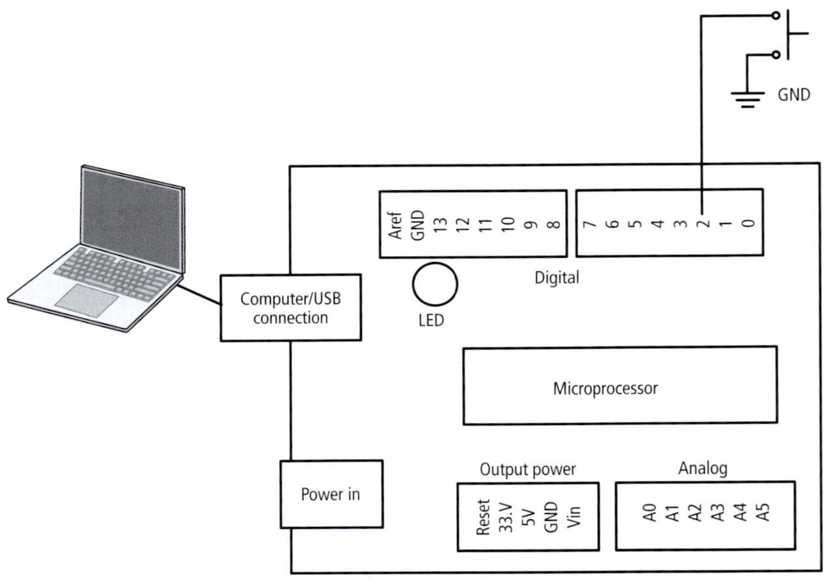

6 To run the accompanying SN095 code, wire a normally open pushbutton to the Arduino as shown between digital pin No. 2 and ground.

normally open button is pushed, the onboard LED blinks; it stops when the button is released.

In the code, note that any wording between /* and */ is a comment to help explain the code, but is not part of the code itself and can be deleted. Also, lines of code that start with // are also comments; they help explain that part of the code but can be deleted.

One other modification from the original Button code is using the internal pullup resistor. This ensures the state of the pin, and the code knows when the button is pushed that represents a digital 0. Otherwise we would need to add an external resistor.

Arduino code at first looks a bit complex, but after you've set up a few simple systems you'll start to understand the setup and loop segments. Much of the code used in Arduino model railroad projects follow the basic steps of the code SN095 (opposite page). This is a good sketch to practice on to develop this understanding of the flow.

CODE FOR BUTTON/BLINK TEST (SN095)

```
/*
  SN095 Code Modified by Paul Bradt
  Modification combines the Button with Blink code
    Description of Blink turns LED on and off with 1 sec interval
    Description of Button Code below:
  Button Code Turns on and off the on-Board light emitting diode (LED) connected to digital pin 13,
  when pressing a pushbutton attached to pin 2.
  The circuit:
  - If using a separate LED needs to be attached from pin 13 to ground through 220 ohm resistor
  - pushbutton attached to pin 2 from +5V
  - Using PULLUP INPUT on Pin 2 so do not need resistor for pushbutton
  - Note: on most Arduinos there is already an LED on the board
    attached to pin 13.
  Button code created 2005
  Original button code by DojoDave <http://www.0j0.org>
  modified 30 Aug 2011
  by Tom Igoe
  This example button code is in the public domain.
  https://www.arduino.cc/en/Tutorial/BuiltInExamples/Button
*/
// constants won't change. They're used here to set pin numbers:
      const int buttonPin = 2;      // the number of the pushbutton pin
      const int ledPin =  13;       // the number of the LED pin, 13 is the built in LED on an UNC R3

// variables will change:
      int buttonState = 0;          // variable for reading the pushbutton status
void setup() {
  // initialize the LED pin as an output:
       pinMode(ledPin, OUTPUT);
  // initialize the pushbutton pin as an input:
       pinMode(buttonPin, INPUT_PULLUP); //Using internal resistor to pullup voltage
}
void loop() {
  // read the state of the pushbutton value:
         buttonState = digitalRead(buttonPin);
  // check if the pushbutton is pressed. If it is, the buttonState is LOW:
             if (buttonState == LOW) {
    // This is the code portion from Blink and blinks the LED every second while button is pushed
           digitalWrite(ledPin, HIGH);
           delay(1000);
           digitalWrite(ledPin, LOW);
           delay(1000);
  } else {
    // turn LED on:
           digitalWrite(ledPin, LOW);
  }
}
```

Other basic nomenclature and commands

One of the most common commands is the Delay, (). It stops Arduino from doing anything for the amount of time in milliseconds within the parentheses. Other commands include:

Print: Prints some info to a port.

Println: Normally used in printing data to the serial port when the next character or data point needs to be on the next line.

digitalWrite: Sends either a high or low to a port when defined conditions are met.

Serial baud rate: Establishes the communication port between the Arduino and the computer; for most Arduinos the speed is 9600.

OUTPUT: Configures an Arduino port for output to a device

INPUT: Configures an Arduino port for input from a device

Arduino code has its own nomenclature and symbols used in diagrams and drawings to indicate certain critical commands. We've already looked at symbols indicating a section of code or lines to ignore. Here is that info again with other common examples:

// Comment nonfunctional lines of code

/* Start of long nonfunctional lines of code on multiple lines, with */ at the end

{ } loop of code

; End of line of code

The following are logic command symbols (there are extra spaces needed to make these commands work):

Greater than: >

Less than: <

Equal: =

AND: &&

OR: ||

JMRI and C/MRI

The Java Model Railroad Interface (JMRI, jmri.org) is open-source, free software that allows many types of control on a model railroad. The first release of JMRI occurred in 2002, and it has evolved into a powerful tool. This book will provide some tips on how to use some of the key components of JMRI. Basically, JMRI provides a computer-controlled interface. The software has two main modules: the popular DecoderPro — which is not covered here — allows users to program and configure decoders.

The JMRI module we're concerned with is PanelPro, which allows users to set up several different custom layout interface systems including dispatching, signal, and turnout control. The final goal for many modelers is to use JMRI to set up a computer interface screen that simulates a Union Switch & Signal Centralized Traffic Control (CTC) panel in the PanelPro module. Along with the JMRI website, the JMRI user group provides a useful forum (groups.io/g/jmriusers).

We'll be looking at doing this starting in Chapters 5 and 6, and there are example videos online that show how to set up occupancy detection as well as signal and turnout control. JMRI capabilities enable users to run just about any feature or control associated with a model railroad. Especially for large, modern layouts, JMRI is a powerful tool.

The Computer Model Railroad Interface (C/MRI) is a system developed by Bruce Chubb around 1985. It uses a serial interface to connect various devices to a computer. The original intent was to control signals automatically, and we'll be using it later in this book to provide the base code to run on an Arduino as a C/MRI node that communicates with JMRI. There's also an online user group for C/MRI (groups.io/g/CMRI-Users).

PROGRAMMING TIPS AND HINTS

1. Each Arduino attaches to a specific com port. The port may have to be changed or selected in the tool tab under "port" to get the IDE to recognize the Arduino when uploading a sketch.
2. If you are pasting code into the IDE, do not copy it from Microsoft Word or another word processor. First, put it in a text editor such as Notepad, NotePad++, or some other C/C++ IDE editor, and then copy it from there. Important note: Notepad and Notepad++ are not IDE, and we recommend using an IDE for the advanced tools. More advanced word processing programs add additional formatting information that can cause problems with the Arduino.
3. It is a good idea to test all devices with a basic program to be sure they work before moving to a more complex program — in other words, work on the project in phases. Blink is a good test code.
4. If the final code is complex, get each piece of code working before adding more modules. This way, if there's a problem, it will be easier to find the module where the problem is located. A good practice is to put comments in complex code using /* comment */ to isolate and explain different sections of code.
5. We recommend *not* using the "delay command" for long timing events, because it locks the Arduino and prevents it from doing anything else. Instead use the "millis command" that tracks time intervals between events and still allows other actions to occur. The millis code might be a little more complex, but it allows the Arduino to perform other functions simultaneously. Using the delay command for short events, such as a switch debounce, is recommended.
6. A feature built into the Arduino IDE is the "auto-format command." It can be found under the Tools tab or using "alt-T." This command helps identify missing items and also helps organize the code for improved readability.
7. Another key aspect of Arduino coding is the "loop command." There are a few different types, but common ones such as "void loop" and "for command" perform several operations and then repeat them.
8. Check your wiring twice before applying power. It can be difficult to see which port a wire is plugged into when there are multiple wires.
9. It's hard to know what code is already loaded on an Arduino. One easy way to determine what is loaded on an Arduino is saving code with a descriptive name, date, and even time information. This helps programmers who may need to go back to a previous code version. A helpful trick is to put that descriptive name on a piece of tape and stick it on top of the computer port. This helps when working on (or programming) several different Arduinos.
10. An advantage of the Arduino is that once it is programmed, it remembers the code. So, if a power source is plugged into the power battery port, it will operate the Arduino. According to the Arduino website, any power source that can supply 9-12V DC at a minimum of 250mA will work. The 2.1mm plug must have the center pin providing positive voltage and the exterior of the plug the negative terminal. Some power supplies don't deliver enough current or do not provide stable power. If an Arduino is behaving strangely, try a different power supply.
11. Dennis Drury identified a problem with the current version of the IDE. It will see an inconsistency between an unsigned long statement and long statement.
12. Another item identified by Dennis was that the analog pins 6 and 7 on an Arduino Nano are not set up to be designated digital.
13. One lesson learned from copying code from a word processing program into the Arduino IDE is in the use of quotation marks. Most word processors automatically turn these into curved "smart quotes," but Arduino does not like these. Use simple straight quotes instead.

Some of the above information might not make sense to you now, but will become familiar as you gain experience. Another way to gain knowledge is to join an online or local Arduino user or maker group. They often have knowledgeable people who are happy to assist with problems.

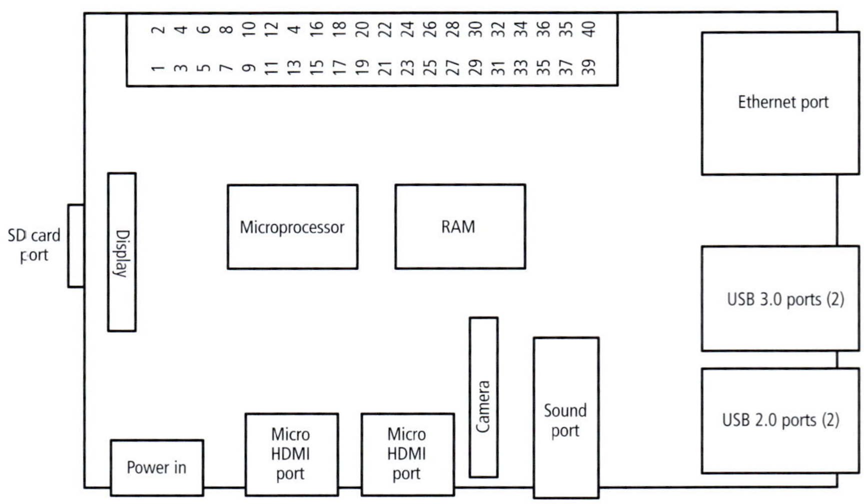

7 The Raspberry Pi 4 (top) resembles an Arduino, but has more computing power. The Pi's basic layout and components are shown in the diagram at right.

Raspberry Pi basics

One of the reasons we chose to use the Raspberry Pi for some projects is its low-cost and the computing power it provides for a permanent computer-based layout interface. The Raspberry Pi 4 is a powerful minicomputer, **7**. It comes with a lot of features, like any other modern computer. It is an experimental/hobbyist device; the original version was developed around 2011 in the United Kingdom to teach programming. For its low cost, however, it has many capabilities and allows users to configure it in many ways. There are several models on the market. For some of the later projects we used a version called the Raspberry Pi 400 — this version is a Raspberry Pi 4 integrated into a keyboard, and in **8** is shown running JMRI.

Once the Raspberry Pi 4 is up and running, it operates just like a normal personal computer. It has a Graphical User Interface (GUI) similar to other computers. This enables you to open programs or access files with the click of a mouse. The Raspberry Pi 4 uses a Debian-based Linux operating system (OS) called Raspberry Pi OS (also

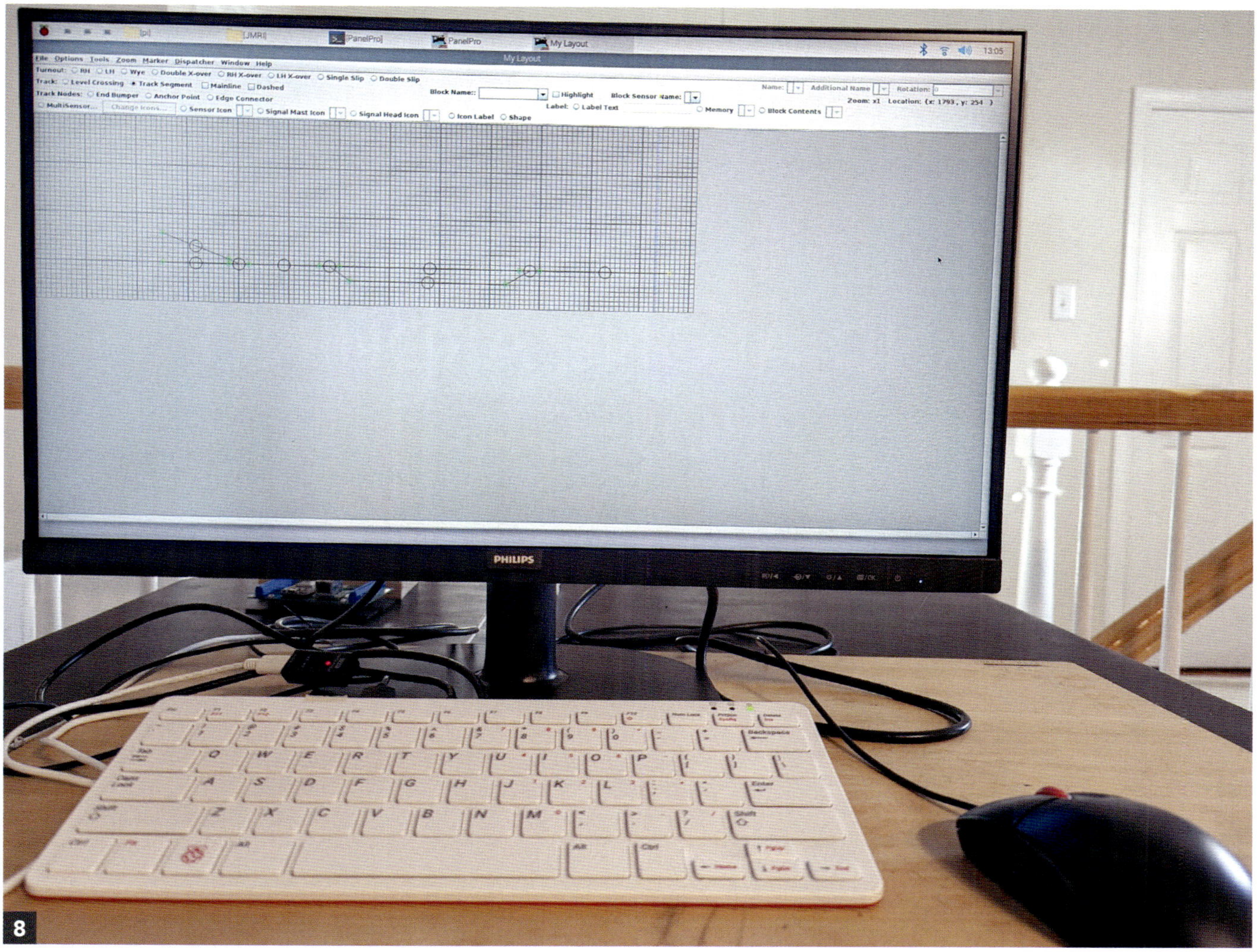

8

This Raspberry Pi 400 is connected to a monitor and keyboard; it's running JMRI (Java Model Railroad Interface).

known as Raspbian) which makes the experience very familiar to those who use either Windows OS or Apple OS.

The Raspberry Pi 4 has a 1.5 GHz, 64-bit Quad core CPU, options of 2, 4, or 8 GB of RAM, an integrated wireless connection, 4 USB ports, an Ethernet port, and 2 micro-HDMI connections. It is a truly powerful device — you can usually find the 4GB versions for around $70.

Here are the general steps to set up the Pi:

1. Insert the SD card.
2. Plug in the monitor.
3. Plug in the keyboard.
4. Plug in the mouse.
5. Start the system.

We've learned a few lessons in setting up Raspberry Pi. A key difference between the Pi and the Arduino is power-supply voltage. The Raspberry Pi uses 5V DC compared to the Arduino's 9-12V. It is critical to use the correct power supply meant for a Raspberry Pi.

The Raspberry Pi may come with an SD card with a pre-installed operating system. However, you can also download the operating system and install it on your own SD card. When formatting an SD card for the Raspberry Pi OS, run the Guiformat program to create an exFAT (also known as 32-bit FAT) SD card and leave all options at default (this website has some helpful info: www.raspberrypi.org/documentation/installation/sdxc_formatting.md).

An excellent way to set up a Raspberry Pi as a JMRI work station was created by Steve Todd. He has set up a download that when installed on an SD memory card per the directions on the site sets up a Raspberry Pi OS with JMRI ready to run! You can find it at mstevetodd.com/rpi.

As of 2024, the Raspberry Pi 5 had just been released. Although we haven't tested any of the projects on a Pi 5, we believe they should work in a similar fashion on this new powerful version.

CHAPTER TWO

STAND-ALONE ARDUINO PROJECTS

To get you into the feel for creating Arduino projects, we've designed a couple of basic stand-alone projects that can simply be installed on a new or existing model railroad without much planning. These don't connect with other major systems (such as control), but they provide a specific animation or activity.

PROJECT 1: Simple signal automation

Signal automation materials list

- 3-color signal, 12V bulbs, Model Power (No. 1677-1)
- 2-color signal, LED, Oregon Rail Supply (No. 114)
- Arduino
- Momentary contact pushbutton switch
- 12V DC power supply for Arduino

1 This Arduino is mounted to the side of the layout. It could also be located under the layout.

2 This three-light signal (using 12V bulbs) is located on one side of the small layout.

3 The two-light LED signal is mounted on the opposite side of the layout from the three-light signal.

This is one of the first projects we implemented on a model railroad back around 2015, and it's still working well after 10 years of service. It simulates the working of an Automatic Block Signal (ABS) system by controlling the color aspect of two signals, **1**, **2**, and **3**. The code is very similar to SN095 in the previous chapter.

A pushbutton activates one 3-color signal, changing it from green to red to yellow and then back to green, along with a 2-color signal on another part of the layout changing from green to red and back to green. The delay command pauses the cycle long enough for a train running at a normal speed to move far enough down the track. One signal is on one side of the small HO oval layout and the second signal is on the opposite side of the layout. As a train passes the 3-light signal, the button is pressed — this starts the sequence of transitioning the signals to match the train's movement as it goes around the loop.

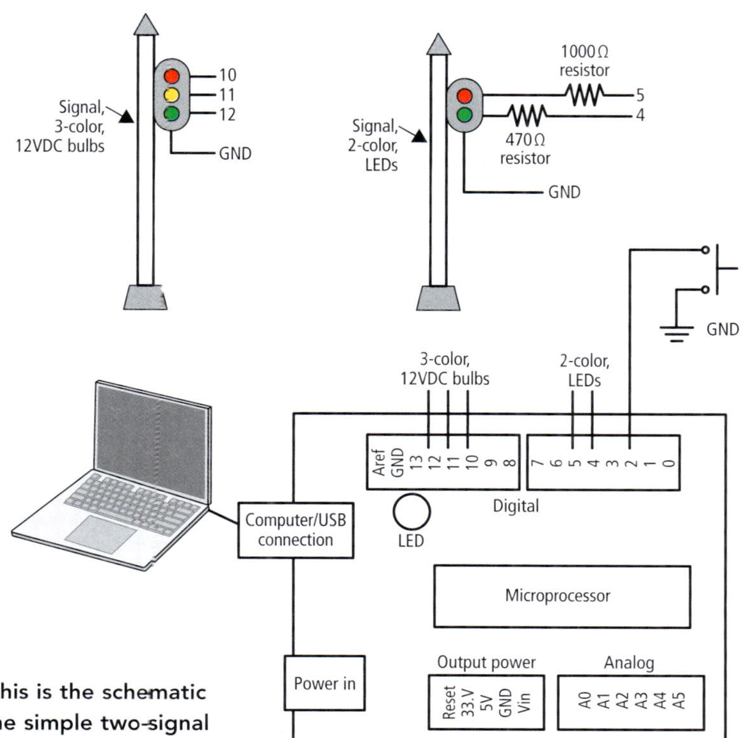

4 This is the schematic for the simple two-signal automation circuit.

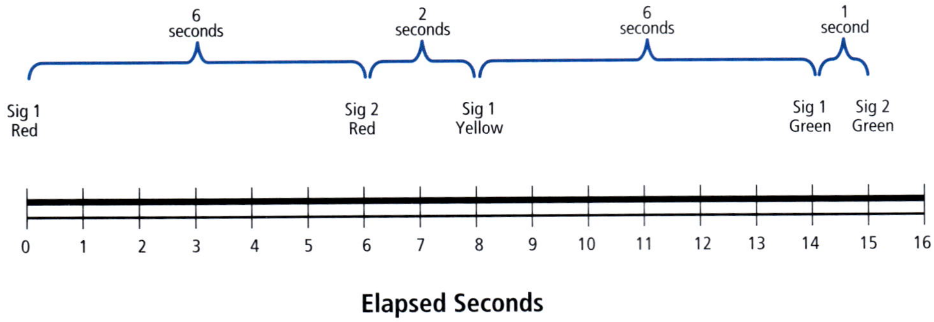

5 This timeline shows the activation sequence of each light in both signals.

CODE FOR BASIC 3-COLOR SIGNAL (SN110)

```
//SN110 Simple Railroad signal automation
/*
  Modified from Blink and DigitalPullup Example code by Paul Bradt
  Turns on a system of five light bulbs or LEDs using a switch
  and then sequences to the next bulb ultimately cycling back to
  first bulb. This can simulate a model railroad signal sequence.
  */
// The setup function runs once when you press reset or power the board
void setup() {
  /* initialize digital pins 4, 5, 10, 11, and 12 as outputs. 2 as input pullup pin.
Input as Pullup does not require external resistor but reverses the logic.   */
  pinMode(4, OUTPUT);   //Green Sig2
  pinMode(5, OUTPUT);   //Red Sig 2
  pinMode(10, OUTPUT); //Red Sig1
  pinMode(11, OUTPUT); //Yellow Sig1
  pinMode(12, OUTPUT); //Green Sig1
  pinMode(2, INPUT_PULLUP);
}
/* The loop function runs forever waiting
for an input from switch
 */
void loop() {
  if(digitalRead(2) == LOW){
    lightSignal1();
  }
}
//This loop cycles when switch pushed turning the lights off in sequence
void lightSignal1(){
    digitalWrite(12, LOW); //Green Sig1
    digitalWrite(10, HIGH); //Red Sig1
    delay(6000);  //Delay 6 seconds
    digitalWrite(4, LOW); //Green Sig2
    digitalWrite(5, HIGH); //Red sig2
    delay(2000); //Delay 2 seconds
    digitalWrite(10, LOW); //Red Sig1
    digitalWrite(11, HIGH); //Yellow Sig1
```

```
    delay(6000); //Delay 6 seconds
    digitalWrite(11, LOW); //Yellow Sig1
    digitalWrite(12, HIGH); //Green Sig1
    delay(1000); //Delay 1 Second
    digitalWrite(5, LOW); //Red Sig2
    digitalWrite(4, HIGH); //Green sig2
}
```

Although this is a simple project and only simulates block control of signals, it works very well and provides animation. It can be used on a small loop layout as we did, or could be used on a large layout — perhaps installed where trains leave a town on a long main line. Our installation has been very rewarding, and has been especially popular with the grandkids as they love to push the button and make sure a train stops before it goes past the red light.

The Arduino was mounted on the side of the layout in a small plexiglass housing. The signal wires were connected to the Arduino, along with a pushbutton per the schematic in **4**.

The diagram in **5** shows the sequence of events and the elapsed time along with the time between events. The elapsed time is needed to develop the flow of events and set up the segments of time between events for the Arduino code.

This is a relatively basic set of code and uses the delay command to start and stop events. It works well to simulate what would be a triggered set of events.

LESSONS LEARNED

We initially developed this code on a computer that later no longer functioned. We hadn't saved the code, so to write this we had to redevelop the code including the timing aspects of the light sequence. Learn from us by saving all code on a portable drive or other backup device.

A very helpful trick is to put a descriptive name of the code on a piece of tape, and stick it on top of the computer port of the Arduino. This way you can tell what code is on the Arduino.

This is a prototype three-light block signal similar to the model in the basic signal project. *Gordon Odegard*

This is a prototype three-head searchlight signal at an interlocking. *Jim Hediger*

PROJECT 2: Simple stand-alone crossing signal with sound

This project demonstrates some of the unique capabilities of the Arduino, expanding beyond the use of controlling lights. It brings in a piezo buzzer device to simulate the warning bells, plus two flashing signals at a railroad crossing. This is a nice stand-alone animation, **6**. The system is automatic and self-contained, as the triggering devices are two infrared (IR) sensor boards.

To simulate the crossing-bell sound, we decided against a conventional sound board (it would have been cost-prohibitive to install at several crossings). Instead, we decided to try a piezo buzzer — available for under $1 —driven by the Arduino tone command. We were very pleased with the resulting warning-bell sound from the piezo buzzer.

Another important aspect of this project is the concept of developing part of it, getting it working, then adding the next part. For complex projects, this phased approach is a good choice to ensure success. This project was completed in three different phases. It also illustrates how sometimes the original plan may not quite work out as expected, with the phased approach helping revise and develop a good final solution.

The first phase was to develop the piezo buzzer tone and frequency, along with determining how the blinking LEDs would be synchronized with the piezo buzzer warning bell.

The second phase was adding the infrared sensors, which detect a train approaching the crossing from either direction. The sensors control the warning bell along with the blinking LEDs.

The final phase was wiring the actual crossing signals and installing them on a small extension module of an HO layout.

Using LEDs, the following circuit and code (see page 21) was tested and worked very well. The piezo buzzer isn't overly loud, so it will not overwhelm the layout. You can find details on setting up the piezo buzzer to produce sound here (www.programmingelectronics.com/an-easy-way-to-make-noise-with-arduino-using-tone/).

We started by making sure the piezo buzzer worked, then configuring the tone and frequency to make it sound like a bell. We didn't have on hand a 100-ohm resistor as recommended by the website, so we substituted a 220-ohm resistor. After adjusting the parameters in the tone code an acceptable bell-like emulation was achieved. The two pairs of red LEDs alternately blink and stay in time with the sound. This could have been a problem with a conventional sound board due to timing differences between the Arduino and sound board.

The schematic in **7** shows how we built up the phase 1 prototype to test the sound on the piezo buzzer. One lesson learned when setting up the buzzer was that to increase its volume, it really needs to be attached to wood or another solid surface.

Crossing signal materials list

- Railroad crossing flashers, Walthers 2-Pack (No. 949-4333)
- Piezo buzzer (available online from several sources)
- Infrared (IR) sensor boards (2); many are available — we used Gikfun Obstacle avoidance IR Infrared Sensor Module Reflective Photoelectric Light Intensity DIY Kit for Arduino UNO (Pack of 5), No. EK1254x5
- Arduino Uno
- Miscellaneous: resistors, wires, terminal strips

Here's the completed crossing, with crossbucks and signals mounted on an HO layout. The signals, from Walthers, use red LEDs.

6

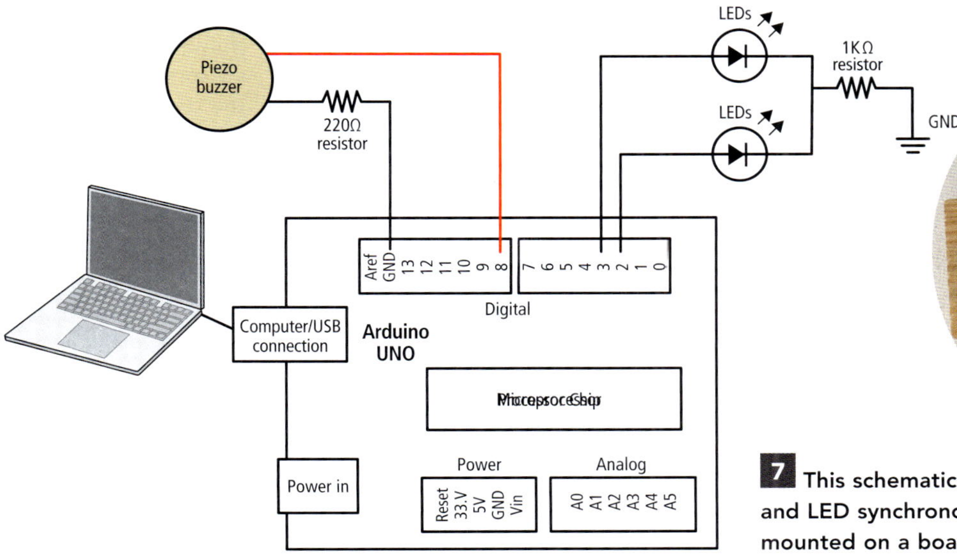

7 This schematic is for the phase 1 Piezo buzzer and LED synchronous test, with the test parts mounted on a board (right).

CODE FOR CROSSING SIGNAL (SN160)

```
//SN160 Phase 1 Crossing Signal Baseline
//Needs input section of code
//A sketch //using tone() function
//Code from
//https://www.programmingelectronics.com/an-easy-way-to-make-noise-with-arduino-using-tone/
//Specify digital pin on the Arduino that the positive lead of piezo buzzer is attached.
int piezoPin = 8;
#define LED_1 1
#define LED_2 2
void setup() {
  pinMode(LED_1, OUTPUT); //Red LED 1
  pinMode(LED_2, OUTPUT); //Red LED 2
}//close setup
void loop() {
  /*Tone needs 2 arguments, but can take three
    1) Pin#
    2) Frequency - this is in hertz (cycles per second) which determines the pitch of the noise
made
    3) Duration - how long the tone plays
  */
    digitalWrite(LED_1, HIGH);
  digitalWrite(LED_2, LOW);
    delay(200);      // wait for a .2 second
  digitalWrite(LED_1, LOW);
  digitalWrite(LED_2, HIGH);
    // Section of code that simulates the crossing bell
  tone(piezoPin, 1000, 100);
    delay(200); //wait for 0.2 second then start again
}
```

8 **The IR sensors have been added to a protoboard on a wood board below the phase 1 board.**

9 **This schematic shows how the IR sensors are wired to the Uno.**

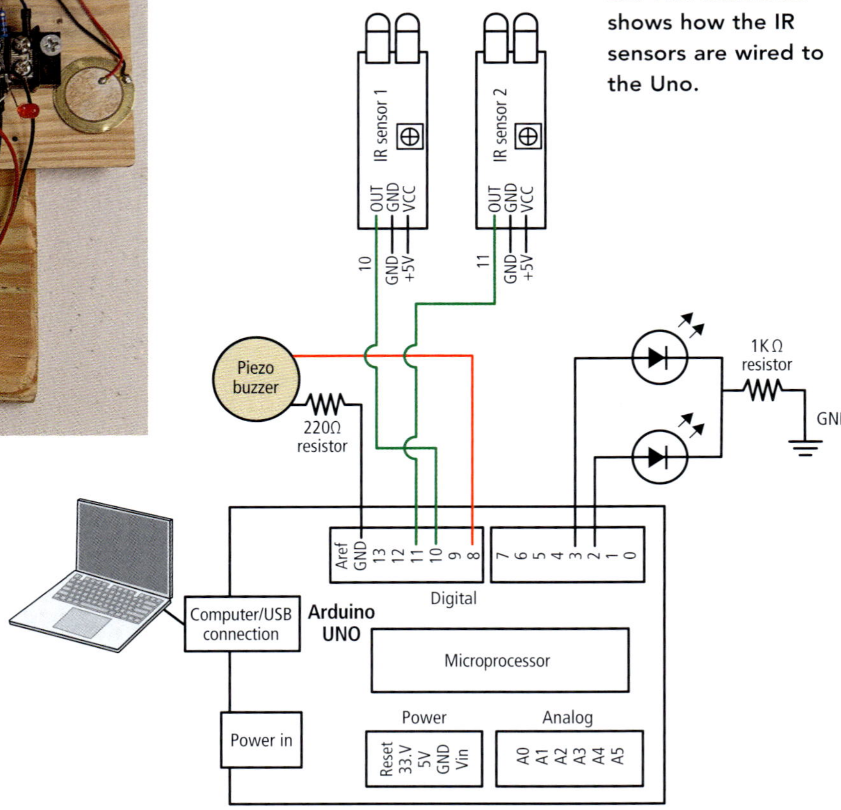

The next phase is adding the IR sensors, **8**. They were inserted into a protoboard attached to another piece of wood connected to the phase 1 version (they will be located between the rails upon final installation). After wire connections were made to the Arduino, the phase 2 version of this project, **9**, was ready for code (below).

CODE THAT INCORPORATES THE TWO INFRARED SENSORS (SN165)

```
/*
  SN165 Phase 2 Two Switch input along blinking LEDs and Piezo sound generation with tone
  Modified by Paul and David Bradt
  Part of this code is based on this example code is in the public domain.

  https://www.arduino.cc/en/Tutorial/BuiltInExamples/StateChangeDetection
*/
// this constant won't change:
const int intTrack10 = 10;   //IR Sensor 10
const int intTrack11 = 11;   //IR sensor 11
int piezoPin = 8; //Setting up peizo transducer to make sound
// Variables will change:
int sensorVal_10 = 0;   // counter for the number of button presses
int sensorVal_11 = 0;   // current state of the button
void setup() {
  //configure pin 0 and 1 as an input and enable the internal pull-up resistor
  //configure the LED outputs
  pinMode(intTrack10, INPUT_PULLUP); //IR sensor Track10
  pinMode(intTrack11, INPUT_PULLUP); //IR sensor Track10
  pinMode(2, OUTPUT);//Red LED2
  pinMode(3, OUTPUT);//Red LED3
  Serial.begin(9600);
}
```

```
void loop() {
    digitalWrite(1, LOW); //Red2
    digitalWrite(0, LOW); //Red3
   sensorVal_10 = digitalRead(intTrack10);
   sensorVal_11 = digitalRead(intTrack11);
   //print out the value of the pushbutton
   Serial.print("Track 10 value: ");
   Serial.println(sensorVal_10);
   delay(50);
   Serial.print("Track 11 value: ");
   Serial.println(sensorVal_11);
   delay(50);
   // Keep in mind the pull-up means the pushbutton's logic is inverted. It goes
   // HIGH when it's open, and LOW when it's pressed.
  if (sensorVal_10 == LOW || sensorVal_11 == LOW){
     digitalWrite(2, LOW);  //Red2
     digitalWrite(3, HIGH); //Red3
delay (200);
     digitalWrite(2, HIGH); //Red2
     digitalWrite(3, LOW);  //Red3
// Section of code that simulates the crossing bell
   tone(piezoPin, 1000, 100);
delay (200); //Pause then start again
  }   else{
     digitalWrite(2, LOW); //Red2
     digitalWrite(3, LOW); //Red3
   }
}
```

Building this project in phases was helpful. When we started on phase 3 we knew the circuit and code worked well. However, we ran into two issues that needed to be resolved. The first was the location of the Arduino (under the layout, on the fascia, or inside a structure atop the layout). We chose to house the Arduino inside a building, which allowed the piezo buzzer to be as close as possible to the actual crossing and not under the table where the sound might be very muted.

The second item was a major issue. When we started testing the actual signals with the circuit, we discovered we'd wired the circuit to the LEDs with common ground (negative), but the signals were common positive. In other words, the common wire between the LEDs was not the negative but the positive connection. We needed to move the resistors from the negative or ground to the ports that were used to turn the LEDs on or off. The code

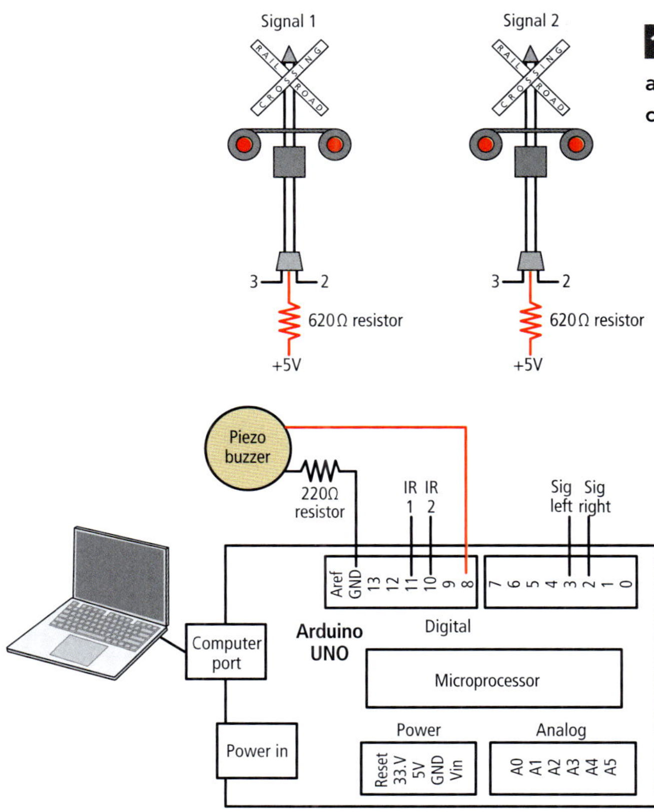

10 **Phase 3 is the addition of the crossing signals.**

also needed to be modified so that the resting state of the ports to the LED signals was high and not low.

In this case we were initially confused on how to do this, but a site showed how we could reverse the connections and the crossing signal would still work by using the digital pins as a ground or negative connection (arduino.stackexchange.com/questions/51108/how-to-use-digital-pin-as-ground#:~:text=If%20some%20of%20your%20devices,Arduino%20pin%20driver%20can%20sink).

Figure **10** shows the final schematic implementing the common positive or anode version.

You can see the Arduino and piezo buzzer located inside the freight station in **11**, and **12** shows the connections underneath the table, the 3D printed resistor terminal block, and the 3D printed wire passthroughs.

CODE WITH OUTPUTS OPPOSITE FOR COMMON POSITIVE CROSSING SIGNAL LIGHTS (SN166)

```
/*
  SN166 Phase 3 Two Switch input along blinking LEDs and Piezo sound generation with tone
This version Swapped HIGH and LOW on Outputs for LEDs for common positive signals
  Modified by Paul and David Bradt
  Part of this code is based on this example code is in the public domain.
  https://www.arduino.cc/en/Tutorial/BuiltInExamples/StateChangeDetection
*/
// this constant won't change:
const int intTrack10 = 10;  //IR Sensor 10
const int intTrack11 = 11;  //IR sensor 11
int piezoPin = 8; //Setting up peizo transducer to make sound
// Variables will change:
int sensorVal_10 = 0;  // counter for the number of button presses
int sensorVal_11 = 0;  // current state of the button
void setup() {
  //configure pin 0 and 1 as an input and enable the internal pull-up resistor
  //configure the LED outputs
  pinMode(intTrack10, INPUT_PULLUP); //IR sensor Track10
  pinMode(intTrack11, INPUT_PULLUP); //IR sensor Track11
  pinMode(2, OUTPUT);//Red LED2
  pinMode(3, OUTPUT);//Red LED3
  Serial.begin(9600);
}
void loop() {
   digitalWrite(1, LOW); // Red2
   digitalWrite(0, LOW); //Red3
  sensorVal_10 = digitalRead(intTrack10);
  sensorVal_11 = digitalRead(intTrack11);
  //print out the value of the pushbutton
  Serial.print("Track 10 value: ");
  Serial.println(sensorVal_10);
  delay(50);
  Serial.print("Track 11 value: ");
  Serial.println(sensorVal_11);
  delay(50);
  // Keep in mind the pull-up means the pushbutton's logic is inverted. It goes
  // HIGH when it's open, and LOW when it's pressed.
 if (sensorVal_10 == LOW || sensorVal_11 == LOW){
    digitalWrite(2, LOW);  //Red2
    digitalWrite(3, HIGH); //Red3
delay (300); //300 msec between LED flashes
    digitalWrite(2, HIGH); //Red2
    digitalWrite(3, LOW);  //Red3
```

```
// Section of code that simulates the crossing bell
  tone(piezoPin, 1000, 100);
delay (300); //Pause then start again after 300 msec
 }   else{
    digitalWrite(2, HIGH);   // Red2
    digitalWrite(3, HIGH);   //Red3
  }
}
```

11

We placed the crossing circuit and buzzer inside an adjacent freight station.

12

The resistors and terminal strip are located under the layout.

LESSONS LEARNED

As shown here, phased construction of more complex Arduino projects may improve success because as each problem arises you can troubleshoot and solve it and then move on to the next step knowing you have a working system. If the complete system is put together at the start, you may encounter multiple problems without many clues in tracing the issues. Phased construction allowed us to get the piezo buzzer working in phase 1, then the infrared sensors in phase 2, and finally the installation and correction needed for the actual crossing signals in phase 3.

We found when installing the IR sensors in a hole between the rails that there are reflections of the sending LED light bouncing back and hitting the sensing LED. We fixed it by placing a small piece of plastic between the LEDs as shown. The top IR sensor has a piece of plastic and the bottom one does not.

This turned out to be a very easy and relatively inexpensive project to set up. This is a real benefit if you need several crossing signals on your layout.

PROJECT 3: Stand-alone train station animated fast clock

Station clock materials list

- SparkFun MicroView — OLED Arduino module
- SparkFun MicroView — USB programmer
- USB to USB cable
- SN150 Fast Clock (which is slightly modified code for MicroView — OLED Arduino)

The next stand-alone project simulates an analog fast clock using an organic light-emitting diode (OLED) display integrated with an Arduino device. It looks very modern but we really wanted to use this unique Arduino.

We used a MicroView OLED, **13**, and because it is an integration of a display and an Arduino, it provides a creative way to install a fast clock on a model railroad. The original code turns this combination Arduino and display into an analog clock. We decided that this would be an easy way to add a clock to a modern train station.

To program the MicroView it must be plugged into a Sparkfun USB interface device, but once programmed it just needs the supply voltage and ground connections to operate. This website shows how to hook up this device: learn.sparkfun.com/tutorials/microview-hookup-guide/quick-start-tutorials. We kept the protective film on the screen until it was installed in the final location.

One of the neat things about this module is that it's a non-standard Arduino Uno with a built-in display module. Sparkfun's website has an analog clock program that would look very nice as a railroad station clock. We modified the code slightly by speeding up the minute and hour hands so that a simulated 10-hour day can pass in about hour.

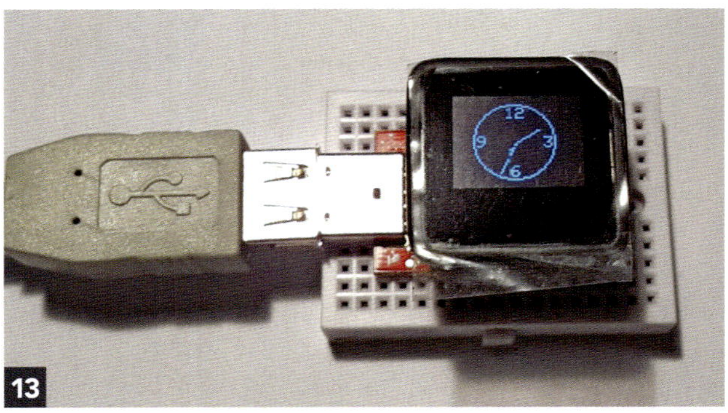

13

The MicroView OLED display/Arduino is set up and running the analog fast-clock program.

We tested a couple of ways to implement the fast clock aspect. Increasing the jump of the second hand worked, but looked very unrealistic, so instead we modified the minute-hand jump. Since it will be on a small railroad, we increased it to a 10-minute jump for every minute. Because the minute-hand fast jump occurs every minute rather than every second, it does not look as unrealistic. If you choose something less than a 10-minute jump, it will not be as noticeable.

The next step was to modify the hour-hand jump to occur at the same time the minute hand reaches the 12. To do this it has to move an hour after 6 minutes, so the minute count is divided by 6. These modifications are in the lines of code below — they're the part that calculate the angle in degrees for the hour and minute hand.

CODE FOR STATION FAST CLOCK (SN150)

```
//SN150 Rev C fast clock Modified by Paul and David Bradt
//Modification 10 times faster on minute hand
//Modification to the hour hand by divide minute calculation by 6
//Define beginning of Railroad workday
//Added in Serial Port display
/**************************************************************
MicroView_Analog_Clock.ino
SFE_LSM9DS0 Library Simple Example Code
Jim Lindblom @ SparkFun Electronics
Original Creation Date: February 28, 2015
https://github.com/sparkfun/MicroView/tree/master/Libraries
Turn your MicroView into an analog clock!
This sketch requires the Arduino time library. Get it from
here: http://playground.arduino.cc/Code/Time
Development environment specifics:
   IDE: Arduino 1.6.0
   Hardware Platform: MicroView
This code is beerware. If you see me (or any other SparkFun
employee) at the local, and you've found our code helpful, please
buy us a round!
```

```
Distributed as-is; no warranty is given.
**************************************************************/
#include <MicroView.h>
#include <Time.h>
#include <TimeLib.h>
// Define how big the clock is. Don't make it larger than 23
// This is the radius of the clock:
#define CLOCK_SIZE 23
// Use these to set the clock's begin time at 7:00 AM
//Begining of the day for your Railroad
#define HOUR 7
#define MINUTE 0
#define SECOND 00
#define DAY 28
#define MONTH 4
#define YEAR 2021
const uint8_t maxW = uView.getLCDWidth();
const uint8_t midW = maxW/2;
const uint8_t maxH = uView.getLCDHeight();
const uint8_t midH = maxH/2;
void setup(){
  Serial.begin(9600);
  // Set the time in the time library:
  setTime(HOUR, MINUTE, SECOND, DAY, MONTH, YEAR);

  uView.begin();     // set up the MicroView
  uView.clear(PAGE);// erase hardware memory inside the OLED
  uView.display();  // display the content in the buffer
  // Draw clock face (circle outline & text):
  drawFace();
}
void loop(){
  drawTime();
}
//Keep track of time and math to draw hours/minute/second arms and the clock itself
void drawTime(){
  static boolean firstDraw = false;
  static unsigned long mSec = (millis() + 1000);
  static float degresshour, fasthour, degressmin, fastminute, degresssec,
              hourx, houry, minx, miny, secx, secy;
  // If mSec
  if (mSec != (unsigned long)second()){
    // First time draw requires extra line to set up XOR's:
    if (firstDraw){
      uView.line(midW, midH, 32 + hourx, 24 + houry, WHITE, XOR);
      uView.line(midW, midH, 32 + minx, 24 + miny, WHITE, XOR);
      uView.line(midW, midH, 32 + secx, 24 + secy, WHITE, XOR);
    }
    // Calculate hour hand degrees (Modified for Fast Clock):
    degresshour = ((((hour() + fasthour) * 360) / 12) + 270) * (PI / 180);
    fasthour = (hour() - HOUR + minute()/6);
    // Calculate minute hand degrees Modified for Fast Clock):
    degressmin = (((minute() * 3600) / 60) + 270) * (PI / 180);
    //3600 is 10 times on minute hand
    fastminute = (minute() *10);
    // Calculate second hand degrees:
```

```
    degresssec = (((second() * 360) / 60) + 270) * (PI / 180);
    int accelerated_minute = minute() * 10;
    Serial.print("The accelerated clock time is ");
    Serial.print(fasthour);
    Serial.print(":");
    Serial.print(fastminute);
    Serial.print(":");
    Serial.print(second());
    Serial.println();
    // Calculate x,y coordinates of hour hand:
    hourx = cos(degresshour) * (CLOCK_SIZE / 2.5);
    houry = sin(degresshour) * (CLOCK_SIZE / 2.5);
    // Calculate x,y coordinates of minute hand:
    minx = cos(degressmin) * (CLOCK_SIZE / 1.4);
    miny = sin(degressmin) * (CLOCK_SIZE / 1.4);
    // Calculate x,y coordinates of second hand:
    secx = cos(degresssec) * (CLOCK_SIZE / 1.1);
    secy = sin(degresssec) * (CLOCK_SIZE / 1.1);
    // Draw hands with the line function:
    uView.line(midW, midH, midW+hourx, midH+houry, WHITE, XOR);
    uView.line(midW, midH, midW+minx, midH+miny, WHITE, XOR);
    uView.line(midW, midH, midW+secx, midH+secy, WHITE, XOR);
    // Set firstDraw flag to true, so we don't do it again.
    firstDraw = true;
    // Actually draw the hands with the display() function.
    uView.display();
  }
}
// Draw the clock face. That includes the circle outline and
// the 12, 3, 6, and 9 text.
void drawFace(){
  uView.setFontType(0); // set font type 0 (Smallest)
  uint8_t fontW = uView.getFontWidth();
  uint8_t fontH = uView.getFontHeight();
  //uView.setCursor(27, 0);
  // points cursor to x=27 y=0
  uView.setCursor(midW-fontW-1, midH-CLOCK_SIZE+1);
  uView.print(12);  // Print the "12"
  uView.setCursor(midW-(fontW/2)-1, midH+CLOCK_SIZE-fontH-1);
  uView.print(6);  // Print the "6"
  uView.setCursor(midW-CLOCK_SIZE+1, midH-fontH/2);
  uView.print(9);  // Print the "9"
  uView.setCursor(midW+CLOCK_SIZE-fontW-2, midH-fontH/2);
  uView.print(3);  // Print the "3"
  uView.circle(midW-1, midH-1, CLOCK_SIZE);
  //Draw the clock
  uView.display();
}
```

This is a unique Arduino, and using the code to set it up for a fast clock is the perfect application for this integrated display device. The next section shows how this clock was incorporated into a representation of Denver Union Station using the Walthers N scale Union Station as the starting point/core building block, **14**.

I've always admired the iconic Denver Union Station and decided to create an N scale version by modifying the Walthers Union Station Building, adding a similar version of the unique glowing sign and clock to one side of it. While the model is not an exact match for the building, it resembles it enough for my needs.

14 The digital (simulated analog) fast clock is operating in the upper fascia of an N scale model of Denver Union Station.

15 The light-color areas are the 3D-printed additions to the Denver Union Station front wall.

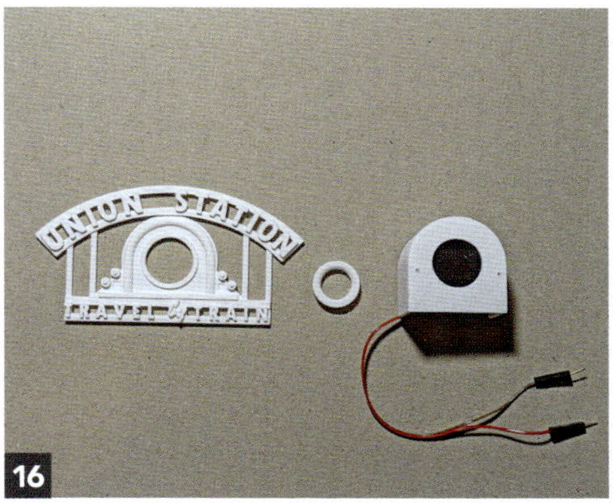

16 This shows how the key parts fit together between the station sign, alignment ring (middle), and the housing for the OLED clock.

17 The clock is retained in the housing by two screws and a piece of styrene.

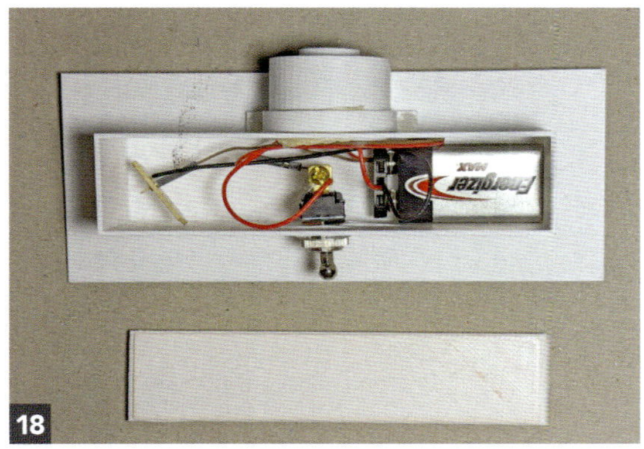

18 The clock and housing are fitted into the roof assembly, along with the battery and switch.

Photo **15** shows the 3D pieces I printed to create the arched window and raised sections of the building. It also shows the clock location at the top of the building. The end sections of the Walthers kit were shortened to better resemble the Denver station. The depth of the station was narrowed due to the foot print limitations on the layout.

You can see the 3D pieces including the sign, alignment disk, and clock housing in **16**, and **17** shows how the clock was retained in the housing.

All that's needed to power the clock is a 9-12V source connected to the positive and ground connections to the SparkFun MicroView. We used a 9V battery for our installation.

Photo **18** shows the upper roof structure, which contains the clock housing, clock, on-off switch, and battery for power.

The clock is installed on the track side of the building, although the prototype station has one on street side too. If you want an installation with a second clock, it could easily be added to the street side with one switch that turns on power to both of them. This should keep them synchronized.

LESSONS LEARNED

The projects in this chapter show off the great capabilities of the Arduino microcontroller as a stand-alone system. These details can easily be added to any layout, and for the most part only need power to help animate a layout with lights, sound, and graphics. They're a great way to get comfortable with Arduino technology and get started with the basics. The next chapters provide examples of integrated systems that can provide several different functions.

CHAPTER THREE

WELDING SHOP WITH LIGHTING AND SOUND

This project ties together an Arduino, sound board, 3D printing, and some kitbashing to create a unique building with simulated welding lighting and sound effects. Many modelers have a specific model that they've always wanted to eventually build. For us, the Pingree Grove (Ill.) machine shop, published in the March 1972 *Model Railroader*, was a "someday" model. Its odd shape is interesting, and although the prototype wasn't rail-served, we figured it would be plausible to model it along a rail siding.

PROJECT: Simulated welder and torch

Pingree Grove machine shop

DESCRIBED AND DRAWN
BY ELMER CERNY

MOST people, when they approach a
railroad crossing, look both ways —
once. I, and probably a lot of other model
railroaders, look both ways twice: once
for trains and the second time for rail-
road interest. I look for buildings that
can be added to my layout, particularly
small to medium-size ones. Sometimes
they are modeled exactly but I'll also
allow the model to be altered slightly.
My limits of freedom in this are:
• I can situate the building in a dif-
ferent but still plausible location.
• I can change the building in time,
making it look newer or older and more
weathered.
• I can change the appearance, but
only to the extent that I could reasonably
change the prototype if I owned it. For
example, I might change the type of
business. I might change the sign and
put up a different name. I could paint
the building a different color, but I
don't allow myself to substitute wood sid-
ing for brick.
I discovered this machine shop build-
ing in a small town about 8 miles west
of Elgin, Ill. It is located about 100 feet
from the Milwaukee Road's line. As I
studied it I considered several points
about it:
• Does this building have interest?

62 Model Railroader

Materials list for lighting effects

» Arduino Nano and plug-in board (screw terminal strips)
» SparkFun Wav Trigger
» Small speaker
» Arduino Uno
» Miscellaneous: wire, terminal strips, momentary-contact DPDT switch, white LED, small 12V bulb

Materials list for structure

Woodland Scenics/DPM:

» 11200 City Cab Co. (walls: 112-2, 112-4, 112-5, 112-6, and 112-7)
» 30106 Dock level freight doors
» 30139 Two-story rectangular windows, 2
» 30111 Two-story blank wall

JTT:

» 97480 Wood roof shingle sheet

1

The Pingree Grove machine shop, originally featured in the March 1972 *Model Railroader*, served as inspiration for this kitbashing project. An Arduino controls interior welding and cutting-torch lighting (visible in the windows above), as well as sound. The effects can be applied to any industrial building.

We wanted animation for this building, so we decided to try to simulate the visual effects of an arc welder and cutting torch using light, combined with sound, using an Arduino and sound board. The resulting flickering lights can be readily seen through the building's windows, **1**. You can, of course, apply these Arduino-based effects to almost any other structure model, even if you don't want to build this exact building. If you're going to do that, you can skip ahead to the section on animation. We'll start by describing how we built our structure.

Building construction

The starting point for this project is the Woodland Scenics (former Design Preservation Models, DPM) City Cab Co. injection-molded kit. It's

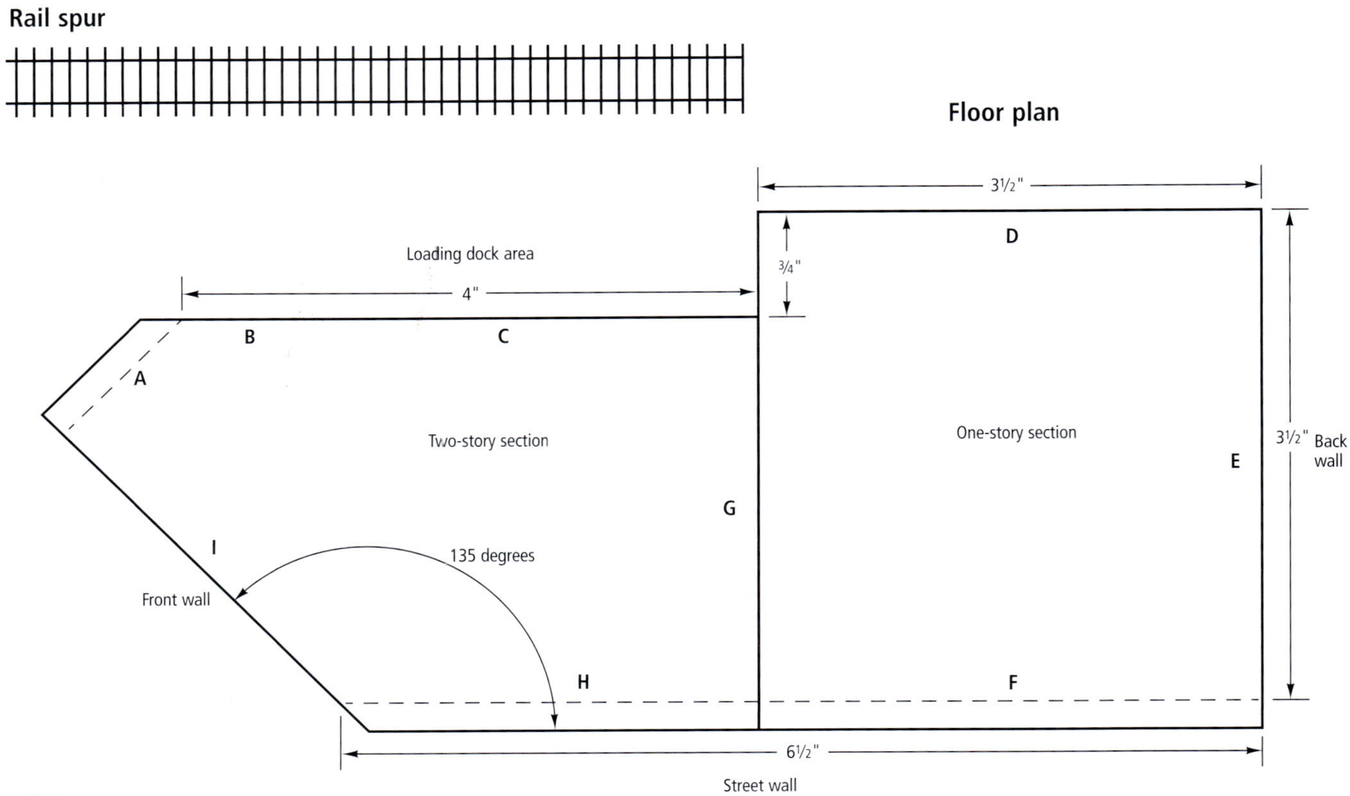

2 The building's floor plan includes basic dimensions and angles. The letters indicate the wall sections; they're keyed to fig. 3. The plan is altered from the original article to allow for using kit parts and to include a loading dock and rail siding.

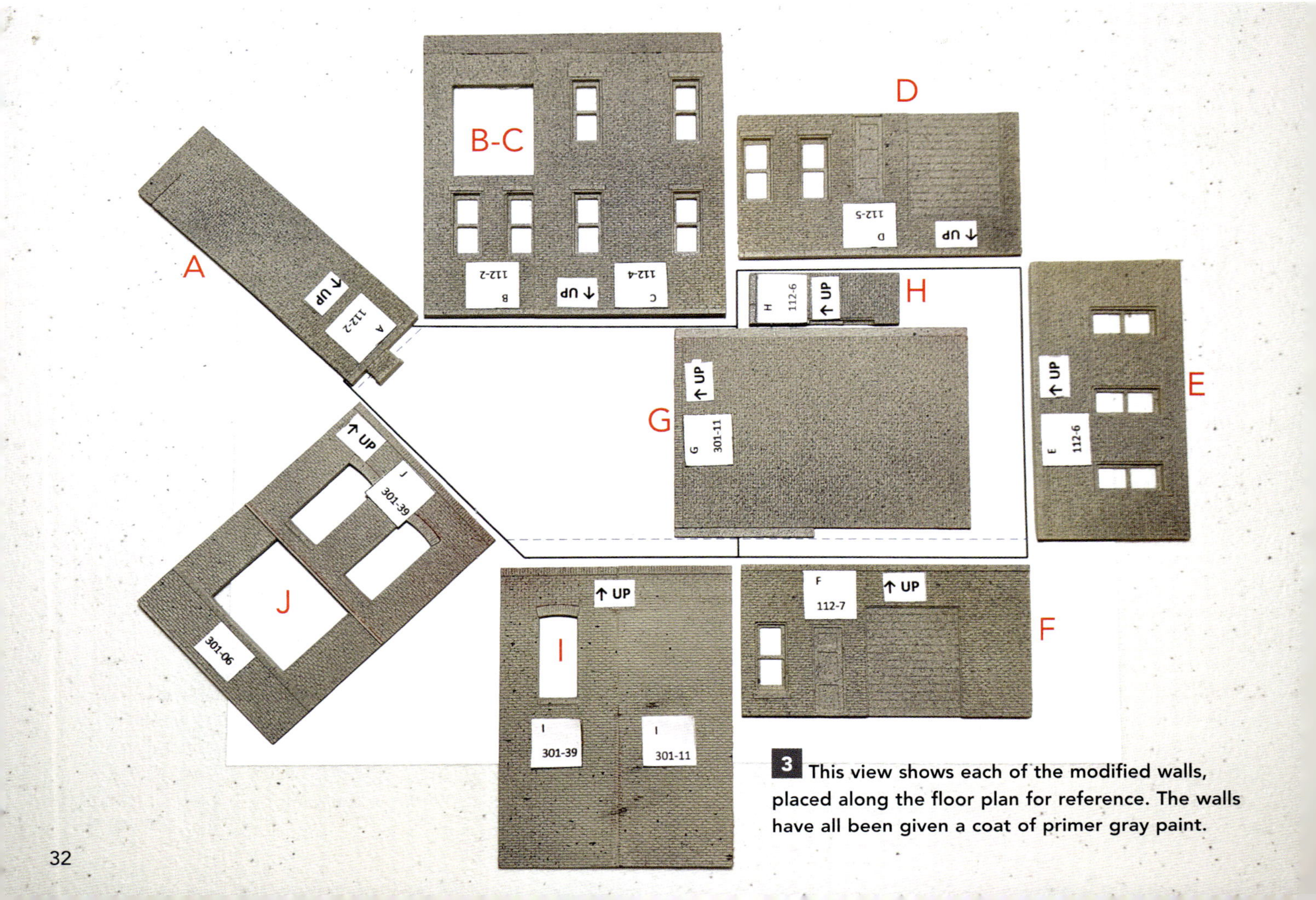

3 This view shows each of the modified walls, placed along the floor plan for reference. The walls have all been given a coat of primer gray paint.

4

On walls B-C and A, add a section of brick at the bottom so their height matches the modular sections.

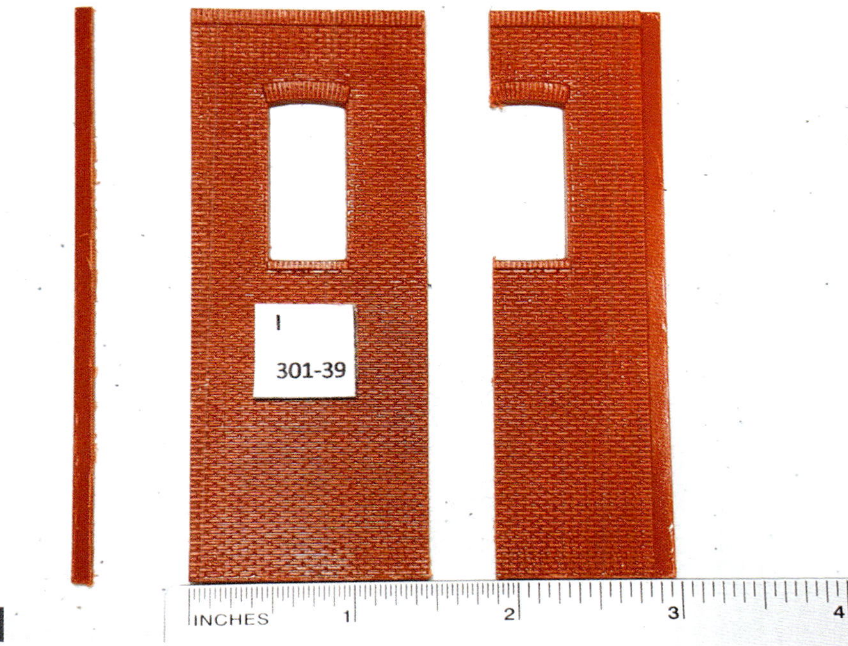

5

Wall I is combined as shown from parts of 301-39 and 301-11. Cut 301-39 along the edge of the right window as shown.

similar to the Pingree Grove shop as it also has a two-story section along with one-story garage area. At first we thought we could use it as-is, but after reviewing the walls and the shape of the prototype Pingree Grove building, we knew we needed to make some changes. Fortunately, Woodland Scenics/DPM also has a line of modular walls that can be used to create the modified walls. The brick pattern and windows are similar to the City Cab walls.

You can see in **2** the original outline from the article, with the dashed lines showing the approximate dimensions of the modified building. It also shows the track and loading dock (not on the prototype, but added to make it a rail-served industry). Each wall is lettered for organization. The two-story loading dock wall is made up of two sections, B and C.

The photos and descriptions show how each wall was modified. Standard plastic construction methods were followed. The walls were all cut with a metal straightedge and a hobby knife following the drawings and photos. The dimensions listed are approximate; adjust them to suit your available space and to match the exact fit of the parts.

Parts from the City Cab kit have a "112" prefix, and parts from the modular section kits have a "301" prefix. The modified wall sections are all shown together in **3**, placed on the floor plan to illustrate how everything fits together. Each is labeled with the parts used to make them.

Three walls of the two-story section need significant modifications: the front wall (J), loading dock wall (B-C), and the street side wall (I). For the other walls (A and G), the only modifications are to cut them to the right size. Walls B-C and A require a small section added to the base to make them the same height as the modular wall sections, **4**.

Walls A and B are made from part No. 112-2. Section A is approximately

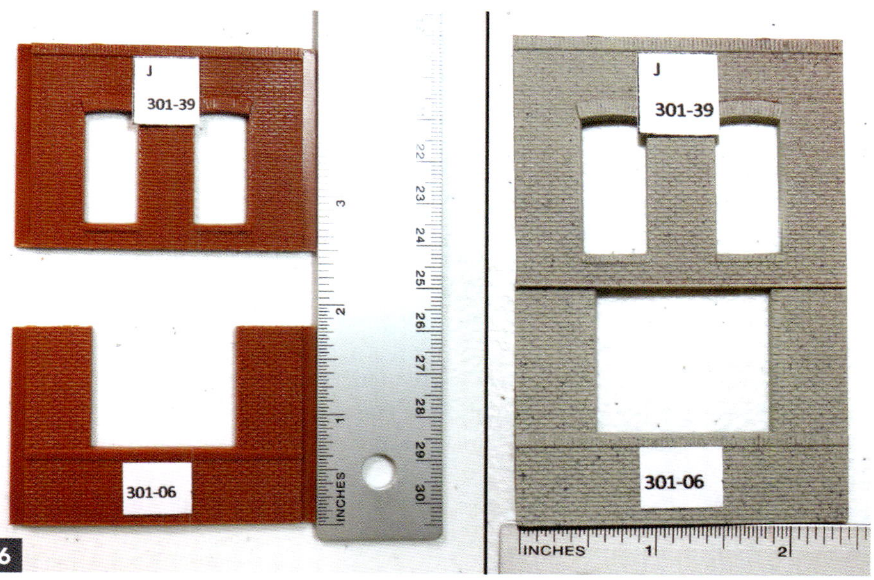

6

The top of Wall J is from 301-39 and the bottom is from 301-06, with the top cut off as shown. A strip of .025" x .100" styrene is added between the sections so the wall matches the height of the other two-story walls.

7 We used 3D printing to make a floor/foundation and roof for the two-story section (top). You can also cut these pieces from heavy styrene. Rubber bands keep the wall sections together during assembly (bottom).

1¼" wide; section B is approximately 1⅜" wide.

The B-C wall is made from two pieces: The section from 112-2 (approximately 1⅜" wide) is labeled B from the previous step. The section from 112-4 (approximately $2\frac{7}{16}$" wide) is labeled C. Cut off the left side. A freight door opening is cut out of section B — do this prior to assembling the two walls. We found a freight door in our scrap bin that fit the opening. The assembled wall is about $3\frac{13}{16}$" wide.

Wall G is made from 301-11; it has a notch cut out for the one-story section.

Wall I is made from a section of 301-39 and 301-11, **5**. On 301-39, remove the recessed tab on the left side of the wall. Use the right window as a guide to make the cut at the edge of that window (section I is about 1½" wide). Add a piece from blank wall section 301-11. Start with removing the recessed edge or tab on the left side, then make a cut a little over 1⅜" from the same left side. The assembled wall is about 2⅞" wide.

Wall J is made from the top section of 301-39 (two-story with windows) and the bottom section of 301-06 (one-story loading dock), **6**. The bottom section is just over 1¾" tall and the top section is approximately 1⅞" tall. Add a strip of .025" x .100" styrene, $2\frac{7}{16}$" long, between the two sections to form the top of the freight-door opening. This also makes the wall match the height of the other walls.

Wall D (railroad-side short wall), 112-5, must be cut to 3⅝" wide. The left side, E, 112-6, must be cut to just under 3⅝" wide. The right side, H, 112-6, is about ⅝" wide. Wall F, 112-7, is just over 3½" wide. The one-story walls need a chamfer or bevel on the inside of the walls so they fit together well.

When we began assembling the modified wall sections, it was difficult to get them to match exactly because of the odd angles and differing wall heights. Making a floor/base for the two-story section of the structure helped this and provided a solid foundation. We decided to 3D print the floor and the roof to match the unique shape of the two-story section. This also made it a lot easier to hold the walls at the correct angle to assemble the non-square two-story section of the building. You can also certainly make a floor and roof in conventional fashion with sheet styrene, foam core, gatorboard, or other material, **7**.

Space precludes going into great detail on how we 3D printed the base, but feel free to email us if you'd like detailed information (see page 5).

The roofs were finished using texture paint, then painted black.

Assembly and painting

Test-fit all pieces to ensure they fit together well, and fill any gaps with modeling putty or small strips of styrene. Spray-paint the walls with an undercoat of light gray, then add a very light mist or spatter of black paint. This will help with later weathering.

Glue the walls together, using square styrene strips to reinforce the joints. We started with the two-story section, with the assembly sequence being street wall (I), then the blank wall (G) and the trackside wall (B-C), as they meet at 90-degree angles. The floor and rubber bands helped hold the angled assembly together and kept the walls aligned until the glue dried, **7**.

Add the last two walls: the front wall (J), which needed a shim, and chimney wall (A). The roof and another rubber band helped keep things aligned.

Move to the one-story section starting with the street-side wall. The assembly sequence was street wall (F), back wall (E), track wall (D), and then finally the small wall (H), **8**. A shim of .125"-square styrene was added on the small wall (H) where it mates with the two-story section to complete the building. Atop the small wall we added a styrene assembly to match the roof section.

Add end caps to cover the recessed edges on the top part of the blank two-story wall and the left edge of the front wall. The end caps included with the DPM modular walls are too wide and need to be cut in half.

8

Add the single-story section to the two-story structure. You may have to fill gaps at the walls or roof with styrene strip. Styrene strips also reinforce the corner joints.

9

This view shows the assembled structure including the canopy on the front side, made from JTT shingles, and the sign, which we made in a word-processing program and printed.

The peeling paint on the prototype, visible in **1**, is distinctive. We used a common method to simulate peeled paint. To do this, before painting the finish color, lightly dab rubber cement in places where the paint has peeled off. We tried to match the photos of the real building.

Once the rubber cement dries, spray the final coat of white paint over the entire building. When that dries, rub off the areas of rubber cement, exposing the gray beneath it. We did some additional touchup to try to duplicate the images in the original article, **9**.

Paint and insert the separate windows on the modular walls. The building is now ready for details and animation.

10 This is the assembly for the arc welder. You can locate the toggle switch on the layout fascia or a nearby control panel.

Adding Arduino-based animation and sound

This Arduino project was inspired by an arc welder simulator by Steve Spence that we found online (circuitcrush.com/arduino/2016/11/05/arduino-model-railroading-arc-welder.html).

We'll add two Arduino configurations. The first version, designated SN220, is based on Steve's arc welder and runs on an Arduino Uno. It operates the same random arc welding light when an on-off pushbutton switch (SPST) is pressed. The second version, SN230, uses an Arduino Nano and a momentary-contact DPDT switch to operate either an LED arc simulator light or a small light bulb to simulate a cutting-torch burn.

For SN220, this project modifies the random "always on" for the arc weld light from Steve's version to be on only when the switch is activated. One other change is that it no longer flashes continuously, but will turn off when the switch is off. There is some randomness to the flashes, and it turns off for a short time then starts back up after a slight delay when the switch is activated. The switch connection can be brought out to a control panel or layout fascia, **10**. The circuit connections are shown in **11**.

The SN 220 code (page 37) has two main parts: the first sets up the configuration, and the second part monitors the switch position and then randomly blinks the LED to simulate an arc welder.

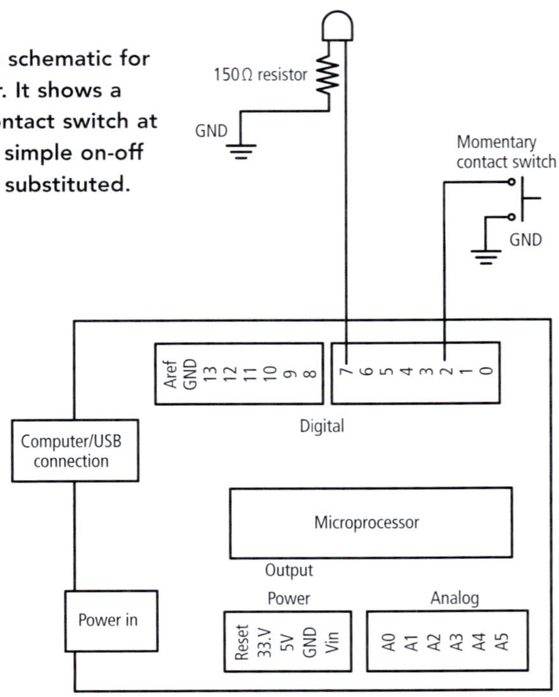

11 Here's the schematic for the arc welder. It shows a momentary-contact switch at upper right; a simple on-off toggle can be substituted.

CODE FOR SIMULATED ARC WELDER (SN220)

```
/*SN220 Code by Paul Bradt and David Bradt based on these original codes:
  Input Pull-up Serial
  created 14 Mar 2012
  by Scott Fitzgerald
  This example code is in the public domain.
  http://www.arduino.cc/en/Tutorial/InputPullupSerial
  and Simulation of an Arc welder
  By Steve Spence
  https://circuitcrush.com/arduino/2016/11/05/arduiro-model-railroading-arc-welder.html
*/
//This Rev takes out Randomness and adds a switch
void setup() {
  //start serial connection
  Serial.begin(9600);
  //configure pin 2 as an input and enable the internal pull-up resistor
  pinMode(2, INPUT_PULLUP);
  pinMode(7, OUTPUT);
}
void loop() {
  //read the pushbutton value into a variable
  int sensorVal = digitalRead(2);
  //print out the value of the pushbutton
//This section emulates the Arc Welder
  if (sensorVal == LOW) {
    int i, count;
    count = random(5, 9); //How many time LED blinks
    for (i = 0; i < count; i++) {
      digitalWrite(7, HIGH); // set the LED on
      delay(50); //Delay for how long LED stay on
      digitalWrite(7, LOW); // set the LED off
      delay(50); //Delay For how long LED turn back on
    }
    delay(800);
    Serial.println(count);
  }
  else {
    digitalWrite(7, LOW);
  }
}
```

Nano-controlled arc welder and cutting torch (SN 230)

This project adds a small bulb to simulate a cutting torch. The bulb is rated at 12V, so when operated at a lower voltage it tends to appear slightly red, similar to a cutting torch. It also uses a momentary-contact switch that precisely controls the time the arc light is lit or the torch light is on. We used a Nano to show two things: it's a much smaller package than the Uno, and it has a plug-in board that uses screw terminals, providing a more robust connection than push-in connectors, **12**. The circuit is shown in **13**.

As with the SN220 code, the SN230 code (page 39-40) has two main parts. The first sets up the configuration and the second part monitors the switch position. Depending on which side the switch is set, it either randomly blinks the LED to simulate an arc welder or the light bulb to simulate a cutting torch. You can see how the arc and torch look through the windows of the weld shop in **1**.

12 The torch effect uses an Arduino Nano, with a 12V bulb (lighted at lower right).

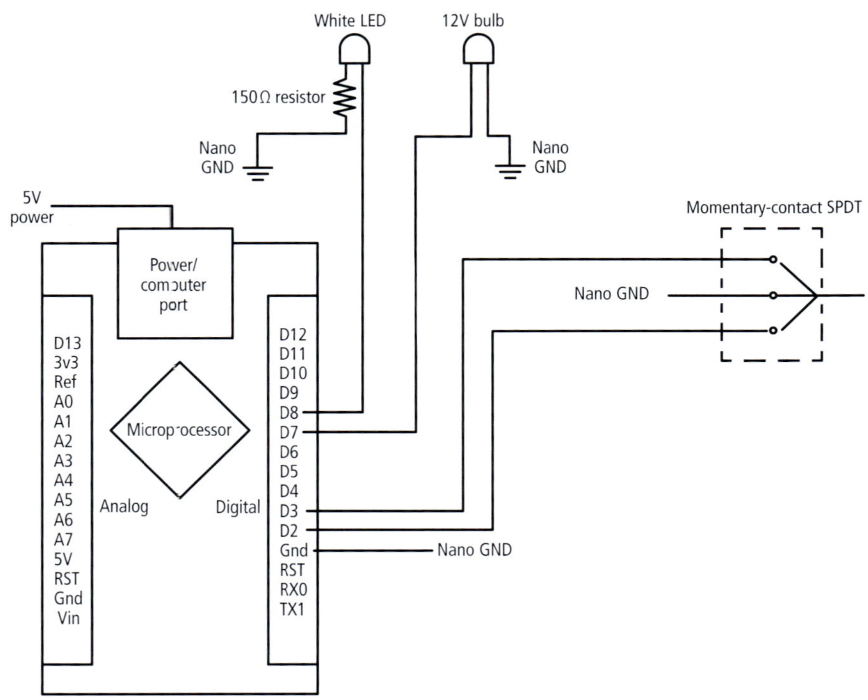

13 Here's the schematic for the Nano lighting effect.

CODE FOR SIMULATED ARC WELDER AND CUTTING TORCH (SN230)

```
/*SN230 Rev B Code by Paul and David Bradt based on these original codes:
  I arduino.cc/en/Tutorial/InputPullupSerial
  Simulation of an Arc welder
  By Steve Spence
  https://circuitcrush.com/arduino/2016/11/05/arduino-model-railroading-arc-welder.html
*/
unsigned long start_Torch_Millis, start_Arc_Millis, currentMillis;
const unsigned long arc_period = 12280;
const unsigned long torch_period = 46750;
bool sensorVal2 = false, sensorVal3 = false;
//Rev E simulating arc welder with White LED
// More rapid flicker
void setup() {
   //start serial connection
  Serial.begin(9600);
  pinMode(2, INPUT_PULLUP);
  //configure pin 3 as an input and enable the internal pull-up resistor
  pinMode(3, INPUT_PULLUP);
  pinMode(7, OUTPUT);
  pinMode(8, OUTPUT);
  start_Arc_Millis = millis();
  start_Torch_Millis = millis();
}
void loop() {
  currentMillis = millis();
  if (digitalRead(3) == LOW && sensorVal3 == false) {
    sensorVal2 = true;
    Serial.println(3);
  }
if (digitalRead(2) == LOW && sensorVal2 == false) {
    sensorVal3 = true;
    Serial.println(2);
  }
//This section emulates the randomness of a cutting torch
  if (sensorVal2 == true && sensorVal3 == false) {//Cutting Torch Welder
    digitalWrite(7, HIGH); // set the Light on
    delay(55); //Delay for how long Light stay on
    digitalWrite(7, LOW); // set the Light off
    delay(9); //Delay For how long Light turn back on
  if ((currentMillis - start_Torch_Millis) >= torch_period) {
      sensorVal2 = false;
      digitalWrite(7, LOW);
      start_Torch_Millis = millis();
    }
  }
  //This section emulates the randomness of an Arc Welder
 if (sensorVal3 == true && sensorVal2 == false) {//Arc Welder
    digitalWrite(8, HIGH); // set the LED on
    delay(55); //Delay for how long LED stay on
    digitalWrite(8, LOW); // set the LED off
    delay(9); //Delay For how long LED turn back on
```

```
if ((currentMillis - start_Arc_Millis) >= arc_period) {
      sensorVal3 = false;
      digitalWrite(8, LOW);
      start_Arc_Millis = millis();
    }
  }
  delay(10);
}
```

Arc welding and torch sound

The next step is connecting the WAV Trigger, which will simulate the sound of the torch and welder. Combining the sound and light is a bit tricky, since they need to be synchronized. The two systems that are combined are the Arduino Nano project above and the WAV Trigger described here.

The WAV Trigger is a very nice device produced by Sparkfun that stores various sounds and then plays them back when triggered. It's relatively easy to use, but getting the sound set up is somewhat advanced. We purchased some sound files online; you may be able to make recordings of an arc welder or cutting torch or find sound files from other sources. You can, of course, use a Trigger to provide any number of sounds on a layout.

The simple setup of the WAV Trigger, activation switch, power supply, and speaker are shown in **14**. This setup is perfect if you only want to play sounds without any light simulations. The Trigger plays the WAV file loaded on the micro-SD card. It is controlled by a switch connected between the trigger 1 (T1) and the adjacent ground pin. The file name has to be in the "001_xxx.wav" configuration.

The advanced configuration with the WAV Trigger combined with the Arduino Nano welder/torch from the previous section is in the circuit shown in **15**.

One of the key aspects is timing the activation to ensure the arc-weld light simulation matches the arc-weld sound file (also true for the cutting torch). The solution is simply to use the same switch to activate both at the same time. We did that by using a momentary-contact double-pole, double-throw (DPDT) switch. This means there are two connections and two switches combined.

You need to obtain a sound file, then adjust its loudness and duration so it provides the right volume without overwhelming the area. We purchased sound files for a welder and cutting torch from www.soundsnap.com/tags/welding.

For other projects, we have captured audio files with a cell phone. This works well, but the resulting files have to be converted to WAV format. There are websites that do this easily; we used www.zamzar.com/convert/m4a-to-wav/.

Modify the sound so it matches the length of the welding and torch lights. The time the lights run can also

14 **The WAV Trigger is in the middle, with its activation switch, power-supply connection, and speaker (right).**

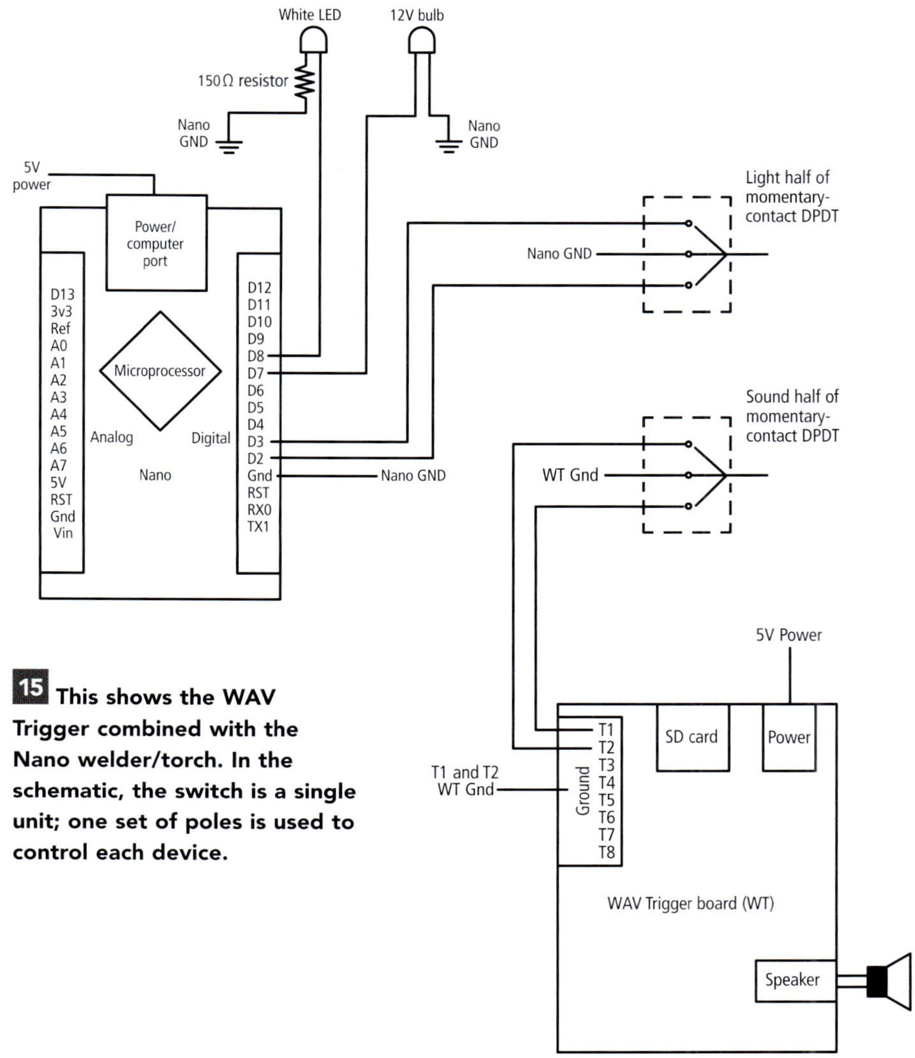

15 **This shows the WAV Trigger combined with the Nano welder/torch. In the schematic, the switch is a single unit; one set of poles is used to control each device.**

16 **Below is the control screen for the Audacity software, which makes it easy to modify sound files. The "Time Shift" tool is highlighted at top.**

be modified in the Arduino code. The tool used to modify the sounds' length and other parameters is a program named Audacity, which must be set up so it starts and plays about the same time as the arc welding starts (www.audacityteam.org/about/).

Once you load the sound files into Audacity, you can use it to make modifications like shifting the timing, shortening or lengthening the sound to fit the LED (arc) or bulb (torch) timing, increasing the volume, adding reverb, and other cool features, **16**.

These projects are presented to spur your own ideas for lighting and sound effects that you can add to your layout. The possibilities truly are extensive, and we hope this project inspires to you develop your own animation effects.

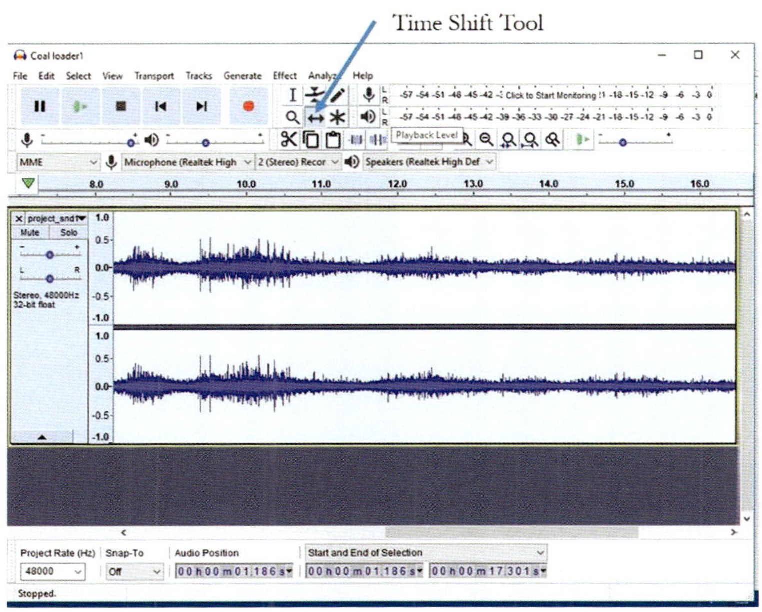

CHAPTER FOUR

INTEGRATED ARDUINO LAYOUT PROJECTS

The two projects in this chapter use Arduinos tied to the layout control system to provide automatic reverse-loop control for standard DC layouts and an Automatic Block Signal (ABS) system for DCC layouts. With this higher level of integration comes more sophistication. These projects provide examples that, even if you don't use these exact applications, you can use them as inspiration for developing your own experiments and projects.

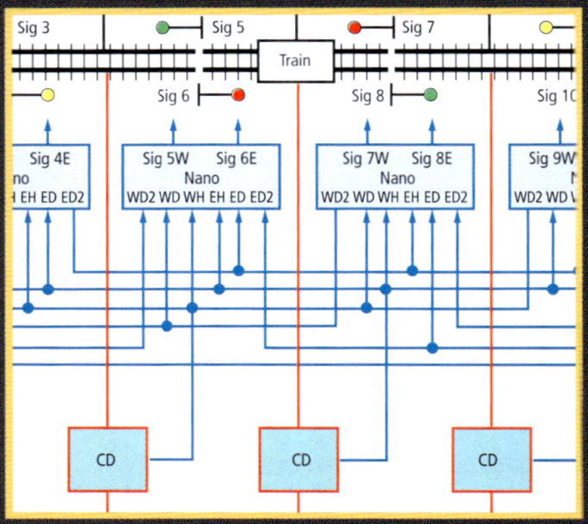

PROJECT 1: Automatic reversing loop control for standard DC

Materials list

- » SparkFun RedBoard Qwiic DEV-15123
- » SparkFun Qwiic Quad Relay COM-165660
- » SparkFun Qwiic Cable, 50mm PRT-14426
- » TRCT5000 IR sensor

The Sparkfun Qwiic Arduino and Cable are the base for the reversing-loop project.

Labeling all of the components helps make later troubleshooting much easier. The Arduino (top center) is labeled with its code; the quad relay is at right. Terminal strips simplify many wiring connections, especially for changing from heavy- to light-gauge wire.

This project shows how we automated the reverse loop operation at one end of a DC-controlled layout. We had a small N scale display layout that used a standard DC power pack and wanted to set it up so that a train could enter the loop and proceed through it without stopping while the polarity and loop turnout changed automatically.

Reverse loops present a wiring challenge because as the track circles around, the inside and outside rails meet — without rail gaps, the result is a short circuit. With Digital Command Control (DCC) there are several automatic reverse-loop solutions for this, but for standard DC control we wanted to try a different approach.

We developed this system using a quad relay to change both the track polarity and operate the turnout at the entry to the loop. It uses an Arduino Sparkfun Red Board Qwiic, **1**, and the Sparkfun Quad Relay Qwiic board, along with an infrared (IR) sensor for train detection, **2**, **3**. The loop track needs to be isolated by double rail gaps at the ends of the entry turnout.

Here's how it works: A train arrives at the reverse loop on the main line. It continues on the straight section of the reverse loop into the curved section. When the train covers the IR sensor, the Arduino senses the train in this second section and flips the polarity of the main line, which allows the locomotive to continue past the turnout and back the way it came. The system also changes the direction of the turnout.

The Quad relay is the key to making this operation happen. It is used to both operate the turnout and reverse polarity of the track. It uses two of the relays in a similar method as a double-pole, double-throw (DPDT) switch. The Qwiic connection streamlines and minimizes the number of wires required to connect to the Arduino Redboard Qwiic board. You'll need to follow the instructions on the Sparkfun site to have the Arduino IDE see the board, as it is not a standard Arduino.

The accompanying SN184 code (page 44-45) monitors the IR sensor so that when the sensor is covered by the train passing above it, the code triggers the track polarity to switch and also triggers the reverse-loop turnout to switch. Once the train arrives at its destination, the operator can flip the reset switch, which changes the turnout and polarity of the starting-point track back to the original configuration.

The code has three main parts. The first part sets up the configuration, the second part starts the loop that repeats, and the third part monitors the IR sensor and the reset switch, then changes the track polarity and the turnout based on the inputs. You may need to download and install the two libraries on your computer: The Wire library may already be included., and the Sparkfun Quad Relay library can be obtained following the instructions on the Sparkfun site.

There are a number of track configurations that you can use with this application — use your imagination and figure out how you can apply it to a new or existing layout. Just be aware that the section that reverses polarity is the block approaching the loop, not the loop itself. And remember that the IR sensor should be located so that the entire train is within the block when the locomotive hits the sensor (otherwise the turnout will change while under the train). See Wiring Your Model Railroad, by Larry Puckett (Firecrown) for more information on reverse loops and wiring.

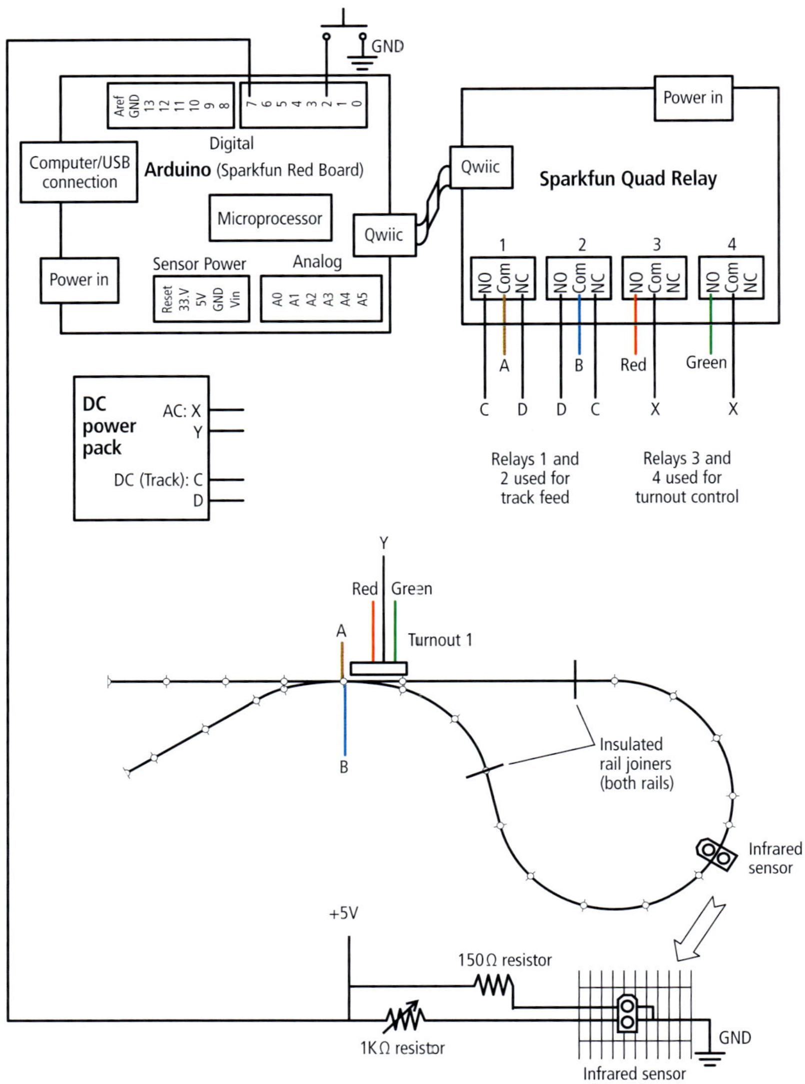

3 This schematic shows the wiring for the project. Compare this to the photo of the components in 2.

CODE FOR REVERSE LOOP (SN184)

```
//SN184 N scale DC reverse loop automatic control
// Using Qwiic Arduino
//Modified Qwiic Quad Relay code from Sparkfun site by Paul Bradt
#include <Wire.h>
#include "SparkFun_Qwiic_Relay.h"
#define RELAY_ADDR 0x6D
int stateSwitch1 = 2;
int stateSwitch3 = 2;
unsigned long previousMillis = millis();
Qwiic_Relay quadRelay(RELAY_ADDR);
void setup() {
  Wire.begin();
  Serial.begin(9600);
//Sets up Relays in standard mode
  if (!quadRelay.begin())
    Serial.println("Check connection to the Qwiic Relay.");
```

```
else
    Serial.println("Ready to run");
  quadRelay.turnRelayOff(1);
  quadRelay.turnRelayOff(2);
  quadRelay.turnRelayOff(3);
  quadRelay.turnRelayOff(4);
  pinMode(2, INPUT_PULLUP); //Reset switch
  pinMode(7, INPUT); //IR Sensor Input
}
void loop() {
  unsigned long currentMillis = millis();
  int val1 = digitalRead(7);
  //Give the user a good indicate that IR at 7 pin is working
  if (val1 == 0){
    digitalWrite(13, HIGH);
  }else{
    digitalWrite(13, LOW);
  }
//Monitors IR sensor and changes relays to reverse-return mode
  if (val1 == 0 && stateSwitch1 == 2 && stateSwitch3 == 2 && currentMillis - previousMillis >=
4750) {
    quadRelay.turnRelayOn(1);
    quadRelay.turnRelayOn(2);
    quadRelay.turnRelayOn(3);
    delay(200);
    stateSwitch1 = 1;
    stateSwitch3 = 1;
    Serial.println("Turning 1 to 3 relay to on.");
    previousMillis = currentMillis;
   }
 if (stateSwitch1 == 1 && digitalRead(2) == LOW && currentMillis - previousMillis >= 4750) {
    quadRelay.turnRelayOff(1);
    quadRelay.turnRelayOff(2);
    quadRelay.turnRelayOn(4);
    delay(200);
    quadRelay.turnRelayOff(4);
    stateSwitch1 = 2;
    Serial.println("Moving to reset mode.");
    previousMillis = currentMillis;
  }
//Monitors Switch and changes back to standard mode
  if (stateSwitch3 == 1 && currentMillis - previousMillis >= 250) {
    quadRelay.turnRelayOff(3);
    stateSwitch3 = 2;
    Serial.println("Time delay turning 3 Quad Relay off.");
    previousMillis = currentMillis;
  }
}
```

Lineside signals, **5**, have long been popular with model railroaders. They provide colorful animation on a layout, and can enhance operations as well. We were looking for an easy-to-install signal system that would follow prototype practice with a minimum of difficulty or expense. The Arduino-based Automatic Block Signal (ABS) system for DCC layouts, devised by Dennis Drury and described here, meets these criteria.

You can use this system for a long main line with several blocks, or a simplified installation of just a couple of blocks between towns on a small layout. The drawings show how the connections work between blocks for a long installation.

Most LED model railroad signals are based on common-anode wiring, **6** (the common wire is connected to the anode, or positive, connection on each LED in the signal head), but this project describes a configuration for common cathode signals (more common from European manufacturers). If you're making and wiring your own signal heads, be sure you wire the cathodes together as the common. If you're using common-anode signals, you'll need to modify the code slightly as shown in the box at the bottom of page 53.

This system provides four aspects: red, yellow, flashing yellow, and green. There's also an option in the code to implement approach lighting (where signals are only illuminated if trains are approaching) if desired. Simply un-comment the appropriate sections.

Prototype ABS

Railroads were installing ABS systems prior to 1900. It is a system that divides a main line into a series of blocks; low-voltage electricity passing through the rails is shunted by wheels and axles when a train is present, allowing the system to detect a train in a block. When a train is detected, the system sets signals at the block

Signals add colorful animation to model railroads, and also add to operation. These signals are showing various aspects on multiple tracks on Canadian National at Coteau, Quebec. *Brian Solomon*

boundaries to alert other trains. (Dave Abeles' book *Guide to Signals & Interlockings*, from Firecrown, explains ABS and other systems in detail). With ABS, this usually means that a red signal indicates a train in the next block and yellow a train that's two blocks ahead. Our system adds another aspect, a flashing yellow if a train is three blocks ahead.

Colors (red, yellow, and green) and position (of semaphores) are the primary aspects used on lighted signals. Green is clear, yellow is approach/ proceed prepared to stop at the next signal, and red means stop and proceed at restricted speed. There may be other signal indications as well, such as our flashing yellow (advance approach).

System block diagram and theory of operations

The Arduino Nano microcontroller is the heart of the system, although you could probably substitute an Uno or a Pro Mini. Note that this system is built around the +5V version of the Nano. It receives inputs from

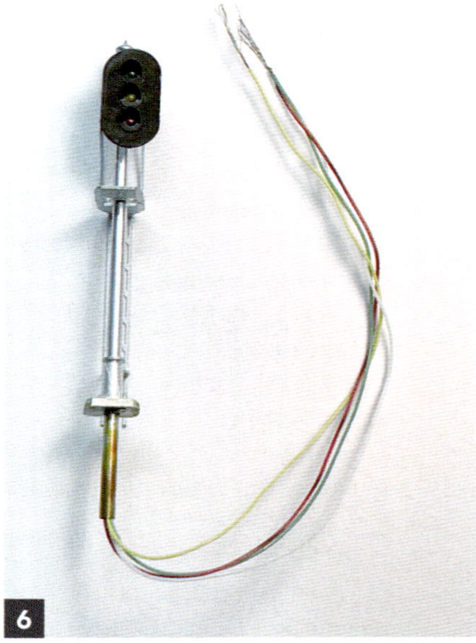

Most model signals using LEDs have a common wire plus a wire for each color LED. Some, like this Tomar model, have anode-common wiring.

current-sensing block detectors ("CD" on the drawing) and uses an internal program file to drive a pair of three-color signals in order to provide the correct signal aspects. This can be used to install either single-track or double-track ABS systems. The system block diagram for a single-track ABS installation is shown in **7**.

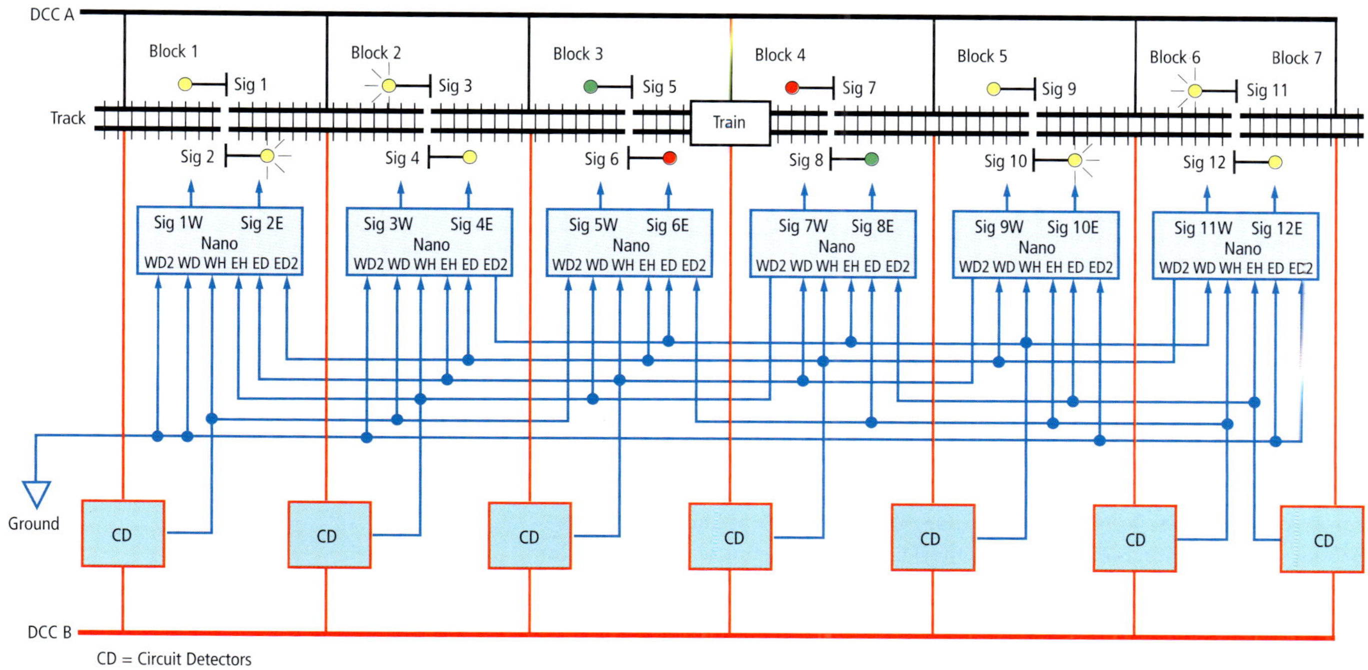

7 This shows the connections required among Arduino boards along a seven-block stretch of main line. The signals are shown how they would display indications with a train in block 4.

ED2	ED	EH	WH	East Signal	WD2	WD	WH	EH	West Signal
High	High	High	Low	Green	High	High	High	Low	Green
Low	High	High	Low	Flashing Yellow	Low	High	High	Low	Flashing Yellow
DC	Low	HIgh	Low	Yellow	DC	Low	High	Low	Yellow
DC	DC	Low	Low	Red	DC	DC	Low	Low	Red
DC	DC	DC	High	Dark	DC	DC	DC	High	Dark

DC=Don't Care
Signals will only be dark if Approach Lighting option is used; otherwise ignore that column

8 Constructing a "truth table" grid helps to show what indications are required for which signals depending upon the presence of logic low (occupied) or high (unoccupied) signal from each block detector.

Each block is fed from the two-wire DCC bus marked "DCC A" and "DCC B." It doesn't matter which side of the DCC signal is fed through the detectors as long as it's consistent throughout the layout. In our sample, DCC A feeds the track directly while DCC B goes through a current detector before it's connected to the track. The current detectors that we used are the cpOD detectors from Model Railroad Control Systems (MRCS) and the BOD-4 and BOD-8 from RR Cirkits, but any current detector can be used as long as it provides a TTL logic low output when the detector is active.

The output from the detector is fed into the inputs on the Arduino called WD2, WD, WH, EH, ED, and ED2. These stand for the West Distant 2, West Distant, West Home, East Home, East Distant, and East Distant 2 inputs. The outputs of the Arduino boards connect to the signals themselves. Note that you will need dropping resistors in line with the wires going between the Arduinos and signal LEDs (some model signals have the resistors built in — check the signal manufacturer's instructions). Use the highest-value resistor that still gives a good brightness level from the LEDs, and remember different colors might require different value resistors. Values Dennis has used successfully

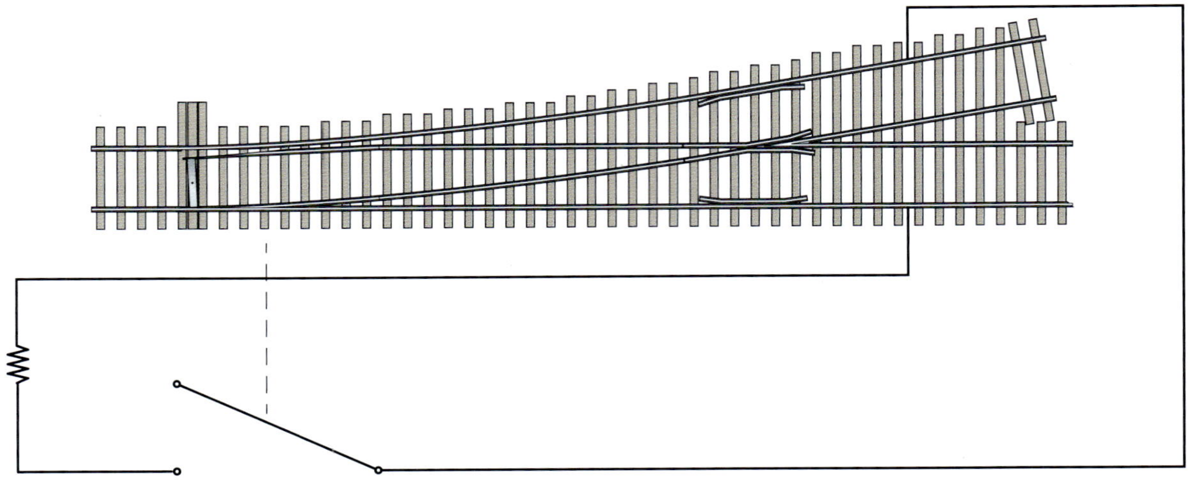

9 If a turnout on the main line is set for the diverging route, it should set the signals to restrictive. To make this happen, wire a resistor as shown with the turnout-control contacts (Tortoise or other) so that when the turnout is set for the diverging track, the resistor is effectively placed across the rails. The detector will then read the resistor as a load (the same as if a train were in the block), activating the appropriate inputs.

range from 330 ohms all the way up to 10K ohms.

Each Arduino provides the signal aspects as follows: If the West Home input is logic low (indicating a train is present), the west signal will be red. If the West Home input is logic high and the West Distant input is low, the west signal will be yellow. If the West Home input is high, the West Distant input is high, and the West Distant 2 input is low, the signal aspect will be a flashing yellow. Finally, if the West Home, West Distant, and West Distant 2 inputs are high, the signal will display green. The same logic holds true for the east signals using the East Home, East Distant and East Distant 2 inputs. (This assumes the approach lighting option is not active.) The truth table spells this out, **8**.

Note that even though there's only one arrow going from the Nano to the signals, that arrow represents four wires, one for each color plus the common. This makes it easy to use a length of Cat-5 ethernet cable to feed two signals. You can also use a length of Cat-5 for the cabling between Nano boards. Six wires will be needed for the East and West Home, Distant, and Distant 2 connections, and the other two will be ground connections to reduce noise.

The diagram in **7** shows what the signals will look like if there is a train in block 4. The train's locomotive is drawing current from the DCC system, so the detector for block 4 will have a logic low output; all other detectors have a logic high output. Go back and follow the previous paragraphs to trace the logic involved in triggering the signals.

Also note the bottom wire in the diagram. The light-blue triangle on the left side of the drawing is a ground connection. This is the same ground that is part of the power feed to the Arduinos and signals. This ground connection is because we don't want a clear signal leading into the end of the track. If the layout is a loop, connect the signal wires so that the West Distant for signal 1 connects back around to block 7. The West Distant 2 for signal 1 would connect to block 6. The same applies for signal 12 connecting back to blocks 1 and 2.

Turnouts

There are no turnouts shown in the block diagrams, but we can account for them. On the prototype, if a turnout is thrown against the main line, the block signals in ABS territory are set to stop governing movement over that section of track. On a layout, it's extremely easy to implement this feature. All that's needed is one set of contacts from whatever turnout controller you happen to be using (such as a Tortoise, Blue Point, or even a slide or toggle switch) as well as a resistor.

In **9**, if the turnout is set for the main, the resistor will be out of the circuit and the detector will function as it normally does. If the turnout is thrown against the main line (as shown), the contacts shown in the diagram effectively wire the resistor across the track. This will draw a small amount of current, which will trigger the detector to show the track as occupied. This in turn triggers the Nano to put the home signals to stop, the distant signals to approach, and the second distant signals to advance approach.

The resistor value needed will likely be around 10K ohms, but test to determine the final value by trial and error based on what brand of detectors you're using.

If you use a manual method of throwing turnouts (such as Caboose

Industries ground throws), this method will not work. In that case you'll need to either add a type of control that includes switch contacts or add some sort of optical detector to provide a means of sensing the position of the throw lever.

Components and wiring

You'll need to provide several components. The first item is a power supply. We recommend a 5V regulated supply, and that it only be used to power the signal system. Each Nano only draws about 2 to 3mA of current, but when adding the current draw of the LEDs and block detectors it's best to allow for 50mA per Nano. This would be an extremely high load, but allowing for that will guarantee that the power supply is never overloaded.

Math shows that this means every 20 signal boards require 1A of current from the supply. Several vendors offer 5V supplies; make sure it's a good quality, regulated supply and that you use good bus wiring practices when connecting the boards — in particular, make sure the +5V and ground are connected to the correct pins on the Arduino.

You'll need wiring to connect the boards to each other. As mentioned, Dennis has used Cat-5 ethernet cable, and it has worked quite well in both connecting the Nano boards to each other as well as connecting the boards to the signals. Use heavier wires (12-16 AWG) for the power and ground connections.

Note that there is no need to run the heavy wires directly to the boards.

10 Block-detection sensors like this BD20 from NCE require no direct connection to the track feeder. Instead, the feeder wire is wrapped around and through the hole in the coil — the detector senses the current draw and sends information to the Arduino.

It's best to run the bus wires to a terminal block, then use lighter gauge wires between the terminal block and the board.

How are trains detected? Whichever detector you choose will need current passing through it to tell the signal system there is a train present, **10**. Locomotives are detected automatically because the motor and decoder always pass some current when on the rails, but in order to have cars detected it will require some extra work. Lighted cabooses and passenger cars will be automatically detected. You may have to add resistors to wheelsets on standard freight cars — resistive wheelsets are available from several vendors. Add one to each non-lighted car. The key is to make sure that any piece of rolling stock in a signal block trips the detector.

There are several manufacturers of model signals using LEDs, and many offer parts and kits to allow you to make your own. As mentioned, most are wired as "common anode," but our code requires "common cathode" wiring.

Also note that this system is a true automatic block, and does not support interlocking, Centralized Traffic Control (CTC), or Absolute Permissive Block signaling (APB).

The code for the system is shown on the following pages.

ABS CODE V1.5 COMMON CATHODE CODE

```
/*
  ABS Signal circuit using the Arduino microcontroller.
  This code implements a single section of bi-directional ABS signals using Arduino NANO board.
  It should work on the UNO, MEGA, Leonardo or Pro MINI boards as well.
  This code is in the public domain and may be shared under the provisions of the Creative Commons
license type BY.
  For more information visit this site:  https://creativecommons.org/licenses/by/4.0/
  Version 1.5a by Dennis Drury  Email cowrr1984@gmail.com
  Version history
  V1.0 Initial Release
  V1.1 Added approach lighting
  V1.2 Changed pin assignments to better match up with the Pro MINI board.
  V1.3 Changed pin assignments to better match up with the NANO board.
  V1.4 Fixed syntax error in the Advance Approach logic and comment error in the Approach Lighting
logic.
  V1.5 Changed millis variables to unsigned long to better match up with the Arduino
recommendations.
  V1.5a Changed input pins due to analog input only on A6 and 7 of the NANO.

                                          Sig_W
                                           0-|
  -----------|------------|------------|----------------|------------|--------
   Blk_WD2      Blk_WD       Blk_WH       |-0  Blk_EH       Blk_ED      Blk_ED2
                                          Sig_E

  The Flashing Yellow section includes modified code from the Arduino.cc website that is in the
public domain
  http://www.arduino.cc/en/Tutorial/BlinkWithoutDelay

*/
// There are six detected blocks
int Blk_WD2 = A0;
int Blk_WD = A1;
int Blk_WH = A2;
int Blk_EH = A3;
int Blk_ED = A4;
int Blk_ED2 = A5;
// There are six signal outputs
// Sig_Wr, Sig_Wy, Sig_Wg, Sig_Er, Sig_Ey and Sig_Eg
const int Sig_Wr = 2;
const int Sig_Wy = 3;
const int Sig_Wg = 4;
const int Sig_Er = 6;
const int Sig_Ey = 7;
const int Sig_Eg = 8;
// There are four internal variables that will change. These are only used for the flashing yellow
// aspects.
int Sig_Wy_f = LOW;
int Sig_Ey_f = LOW;
unsigned long previousMillis1 = 0;
unsigned long previousMillis2 = 0;
// The following variables are the flash rates for the signals.
```

```
// Note these values may need to change depending on the size of your final code and the clock
// speed of your processor.
// The numbers are slightly different because in my experience no two prototype flashing relays
// ever flashed at the exact same rate.
unsigned long interval1 = 800;
unsigned long interval2 = 810;
// The setup routine runs once on bootup or pressing the reset button
void setup()
{
  // Set up the blocks as inputs
  pinMode(Blk_WD2, INPUT_PULLUP);
  pinMode(Blk_WD, INPUT_PULLUP);
  pinMode(Blk_WH, INPUT_PULLUP);
  pinMode(Blk_EH, INPUT_PULLUP);
  pinMode(Blk_ED, INPUT_PULLUP);
  pinMode(Blk_ED2, INPUT_PULLUP);
 // Set up the signals as outputs
  pinMode(Sig_Wr, OUTPUT);
  pinMode(Sig_Wy, OUTPUT);
  pinMode(Sig_Wg, OUTPUT);
  pinMode(Sig_Er, OUTPUT);
  pinMode(Sig_Ey, OUTPUT);
  pinMode(Sig_Eg, OUTPUT);
}
// This loop runs continously
void loop()
{
// Read block occupancy
  Blk_WD2 = digitalRead(A0);
  Blk_WD = digitalRead(A1);
  Blk_WH = digitalRead(A2);
  Blk_EH = digitalRead(A3);
  Blk_ED = digitalRead(A4);
  Blk_ED2 = digitalRead(A5);
// Set West Signal Green
  if (Blk_WH == HIGH && Blk_WD == HIGH && Blk_WD2 == HIGH)
//If approach lighting add "&& Blk_EH == LOW" to if statement
   {
   digitalWrite(Sig_Wr, LOW); digitalWrite(Sig_Wy, LOW); digitalWrite(Sig_Wg, HIGH);
   }
// Set West Signal Flashing Yellow
  if (Blk_WH == HIGH && Blk_WD == HIGH && Blk_WD2 == LOW)
//If approach lighting add "&& Blk_EH == LOW" to if statement
    {
     digitalWrite(Sig_Wr, LOW); digitalWrite(Sig_Wg, LOW);
     unsigned long currentMillis1 = millis();
 if(currentMillis1 - previousMillis1 > interval1)
    {
    // save the last time you blinked the LED
    previousMillis1 = currentMillis1;
    // if the LED is off turn it on and vice-versa:
    if (Sig_Wy_f == LOW)
      Sig_Wy_f = HIGH;
    else
      Sig_Wy_f = LOW;
```

```
// set the LED with the state of the variable:
    digitalWrite(Sig_Wy, Sig_Wy_f);
    }
    }
 // Set West Signal Yellow
  if (Blk_WH == HIGH && Blk_WD == LOW)
//If approach lighting add "&& Blk_EH == LOW" to if statement
   {
   digitalWrite(Sig_Wr, LOW); digitalWrite(Sig_Wy, HIGH); digitalWrite(Sig_Wg, LOW);
   }
 // Set West Signal Red
  if (Blk_WH == LOW) //If approach lighting add "&& Blk_EH == LOW" to if statement
   {
   digitalWrite(Sig_Wr, HIGH); digitalWrite(Sig_Wy, LOW); digitalWrite(Sig_Wg, LOW);
   }
  /*
  Uncomment this section to enable approach lighting
  // Set West Signal to Off
  if (Blk_EH == HIGH)
    {
    digitalWrite(Sig_Wr, LOW); digitalWrite(Sig_Wy, LOW); digitalWrite(Sig_Wg, LOW);
    }
  */
// Set East Signal Green
  if (Blk_EH == HIGH && Blk_ED == HIGH && Blk_ED2 == HIGH)
//If approach lighting add "&& Blk_WH == LOW" to if statement
     {
     digitalWrite(Sig_Er, LOW); digitalWrite(Sig_Ey, LOW); digitalWrite(Sig_Eg, HIGH);
     }
 // Set East Signal Flashing Yellow
  if (Blk_EH == HIGH && Blk_ED == HIGH && Blk_ED2 == LOW)
//If approach lighting add "&& Blk_WH == LOW" to if statement
    {
    digitalWrite(Sig_Er, LOW); digitalWrite(Sig_Eg, LOW);
    unsigned long currentMillis2 = millis();
  if(currentMillis2 - previousMillis2 > interval2)
    {
    // save the last time you blinked the LED
    previousMillis2 = currentMillis2;
    // if the LED is off turn it on and vice-versa:
    if (Sig_Ey_f == LOW)
      Sig_Ey_f = HIGH;
    else
      Sig_Ey_f = LOW;
    // set the LED with the ledState of the variable:
    digitalWrite(Sig_Ey, Sig_Ey_f);
    }
    }
// Set West Signal Yellow
  if (Blk_EH == HIGH && Blk_ED == LOW)
//If approach lighting add "&& Blk_WH == LOW" to if statement
     {
     digitalWrite(Sig_Er, LOW); digitalWrite(Sig_Ey, HIGH); digitalWrite(Sig_Eg, LOW);
     }
 // Set West Siganl Red
  if (Blk_EH == LOW) //If approach lighting add "&& Blk_WH == LOW" to if statement
   {
```

```
    digitalWrite(Sig_Er, HIGH); digitalWrite(Sig_Ey, LOW); digitalWrite(Sig_Eg, LOW);
    }
    /*
    Uncomment this section to enable approach lighting
    // Set signal 2 to Off
    if (Blk_WH == HIGH)
    {
    digitalWrite(Sig_Er, LOW); digitalWrite(Sig_Ey, LOW); digitalWrite(Sig_Eg, LOW);
    }
    */
}
```

COMMON-ANODE VARIATION

If you have common-anode signals and would like to use the ABS Code V1.5 all you need to do is change the digitalWrite statements. For example, in the common cathode sketch it states:

```
// Set West Signal Green
if (Blk_WH == HIGH && Blk_WD == HIGH && Blk_WD2 == HIGH)
//If approach lighting add "&& Blk_EH == LOW" to if statement
{
digitalWrite(Sig_Wr, LOW); digitalWrite(Sig_Wy, LOW); digitalWrite(Sig_Wg, HIGH);
}
```

Change the LOWs to HIGHs and change the HIGHs to LOWs as shown below. Do this for all the set color sections and that's all there is to it.

```
// Set West Signal Green
if (Blk_WH == HIGH && Blk_WD == HIGH && Blk_WD2 == HIGH)
//If approach lighting add "&& Blk_EH == LOW" to if statement
{
digitalWrite(Sig_Wr, HIGH); digitalWrite(Sig_Wy, HIGH); digitalWrite(Sig_Wg, LOW);
}
```

If you prefer, you can contact Dennis Drury via email (cowrr1984@gmail.com) and he will send you the common-anode code at no charge.

CHAPTER FIVE

BASIC DETECTION WITH ARDUINOS AND JMRI

Knowing where trains are on a layout is vital to operations. Engineers need to avoid other trains, and the dispatcher must know where all the trains are to coordinate safe train movements. Hidden track and staging areas can also present challenges for moving trains to avoid collisions. Here are a couple of projects that help us do this — one using a camera, and the other using track-based detectors to relay information to a dispatcher's panel, **1**.

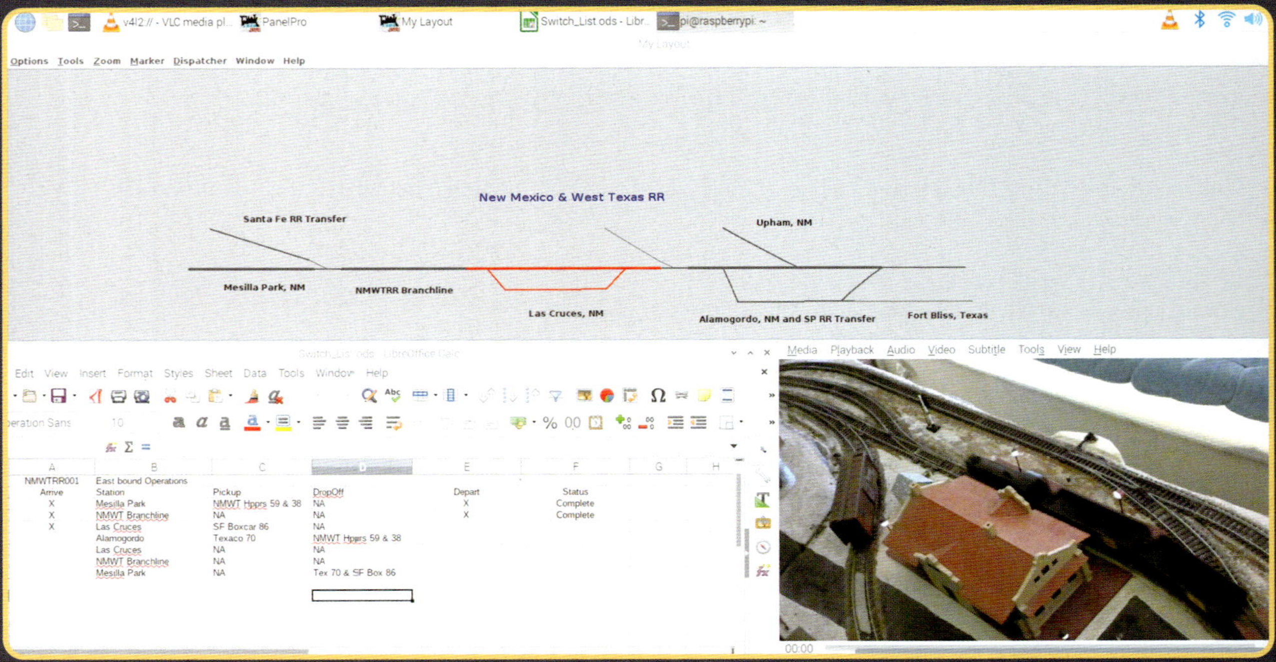

1 **The completed dispatcher's panel/screen shows a schematic of the line (with occupied track in red), along with the train's switch list (lower left) and a remote camera view (lower right). You can incorporate any or all of these features using projects in this and the next chapter.**

PROJECT 1: Dispatcher display with camera system

Materials list

- » Logitech C270 USB camera
- » Raspberry Pi 400 with VLC media player
- » Monitor

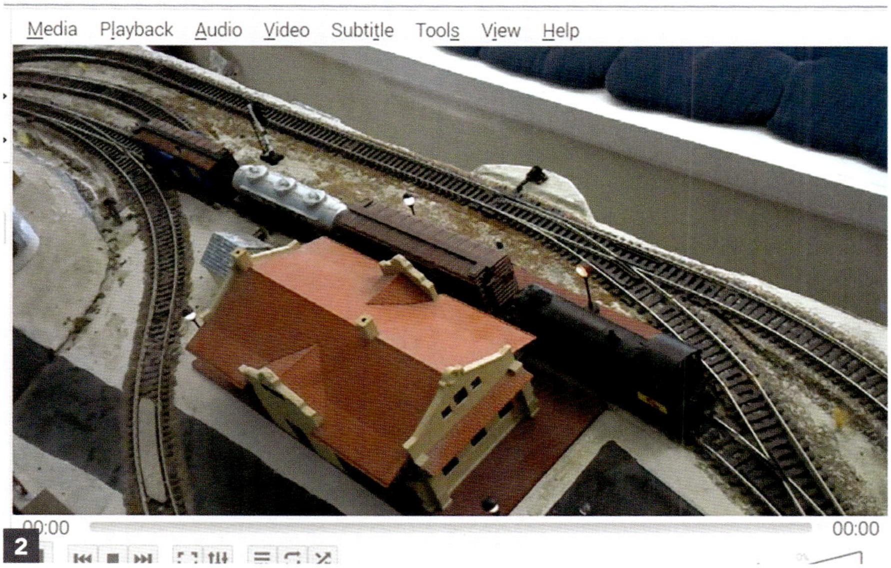

2

A remote camera can be connected through a Raspberry Pi and monitor to provide the dispatcher or train crews with a view of hidden track or staging.

Model railroads — especially large ones — sometimes end up with hidden, hard-to-see, or difficult-to-access locations, especially at staging yards, fiddle yards, or remote areas of a layout. These are all good places to place a remote camera system, **2**, and this easy project shows how. The system uses a special version of the Raspberry Pi 4, designated the Raspberry Pi 400, **3**. The 400 is a Pi 4 that is encased in a keyboard, which simplifies the setup. We chose it since the installation would be set up during an operating session and then moved when finished; with the keyboard integral, this meant one less item to move around.

One other difference is the lack of access to the camera port for a standard Raspberry Pi camera. However, this was not an issue as we opted for a standard USB-connected camera (we considered Bluetooth or Wi-Fi based cameras, but settled on the USB version).

Why the Raspberry Pi? For starters, it's a low-cost computer that can be dedicated to tasking. It comes with a spreadsheet program and word processor, so can be used for scheduling trains and tracking their progress through an operating session. (Later projects will show other ways to use a Raspberry Pi.)

Our Raspberry Pi 400 operating system came with the VLC media player, which is needed for this project. You can see a screen capture from the USB camera video in **2**.

We found the software VLC media player program worked well. It should be loaded on the Raspberry Pi, but if it is not, it is downloadable. You need to use the Linux version.

After it is started and configured, the steps to turn on the camera are very simple: After plugging the camera into the USB port, navigate to "devices" in the VLC media player submenu. If there is more than one device, you may have to test them until you find the correct one. Open "capture device" and select "play." You can set up a monitor or monitors at any location — at the layout near the hidden track, on the layout fascia, or at the dispatcher's desk.

This simple method to add a camera worked very well, and you can easily adapt it to many situations on large and small layouts alike. This concept will be continued in the next project, which involves setting up a small dispatcher's desk on the same Raspberry Pi 400.

3

The Raspberry Pi 400 is built into a keyboard, making it ideal for portable installations.

PROJECT 2: Simple dispatcher's display

Materials list

- » Raspberry Pi 400
- » Arduino Uno
- » Detectors: MRCS cpOD (4)

With this project, we set up a small computerized dispatcher's desk to follow a train through its route and highlight its location on a track diagram. It works in conjunction with DispatcherPro, one of the programs in the free Java Model Railroad Interface (JMRI) open-source software (jmri.org).

This desk is on our HO New Mexico & West Texas Railroad (NM&WT) layout, a fictional bridge route between the Santa Fe and Southern Pacific in southern New Mexico set in the late 1950s-early 1960s. The NM&WT runs from the New Mexico towns of Mesilla Park to Las Cruces and then a final destination of Alamogordo. There is also a siding that reaches Upham, N.M., and a short branch to Fort Bliss in Texas, which is also used as a fiddle yard for Santa Fe/Southern Pacific trains that can be added for additional traffic.

The actual layout is small, consisting of two small interconnected loops, **4**. The layout has additional tracks beyond what's in the schematic, but we don't need to show them for the project. The numbered arrows show a typical local run, starting with the train leaving Mesilla Park (1) heading to the right. It then leaves Santa Fe trackage and crosses from the outer loop to the inner loop (2), entering the NM&WT branch line.

The next stop is Las Cruces (3) to pick up or drop off cars on that siding. Then it heads up over the Imaginario Pass through the Organ Mountains and heads down into Alamogordo (4), at this point on SP trackage. There it switches any cars at the Alamogordo/Upham siding. When complete, the local returns via the same route it traveled to get there. Occasionally the local will stop at Fort Bliss.

This is all accomplished by running multiple laps around the loops, with stations and sidings located along the way. Using the double loop in this way, the local performs as an out-and-back run. This makes operations on a simple track plan much more interesting. This layout is more complex than at first glance — it has four runaround tracks (at each side and each end), allows for continuous running, and can host point-to-point operations.

The layout was originally built with DC block control but later converted to DCC. The outer loop is one block for Mesilla Park. The NM&WT

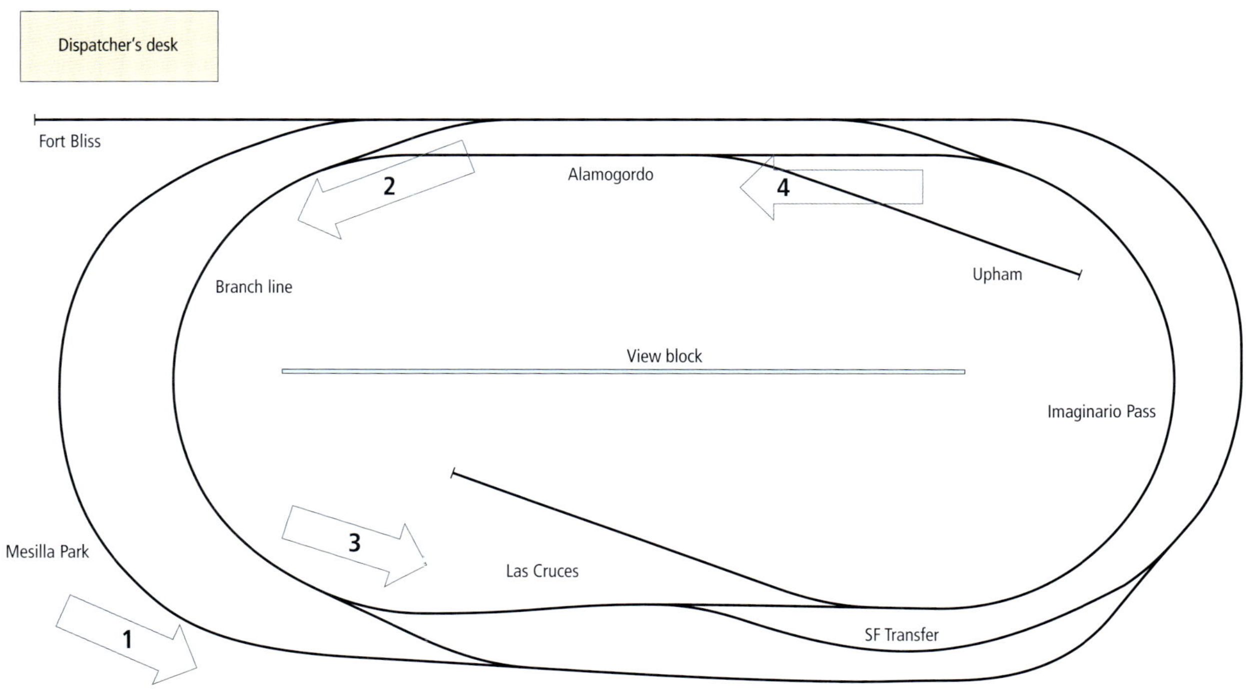

4 **Our layout is simple, with a double oval and multiple sidings, but it allows surprisingly complex operations. Our goal was to add train detection that could be reported on a monitor at a dispatcher's desk.**

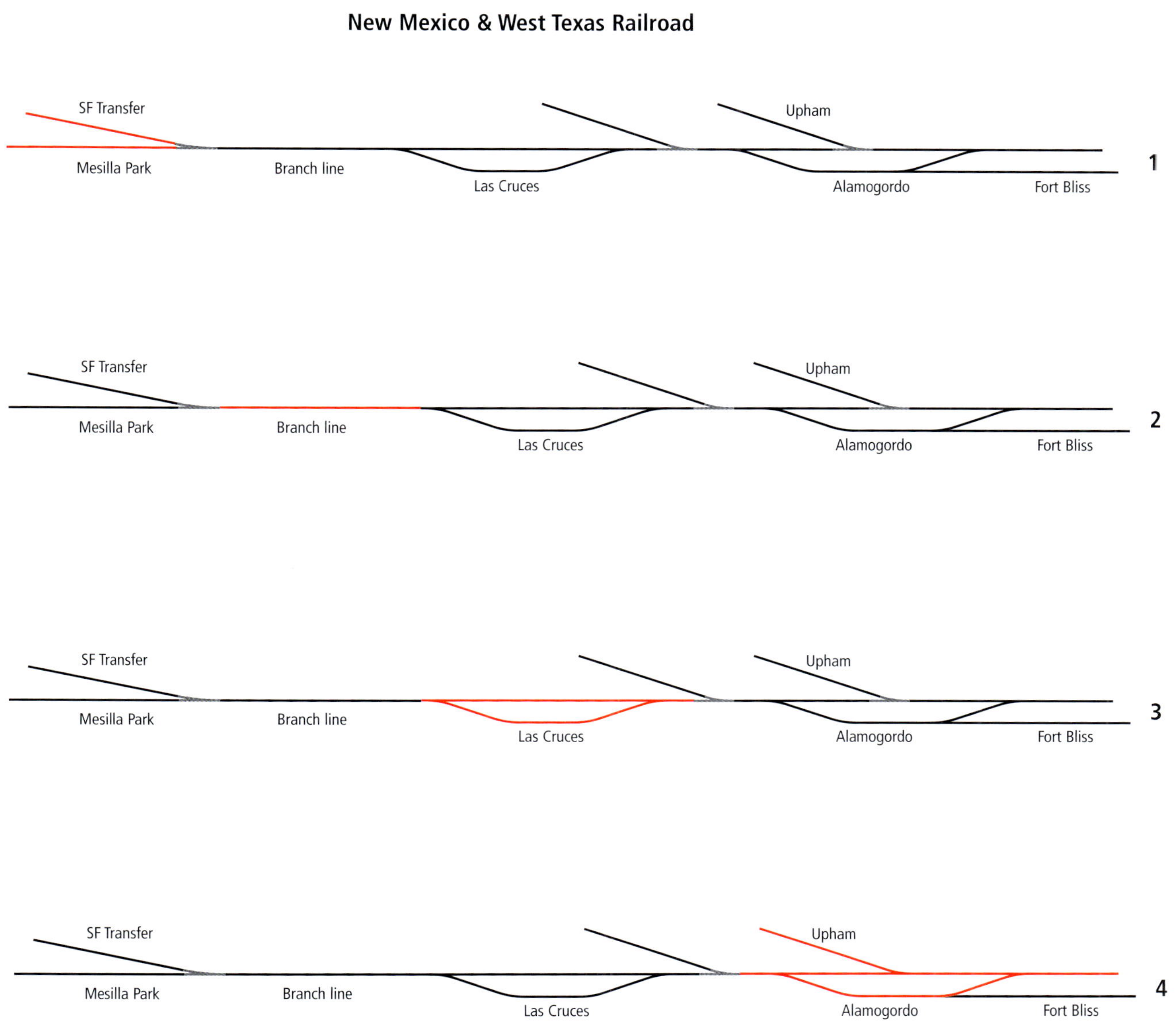

5 Blocks that are occupied turn red. Here's the full progression of a dispatcher's view of a train on our layout, starting at Mesilla Park (top) and progressing through Upham (bottom).

branch line is another block, followed by the Las Cruces block and the Alamogordo block. Each block has one Model Railroad Control Systems cpOD detector monitoring for train occupancy.

This project sets the Arduino up to interface with the real world, and the JMRI system displays the data from the Arduino to show what's happening on the layout. The complete JMRI DispatcherPro desk system is shown in operation in **1** with a switch list in the Calibre calculation spreadsheet program (which is included with the Raspberry Pi operating system), along with a video image of Las Cruces on the other side of the view block (using the USB camera from the previous section), and finally the JMRI track diagram dispatcher panel.

We used the spreadsheet to track the operations on the switch list, and also implemented some random calculations in the spreadsheet for railroad car pickups and setouts to make each run somewhat different. You can modify any part of this to fit your specific layout and situation.

As a train enters each block, that part of the track diagram turns red to show it is occupied, **5**. There's a way to modify this so it looks exactly like a prototype CTC panel; the next chapter shows how to do this.

Setting up JMRI

The basic goal of this project was to set up the dispatcher's monitor to track a train as it traveled on its run. Although our layout is small, you can apply the same steps on a larger layout. We were successful, but we did have challenges along the way. The best way we found to work through these items was to do it incrementally: Get each piece working, and then keep adding to it. Some of the key aspects we discovered are found in the "lessons learned" section on page 64 — you may want to skip ahead and look there first.

Setting up JMRI can be a challenge, but there are many websites and YouTube videos about implementing JMRI. Other helpful places are the JMRI.org site and the JMRI users' group (groups.io/g/jmriusers).

We used a Raspberry Pi 400 (built into a keyboard) for the JMRI dispatcher option. It was connected to a large monitor to display three things: a spreadsheet with a switch list, a video display of a remote location, and the JMRI Dispatcher Panel.

We built a small track to test configurations and code prior to setting it up on the layout. This test track really helped us, and we recommend you do the same before jumping in and installing the system on a full layout — especially if this is your first experience in working with JMRI, detectors, and Arduinos. The test track makes it easy to test and troubleshoot any problems in a controlled location, as opposed to under a layout.

There are four basic steps in setting up this system: downloading the Arduino IDE and setting it up on the Raspberry Pi 400; building the test track with an Arduino; configuring the system and getting communication working; and setting up the route in JMRI. Once you have the test setup working, you can then expand it and migrate it to your layout.

This might seem like a complex and time-consuming process, but it ensures you get a workable solution prior to installing on a layout. It also helps you fully understand how each part of the system interacts with the other. It is important to follow these steps, as each builds on the previous one and might not work well without the prior steps completed. Refer back to Chapter 1 for complete explanations of the various software and components involved in dealing with Arduinos and Pis.

6

The test track is simple — just two straight sections of track divided by insulated joiners — but was extremely helpful in developing the system and getting everything running. The Arduino is at left, with the two block detectors near their tracks. The inbound wires from the DCC system are connected through the terminal strip at bottom.

Step 1: Arduino IDE and Raspberry Pi

One hint as you get started: We found it useful to program the Arduinos on a different computer from the Raspberry Pi. The first step is to download and install the Arduino IDE (software) on the Raspberry Pi. For this project the version used was 1.8.15 (download the software at www.arduino.cc/en/software). The Arduino IDE version recommended for the Raspberry Pi is Linux ARM 32 bit.

Download and install Java and JMRI (www.jmri.org/download/index.shtml) on the Raspberry Pi. The version we used was PanelPro 4.22. The Java version used was 11.09. Good information on how to download JMRI is located at www.jmri.org/download/Install/Raspbian.shtml.

You can also visit Steve Todd's website and download the combination Raspberry Pi operating system (OS) along with Java and JMRI (mstevetodd.com/rpi).

Step 2: Build, wire test track

Our test track is two 9" straight sections connected with insulated rail joiners, with an occupancy detector on each section, **6**. The track is powered by a DCC system, with one feeder wire (yellow) from each block passing through its occupancy detector.

We used MRCS cpOD occupancy detectors, which are relatively simple to use. The version we used has three screw terminals: 5V power, ground, and signal out (which is sent to the Arduino). The track power wire simply passes through the coil on the board, with no hard connection (the coil senses the current load in the wire). Another version of this detector uses five-pin Molex connectors, with two connectors for track power connections.

CODE SN10 OCCUPANCY DETECTOR CODE (SN010)

```
//SN10_Based on Demo Track from previous book Intermediate Projects
//This is set up for two Occupancy Detectors and LED indicators
const int ledPin = 13; //Blk 1 Cutput pin 13 built-in led
int Blk_1 = A1; //cpOPD Blk 1 input
const int Blk2_out = 9; //Red led
int Blk_2 = A2; //cpOPD Blk 2 input
void setup() {
```

```
    pinMode(ledPin, OUTPUT); //LED output
    pinMode(Blk_1, INPUT_PULLUP); //Block 1 detector
    pinMode(Blk2_out, OUTPUT); //LED output
    pinMode(Blk_2, INPUT_PULLUP); //Block 2 detector
  }
  void loop() {
    //This section of code reads the cpOD sensors and turns on LEDs
    Blk_1 = digitalRead(A1);
    delay(25);
    Blk_2 = digitalRead(A2);
    delay(25);
    if (Blk_1 == HIGH)
    {
      digitalWrite(ledPin, LOW);
     }
    if (Blk_2 == HIGH)
     {
      digitalWrite(Blk2_out, LOW);
    }
    if (Blk_1 == LOW)
    {
      digitalWrite(ledPin, HIGH);
    }
      if (Blk_2 == LOW)
     {
        digitalWrite(Blk2_out, HIGH);
     }
  }
```

The SN10 code (page 58-59) is good for testing the operation of the cpODs and making sure they can effectively detect a locomotive. It can be used to set the sensitivity of the cpODs. There are two parts to the code: the first part sets up the configuration, and the second part reads the cpOD when a train is detected and turns on the LED.

One thing we learned from the test-track setup was how many loops of wire should pass through the coil. The illustrated instructions shows a wire looped and passing through the coil twice, but we found one pass through the coil worked well.

Step 3: Configuring and communication

In this part there are two steps that must be followed in the correct order to ensure they work properly. The first is setting up the Arduino as a C/MRI (Computer Model Railroad Interface) device, so it will recognize the occupancy detectors and communicate with JMRI. The second step is to get JMRI on the Raspberry Pi to communicate with the Arduino.

To set up the Arduino Uno to connect with JMRI, use code SN245 (page 61-62), which sets up the Arduino to behave as a C/MRI node. JMRI uses these C/MRI nodes to connect with sensors, signals, and turnouts. In the last section of this chapter you'll find more details that expand on the use of nodes using JMRI. (The term C/MRI is based on Bruce Chubb's system developed in the 1980s.)

The first part of the code sets up the configuration and communication with the Raspberry Pi by configuring the Arduino as a C/MRI node, and the second part monitors the cpODs and then transmits changes to the JMRI code on the Raspberry Pi. There are two libraries that need to be installed to make this work: CMRI.h and Auto485.h.

We now have to set up JMRI to communicate with the Arduino. The first task is to set up a node in JMRI on the Raspberry Pi. A node is like a control point that JMRI recognizes. Start PanelPro, then open "preferences" under the edit tab. This is where you'll set up the node, communication, and other parameters. Since this system only has one Arduino, it only needs one node. We found that designating it "Node 0" worked well. This simple aspect was not clear in many YouTube videos, and caused us some challenges. Dennis Drury recommends using two digits for node IDs. This allows the various tables in JMRI to display in a logical format.

The two screens that you'll need to navigate to set up a node are shown in **7**. There is an option to choose C/MRI emulator instead of serial connection type if you want to experiment before setting up the Arduino to be a C/MRI device.

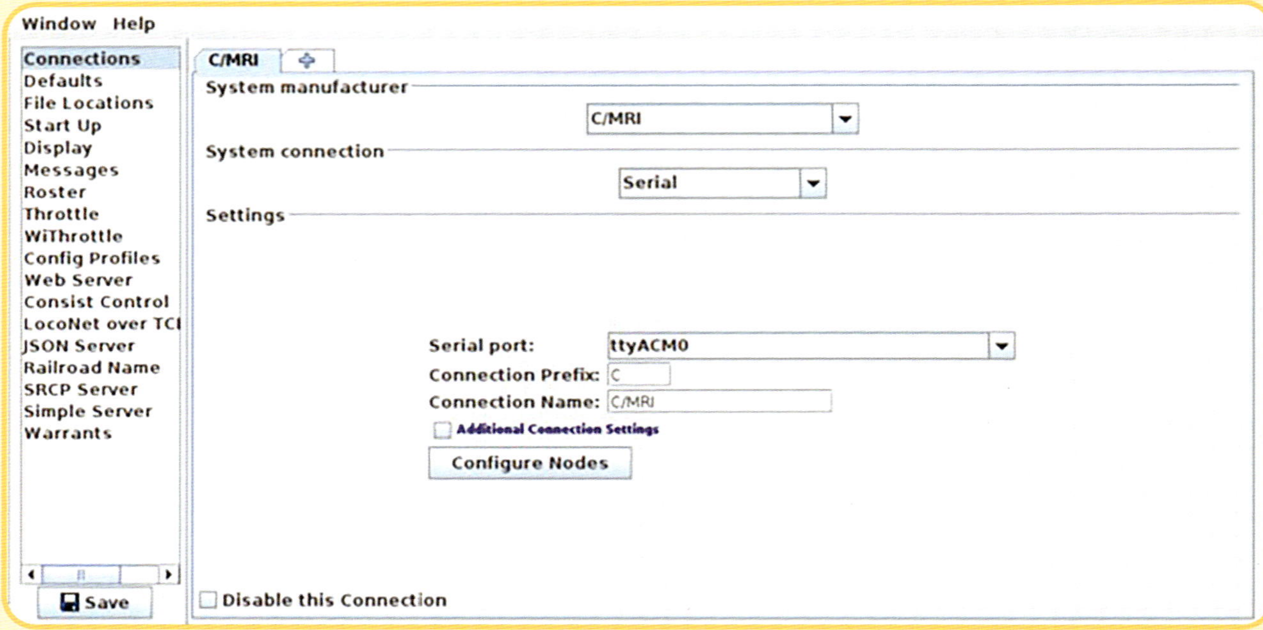

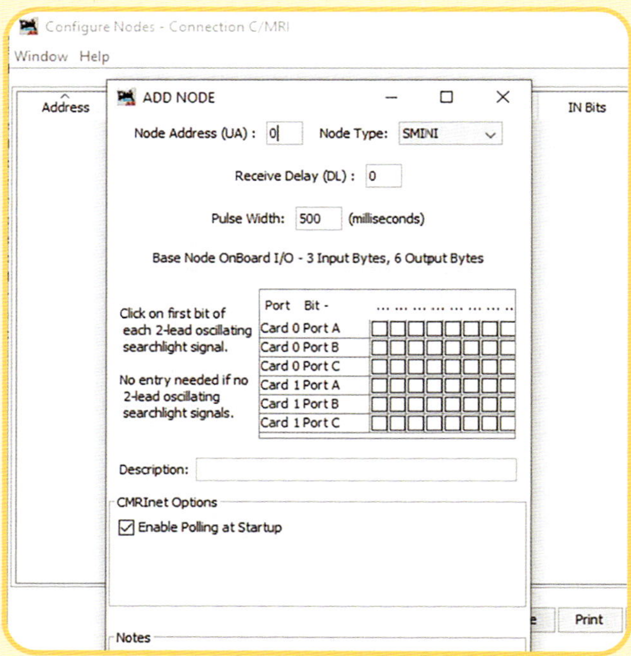

7 To set up a node in JMRI on the Raspberry Pi, start PanelPro, then open "preferences" under the edit tab, above. There is an option to choose C/MRI emulator instead of serial connection type if you want to experiment before setting up the Arduino to be a C/MRI device, left.

CODE FOR CMRI NODE TO INTERFACE WITH DMRI (SN245)

```
//SN 245 JMRI interface code
//Based on code from: www.youtube.com/watch?v=CDdTcNGVFxY
//This sets up a simple single CMRI Node and JMRI configuration
//Using a single SMINI type Node
//Modified by Paul and David Bradt
#include <CMRI.h>
#include <Auto485.h>
#define CMRI_ADDR 0
#define DE_PIN 2
#define L2 13  //On board LED used for troubleshooting detection issues
Auto485 bus(DE_PIN);
CMRI cmri(CMRI_ADDR, 24, 48, bus);
int Occ1 = 6; //cpOD Mesilla Park
int Occ1Reading; // Mesilla Park
int Occ2 = 3; //cpOD Las Cruces
int Occ2Reading; //Las Cruces
int Occ3 = 4;  //cpOD Branch
int Occ3Reading; //Branch
int Occ4 = 5; //cpOD Alamgordo
int Occ4Reading; // Alamgordo
void setup() {
  Serial.begin(9600);
  pinMode(Occ1, INPUT_PULLUP); //cpOD Mesilla Park
  pinMode(Occ2, INPUT_PULLUP); //cpOD Las Cruces
  pinMode(Occ3, INPUT_PULLUP); //cpOD Branch
  pinMode(Occ4, INPUT_PULLUP); //cpOD Alamgordo
  pinMode(L2, OUTPUT);
}
void loop() {
  cmri.process();
  Occ1Reading = digitalRead(Occ1);
  Occ2Reading = digitalRead(Occ2);
  Occ3Reading = digitalRead(Occ3);
  Occ4Reading = digitalRead(Occ4);
  //cpOD detector 1 Mesilla Park
  if (Occ1Reading == HIGH)   {
    cmri.set_bit(1, 0); //Off
    digitalWrite(L2, LOW); //LED off
  }
  if (Occ1Reading == LOW)  //On
{
    cmri.set_bit(1, 1);
    digitalWrite(L2, HIGH); //LED on
   }
  //cpOD detector 2 NMWT Branch
  if (Occ2Reading == 1) //Off
{
    cmri.set_bit(2, 0);
    digitalWrite(L2, LOW); //LED off
  }
  if (Occ2Reading == 0) //On
{
    cmri.set_bit(2, 1);
    digitalWrite (L2, HIGH);
  }
```

```
//cpOD detector 3 Las Cruces
  if (Occ3Reading == 1)     {
      cmri.set_bit(3, 1);
  }
  if (Occ3Reading == 0)
{
      cmri.set_bit(3, 0);
  }
//cpOD detector 4 Alamogordo
  if (Occ4Reading == 1)
{
      cmri.set_bit(4, 1);
  }
  if (Occ4Reading == 0)
{
      cmri.set_bit(4, 0);
  }
}
```

Step 4: Setting up route in JMRI

The next stage is to create the panel in JMRI. To create a layout diagram we used the Layout Editor in PanelPro. Layout Editor allows creating a drawing of the layout/route/track plan. There are a lot of YouTube videos and websites that deal with creating layouts, and the JMRI site covers the basics (www.jmri.org/help/en/html/apps/PanelPro/GettingStarted.shtml).

To draw the layout, you must start with a turnout, bumper, or anchor point first, **8**, then add successive track components. Adding an item to the layout is done by selecting the item at the top of the page, holding the shift key, and then clicking where you want it to go — with a little practice it becomes straightforward. There's an alignment tool to help position everything with the grid, and you can move the components around once they're placed. The drawing method takes some time to get used to, but after a few practice sessions (and some discarded panels) we had the results we needed. The best way to learn this — and the other features — is to just play with it!

Once the plan is set, the next task is to create sensors. Select "Tables," then "Sensors," and the screen in **9** appears. Make sure the sensors correlate to the sensors in the Arduino program. Click on "add" and type in the information for each sensor. Select "CMRI sensors."

The next step is to create a block. Go to tables and select blocks, **10**. When a train is operating on the layout, the status of the sensors and the blocks will show this status change in each one of these tables. This is a good way to test the operation before moving to the next step.

The last step is connecting each block to the appropriate segment on the layout diagram created earlier. A pull-down screen lets you modify it in the layout, **11**.

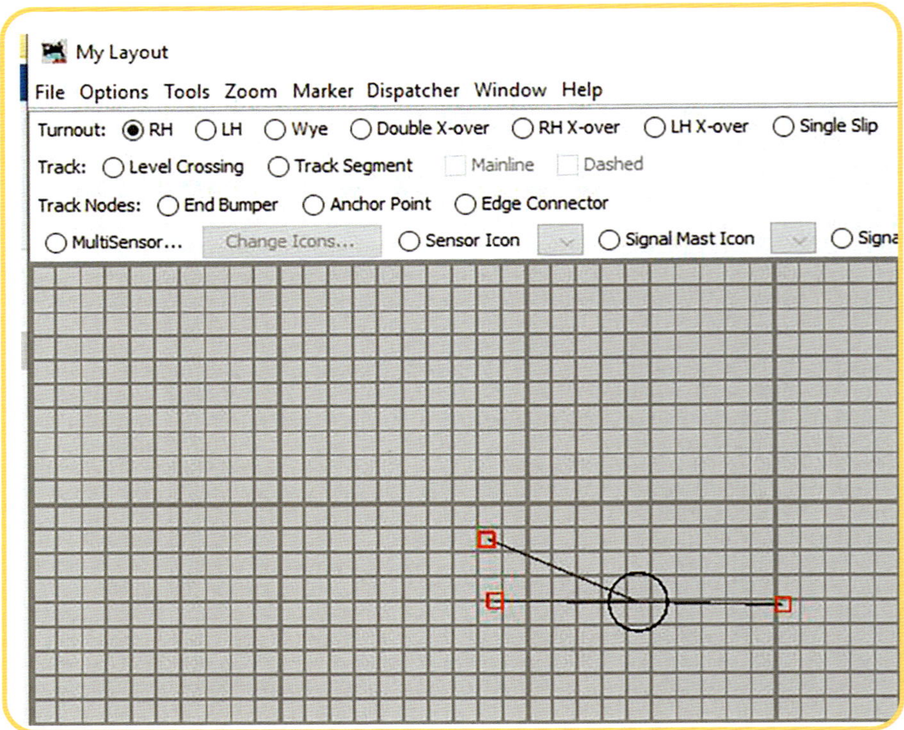

8 **Using Layout Editor in PanelPro, begin drawing the track schematic at an anchor point such as a turnout. You can then add successive track components.**

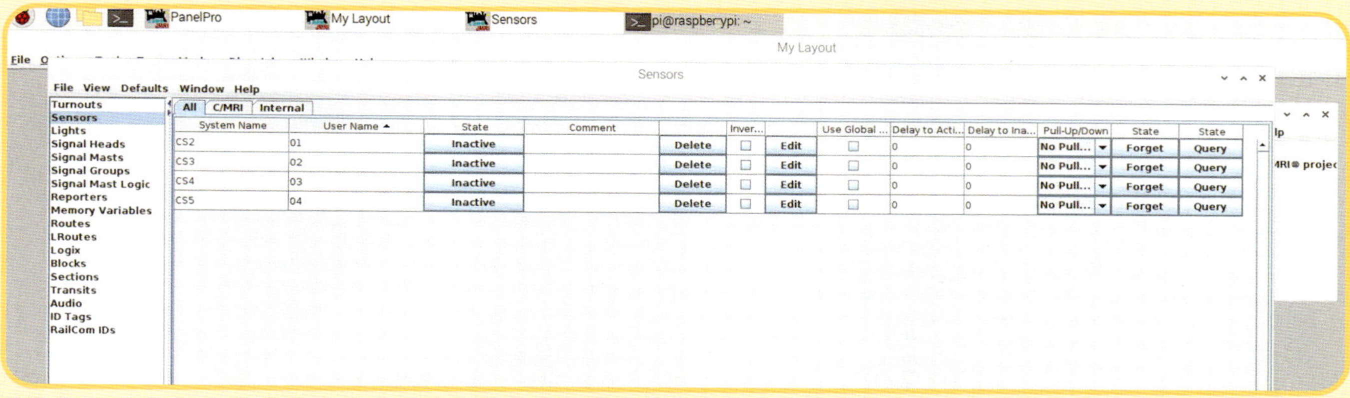

9 Add sensors to the track plan. This is found under "tables," then "sensors." Make sure they match the sensors in the Arduino program.

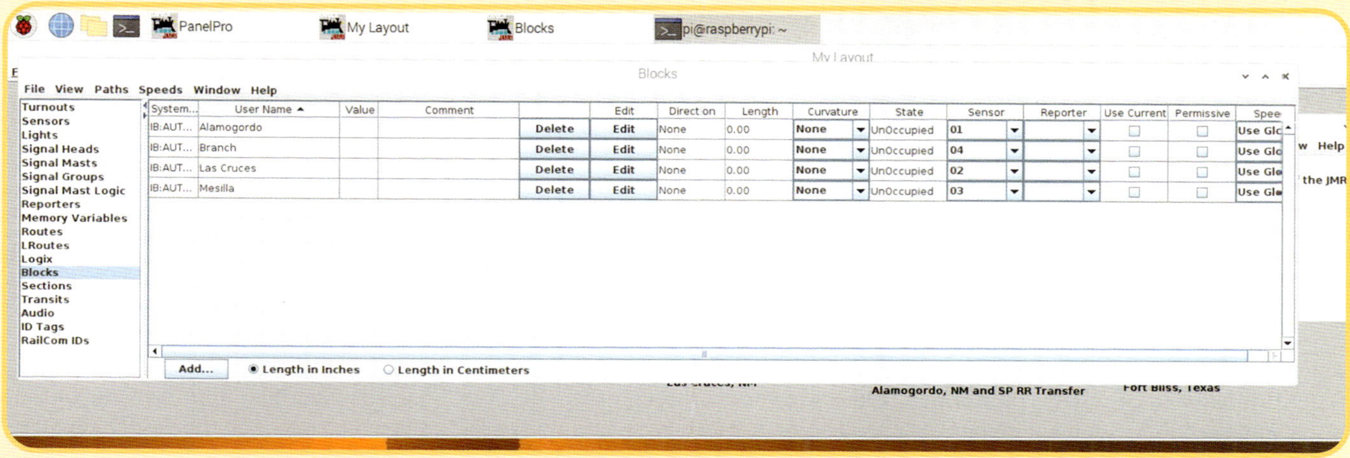

10 Create blocks. This is also under the "tables" tab.

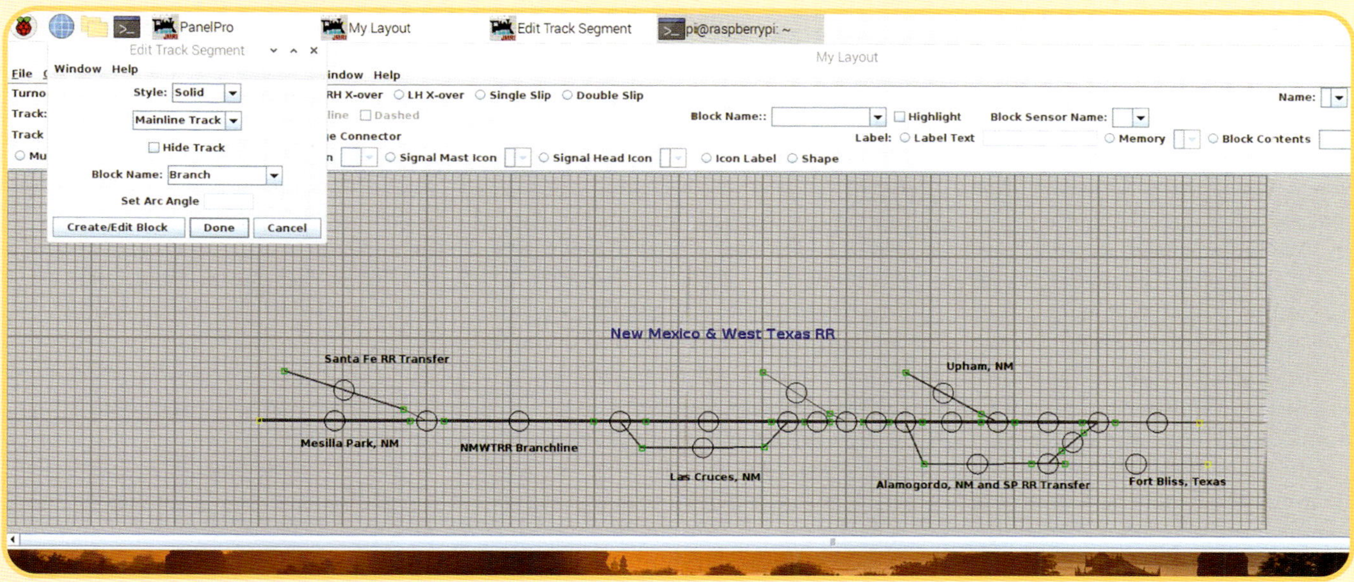

11 Connect each block to the matching area of the track diagram created earlier. A pull-down menu allows you to modify it in the layout.

12 **The Arduino Uno is shown mounted on the side of the layout in a custom 3D-printed housing. The four wires at top (gray, blue, green, yellow) are inputs from the detectors; the terminal strip simplifies wiring. The USB plug at top left is the connection with the Raspberry Pi 400.**

13 **These are the MRCS cpOD detectors. They're shown in their 3D-printed mounting brackets, which are also available from MRCS.**

Lessons learned so far

• Make sure you have the sensors correctly and consistently identified in both JMRI and the Arduino code.

• It is beneficial to name the panel something similar to the Arduino code. This helps to eliminate confusion when troubleshooting and changing variables. It also helps to stick a label on the Arduino with the code file name.

• As you're designing the panel, save the file often — it's good practice to modify the file name with a revision or date. This may be beneficial if you're making significant changes and then discover you want to go back to an earlier version. One thing that confused us at first is that the tables are saved in a panel.

• If the system is behaving strangely, try swapping out components. In our case, we discovered there was a port on the original Arduino Nano that was malfunctioning. Swapping it for another board fixed the problem.

• It can be beneficial to work alongside the Raspberry Pi setup and complete the steps on a normal PC, as well. If you experience a problem, this helps to show if the issue is unique to the Raspberry Pi.

• It can be a challenge to add sensors and blocks to an existing layout, so it's a good idea to plan for blocks and sensors in the initial planning and construction stages of a layout (see Chapter 6).

Final installation

Once we worked through the challenges, it was very rewarding to see JMRI register a block being occupied! You can see the final configuration of the Arduino Uno JMRI mounted on the layout in **12**.

After we configured the Uno on the test track, we installed it on the side of the layout in a custom 3D-printed housing. The housing has slots to feed the wires through to the terminal strip and keep them organized by 5V, ground, and signal from each of the cpODs. We used jumper connections to connect all of the 5V terminals together; the did the same for the ground terminals. We also 3D printed a translucent cover to protect the Arduino. When powered, the LEDs on the board shine through the cover, so we know it's working.

It was also helpful to set up the cpODs on a 3D-printed mounting bracket. It was difficult to attach a cpOD under the table with its included tiny No. 2 wood screws and spacers. However, using a 3D-printed mounting bracket and No. 6 wood screws made it easy. Given the challenges of using existing wiring, we had to move the cpODs a couple of times, and we were glad to have the brackets, **13**.

These brackets can be purchased directly from MRCS (www.modelrailroadcontrolsystems.com/cpod-st-mounting-bracket/). They can be ganged together as they have interlocking tabs on the sides. Also, there is a tab that pops into one of the screw holes to lock the cpOD circuit board in place so it will not move.

This project met our goal of adding a dispatcher's panel to a small layout. The train and turnout operation can be controlled from the dispatcher's desk via standard DCC controls. A second person (engineer) can follow and run the train as well. The dispatcher can track the movements of the train, issue train orders, update the switch list, and watch for any meets coming up with Santa Fe or Southern Pacific trains.

This project only scratches the surface of JMRI and its capabilities. By starting small like this, you will gain confidence in your ability to add a similar system to a larger, more-complex layout.

For us, a future goal is to convert our JMRI panel into a simulated prototype CTC panel, and possibly add signals and turnout controls. The next chapter will show you how to do just that.

CHAPTER SIX

CTC SYSTEM WITH RASPBERRY PI AND JMRI

Previous chapters explained how to add train detection and block signals to a layout. This chapter advances that a giant step, and shows how to design a Raspberry Pi-based Centralized Traffic Control (CTC) system on a new layout, **1**.

1 This system, through JMRI, allows setting up a computer screen that simulates a prototype CTC control panel, as below on Dennis Drury's Klamath Falls Sub layout. Indicator lamps as well as switch and signal control levers and code buttons are all fully operational. With CTC, train movement is governed by signal indications at control points such as sidings, left, as at the west end of Rifle siding Jim Petro's HO Rio Grande layout.
Layout photo: Jim Petro

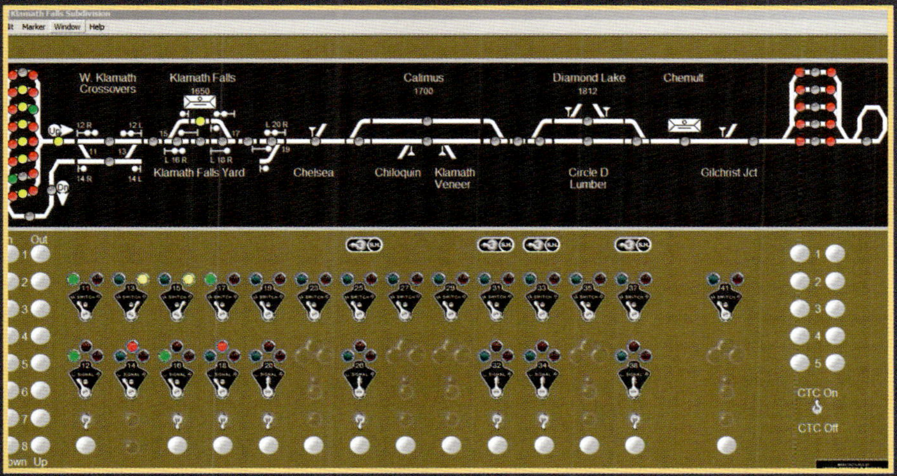

On prototype railroads, Centralized Traffic Control (CTC) allows dispatcher control of mainline turnouts (junctions and passing sidings) and signals to control movement of trains, **2**, relying on block occupancy detection as a guide. A Raspberry Pi together with the Java Model Railroad Interface (JMRI) software described in earlier chapters, along with the Computer Model Railroad Interface (C/MRI), allows doing this on a model railroad.

In this chapter, Dennis Drury explains installing the system, including setting up a computer screen that replicates a prototype Union Switch & Signal Co. dispatcher's panel.

Before embarking on this project, consider whether it makes sense for your layout. If you have a large operation-based layout with lots of scheduled trains, it can be a great addition. For smaller layouts operating fewer trains you may — like the prototype — opt for a simpler system that only uses block signals, such as the ABS system in Chapter 4.

Although implementing a full CTC system like this is much easier than it was a decade or two ago, there's still a significant learning curve and time commitment to doing it. The software now available greatly simplifies wiring, but as the photos and diagrams throughout this chapter show, there's still a large amount of wiring involved, and there's no way to get around it. Multiple signals/signal LEDs, block detectors, nodes, and power supplies all require lots of wire and connections — color-code and label everything, or you'll have an untraceable rat's nest under your layout.

Advanced Raspberry Pi layout control system

Using a Raspberry Pi (www.raspberrypi.org/products/raspberry-pi-4-model-b/) makes this project possible and economical. It will run a JMRI-based system with signals and turnout control. We'll show examples of the steps involved, using two layouts as examples: Dennis Drury's Southern Pacific and Jim Petro's Denver & Rio Grande Western.

You'll need a keyboard and monitor, as well as an interface from the Raspberry Pi to the model railroad. The Arduino-based cpNode system from Model Railroad Control Systems (MRCS, www.modelrailroadcontrolsystems.com/cpnode/) is a good choice. Each one of these nodes provides the basis for inputs and outputs in the blocks of the railroad.

This system implements the C/MRI protocol and is fairly straightforward to set up and use. As originally designed, it used a custom version of the Arduino Leonardo which is now out of production, but MRCS has an updated version that uses an Arduino Pro Mini as well as one using a Mega. The following steps describe how to configure a Raspberry Pi with JMRI to provide signaling. But before getting into that, the following is a description of Dennis Drury's railroad and how it uses JMRI.

Dennis's HO layout is based on Southern Pacific's Klamath Falls Subdivision ("KF Sub") circa 1984, a line that runs from Klamath Falls to Crescent Lake in south-central Oregon. It gives Dennis the chance to model his favorite railroad and also allows him to prototypically include trains of Burlington Northern; Amtrak; Oregon, California & Eastern; Klamath Northern; and his own freelanced short line, the California, Oregon & Western.

Since the prototype was controlled by CTC, Dennis considered CTC control a must for his layout. It's a large layout with three levels and an extensive main line. You can see the layout's CTC dispatcher's panel in **1** (you can see more photos, detailed track plans, and other information on the layout on Dennis's dedicated Facebook page: www.facebook.com/groups/202054440406321).

In looking at the panel, the track is completed from the lower-level staging at the left (which goes through a three-turn helix to get to the next level) through Klamath Falls yard up to the No. 19 switch on the panel. The panel shows, via yellow indicator lights on the schematic, a train departing staging track 3 and heading up the helix, as well as Amtrak's *Coast Starlight,* which is currently in the siding at the Klamath Falls station.

The dispatcher will soon line the *Starlight* out of the siding, where it will cross over to the downhill track. Once that movement is complete, the uphill freight will be lined across into the yard. (None of the lamps to the right of switch 17 are illuminated, since that part of the railroad is still under construction. As track enters service, those sections will become live in JMRI.)

Installing the system

The first thing needed is a Raspberry Pi. A nice thing about using a Cana Kit (Raspberry Pi kit and accessories) on Amazon is it comes with a case, fan, power supply, SD card, and other accessories. You'll also need USB-to-RS485 adapters, **3**, to connect the nodes to the Raspberry Pi.

Download the JMRI program (see Chapter 5). Normally Dennis suggests downloading the program from the JMRI website, but Steve Todd has created a file that provides the Raspberry Pi operating system as well as JMRI along with Java in one convenient package that can be put directly on the SD card used by the Pi (mstevetodd.com/rpi). From the MRCS site you'll need to download the technical guide and the correct Arduino sketch for your specific processor (www.modelrailroadcontrolsystems.com/cpnode-version-2-7/).

Once you've downloaded the material from Steve Todd's website, follow the instructions to put it on an SD card. Insert the SD card in the Raspberry Pi, connect the RS485 adapter to one of the USB ports, connect the monitor, keyboard, and mouse, then apply power. The Raspberry Pi should boot up directly into JMRI, and it will automatically detect the devices connected to the USB ports.

Before you proceed further, you'll need to configure cpNodes. Open the cpNode sketch, **4**. It might seem a bit intimidating at first, but don't worry,

2 **A prototype CTC board uses a combination of levers and buttons to control turnouts and signal indications.**

only a few items need to be configured. The first item is the nodeID, in this case “20.” Each node connected to the Raspberry Pi needs its own unique address. Dennis’s railroad has four nodes, numbered 10 through 13. They don’t need to be numbered in sequence. It’s advisable to use two digits for node IDs — this allows the various tables in JMRI to display in a logical format.

Note that the nodes *must* be connected to the RS485 adapter in a serial manner — they can’t be connected in a “T” in the middle. The nodes do not need to be wired in numerical order. For example, the Raspberry Pi can start with node 12, then 10, 13, and finally 11. Also note that the first node is wired “backward” from the rest, **5**. The TX from the RS485 adapter connects to the RX of the first node, while the RX from the adapter connects to the TX of the first node. From there on, TX connects to TX and RX to RX for the rest of the boards.

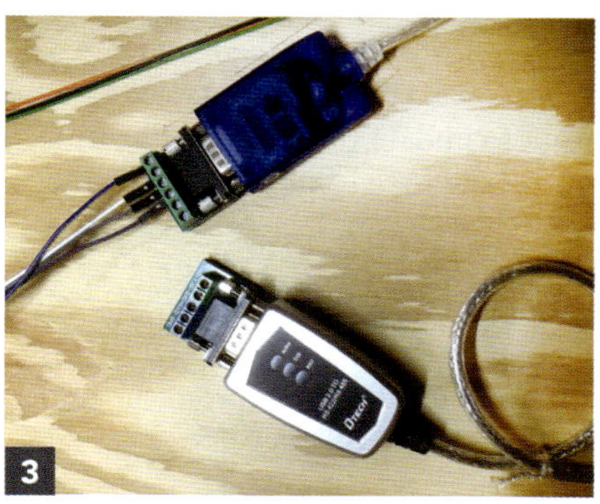

3 **You’ll need USB-to-RS485 connectors to daisy-chain the nodes to the Raspberry Pi.**

The next thing to consider is CMRINET_SPEED, in this case 19200. This speed and 9600 will work with the cpNode hardware as delivered. For a different speed, change out one resistor on the board. See the cpNode schematic for more information (the schematic and technical guide can be downloaded from the MRCS website). You can choose different network speeds, but you need to make sure all nodes have the same speed setting.

If the application needs more than the 16 pins available on the node, you can get IOX boards from MRCS. These boards provide additional inputs and outputs and are configured with the next section of the sketch. Using the IOX boards can provide up to 128 additional input/output pins. These pins are configured in groups of 8 by assigning the characters 0 or 1 to the appropriate IOX addresses. Note that there are jumpers on each IOX to assign the board address. See the technical guide for additional information.

The last item is the base node assignment. In the case shown above, it’s set for 8 output pins and 8 input pins. This can be changed as needed, and not all nodes need the same I/O configuration.

After confirming the correct connection of the nodes to the RS485 card, the next step is to configure JMRI. The Steve Todd image will automatically detect the USB ports. There is a routine called “Poll USB Ports.” Start this and a window similar to **6** will pop up.

On Dennis’s railroad there are three connections: C/MRI, a Digitrax PR3, and a SPROG. For this chapter, you only need to be concerned with the C/MRI connection. In this case the C/MRI system is connected to the ttyUSB0 port. On your system you can verify which port is being used by disconnecting and reconnecting the USB cable and seeing which port changes. Make a note of the port connected to your C/MRI system, as you’ll need that information in the next step.

The JMRI preferences window, **7**, should open automatically if the connections have not been configured.

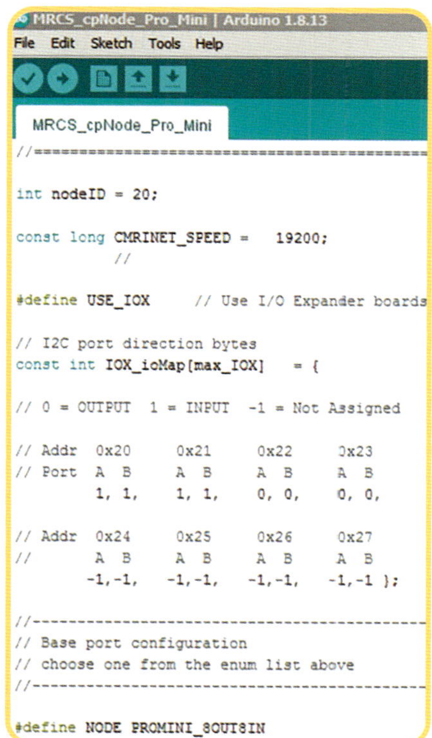

4 **The setup for the cpNode is done using the Arduino IDE. This can be the same computer used to program the other systems described in previous chapters.**

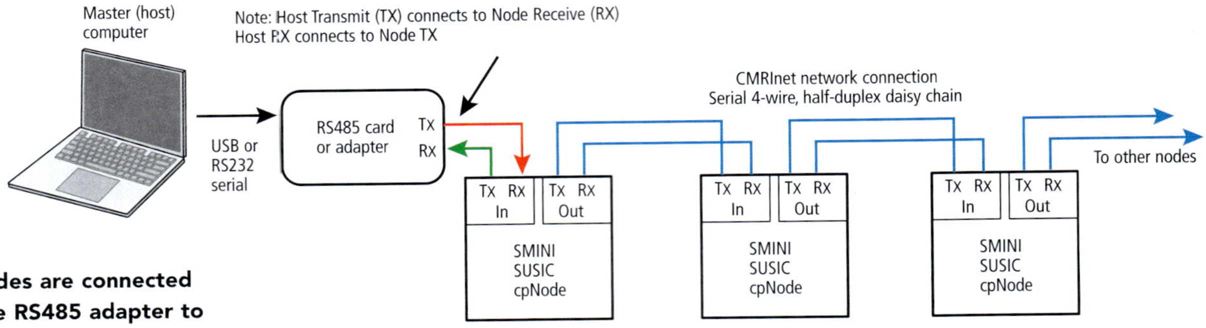

The nodes are connected through the RS485 adapter to the computer as shown. Note the TX to RX connections at the first node, but the remaining connections in the chain are TX to TX and RX to RX.

5 The nodes are connected through the RS485 adapter to the Raspberry Pi as shown. Note the TX to RX connections at the first node, but the remaining connections in the chain are TX to TX and RX to RX.

This is where you tell JMRI what connection is being configured — in this case, C/MRI. Select the connection mode, in this case "serial." Next up is the serial port, recorded in the previous step. On this railroad it's ttyUSB0. The connection prefix and connection name should self-populate. Click in the box that says "Additional Connection Settings" to set the baud rate (this was set in a previous step configuring the node sketches). The node's baud rate is set at 9600, which works just fine. Once this information has been entered, it's probably a good idea to save the preferences. The program will say it needs to reboot, so click OK/yes.

The next step is to create a panel. Under "Panels," select "New Panel" then whichever type of panel you prefer. Dennis created a CTC panel using Panel Editor, but if you prefer a layout diagram instead, then use Layout Editor.

Once the program restarts, enter the data for the nodes. On the main PanelPro window, click "Edit" then "Preferences." When that window opens, click "Configure Nodes," then click "Add Node," **8**. In that image you can see that the configuration uses node address 11, and that it's a CPNODE. The next three items can be left at the default values of Receive Delay 0, Card Size 8 bit, and Pulse Width 500 ms.

Dennis is also using one IOX-32 extension board configured as one input and the other three as outputs. This is described in the cpNode Technical Guide mentioned previously. If desired, you can enter a description such as East End Rock Ridge, or any other text that might help identify where node 11 is located. Dennis left all other options at the default value. Once this is configured, click on the Add Node button and repeat the process for all other nodes that are configured; when they're set, click on Done. It's a good idea to save preferences and reboot the program on a regular basis.

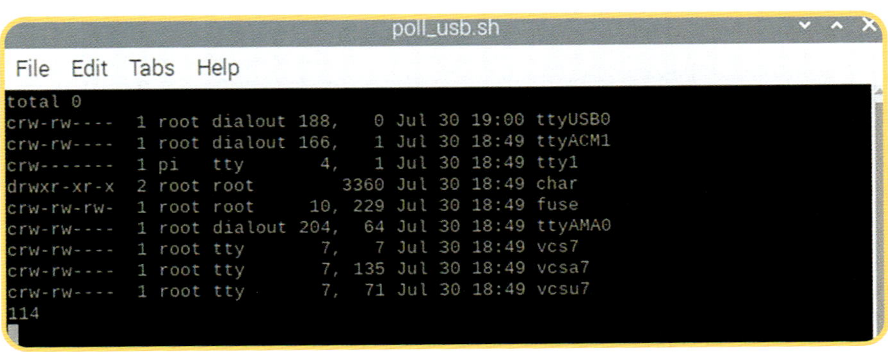
```
poll_usb.sh
File  Edit  Tabs  Help
total 0
crw-rw----  1 root dialout 188,   0 Jul 30 19:00 ttyUSB0
crw-rw----  1 root dialout 166,   1 Jul 30 18:49 ttyACM1
crw-------  1 pi   tty       4,   1 Jul 30 18:49 tty1
drwxr-xr-x  2 root root        3360 Jul 30 18:49 char
crw-rw-rw-  1 root root     10, 229 Jul 30 18:49 fuse
crw-rw----  1 root dialout 204,  64 Jul 30 18:49 ttyAMA0
crw-rw----  1 root tty       7,   7 Jul 30 18:49 vcs7
crw-rw----  1 root tty       7, 135 Jul 30 18:49 vcsa7
crw-rw----  1 root tty       7,  71 Jul 30 18:49 vcsu7
114
```

6 Start the routine "Poll USB Ports" and a window similar to this will open. It will show which devices are connected to which ports, such as ttyUSB0.

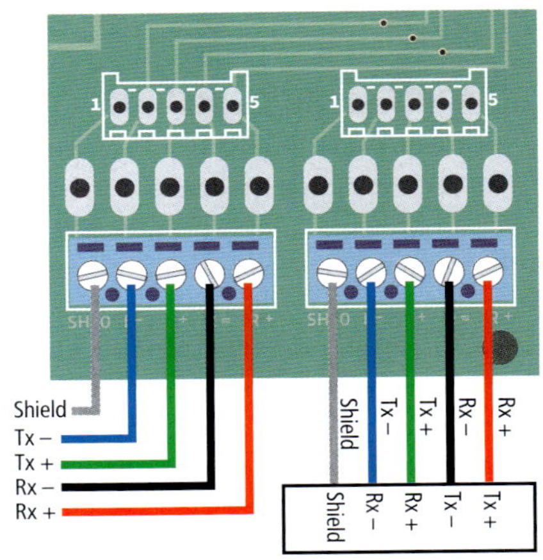

Once all nodes have been entered, you should see a window similar to the one in **9**. These are the three nodes that are currently configured for this railroad. Once construction reaches that point, he will add Node 10, but for right now it's not needed. One last image to add is the C/MRI Serial Command Monitor, located under the C/MRI tab on the main JMRI screen. When the system is powered up and running, each node is polled, which will then generate a response, **10**. The responses are used to update the sensor tables and also show JMRI sending data to the nodes. For example, look at timestamp 22:37:57.659: JMRI is sending a command to node 13, telling the node to change the state of a signal. (IB is short for inbound data from the node; OB is outbound.)

Lessons learned

• When downloading the JMRI image from Steve Todd's website, make sure to get a production version (if in doubt, ask).

- When configuring node sketches, make sure to use the correct one. The Leonardo sketch is markedly different from the Pro Mini one. You can mix and match Leonardo and Pro Mini boards on the same layout, but each one must be programmed correctly.
- Make sure you use the correct TX/RX connections.
- Be certain the baud rate is set correctly and that all nodes match the rate configured in JMRI preferences.
- If using IOX boards, make sure they are configured correctly in the sketch and the "set address" jumpers are in the correct locations.
- Every node needs at least one sensor created in JMRI or the program will not poll that node. In JMRI go to Tools > Tables > Sensors. Make sure the C/MRI tab is selected at the top, then click on "Add" at the bottom (see the cpNode Technical Guide for more information). It's also important to create a panel before adding sensors and turnouts because that's where that information gets saved.

Hardware and installation

The following examples are shown on Jim Petro's D&RGW. There's no way to describe specifics that apply to every model railroad, so we'll look at the processes involved at several control points on Jim's layout. (A control point is a location with a turnout and/or signals that the dispatcher will control, typically the end of a siding or a junction). In following along, you can see what you'll need to do to install a similar system on your own layout.

Jim used the cpNode system from MRCS, described earlier. There are other signal system hardware designs available (LCC, Digitrax SE8c, and others), but the cpNode has certain advantages. A key factor is that it's completely open source, so even if you choose not to purchase the system from MRCS, you can still order the components and build your own.

Previous chapters showed how to divide your railroad into individual blocks and create a drawing of your main line showing these blocks; a section of Jim's is shown in **11**. When adding feeder wires to the track in each section, follow the manufacturers' directions for whichever occupancy detectors you're using. Notice in the drawing that the block numbers are three digits — some software programs have issues with fewer digits. The block boundaries are between signals, except the boundary between blocks BK101 and BK102, which is shown by a line.

The original MRCS cpNode, **12**, used what's called a BB Leo style of Arduino. This was a breadboard version

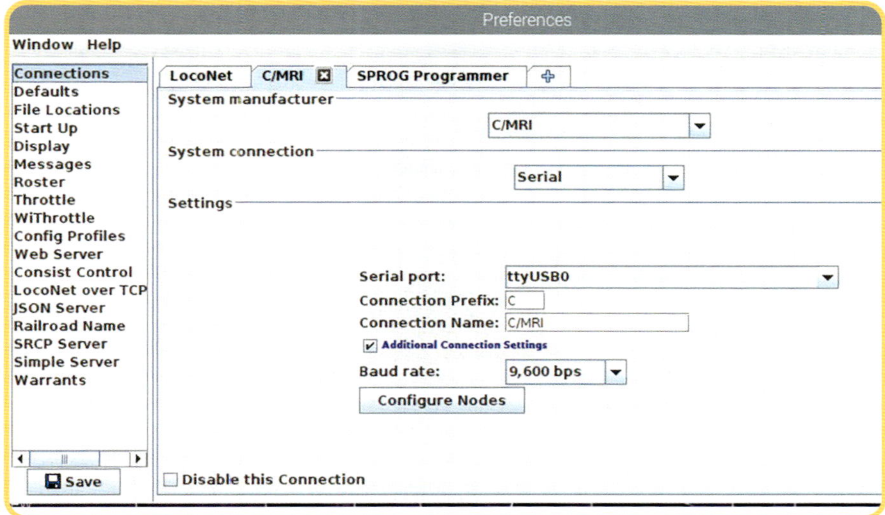

7 **The JMRI preferences window allows specifying which connection is being configured; in this case, C/MRI. Set the connection mode, serial port, and baud rate (speed). Save your preferences and reboot if the program suggests it.**

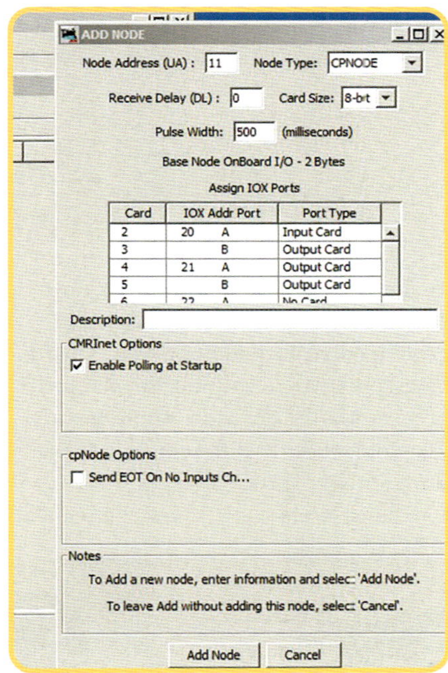

8 **In PanelPro, go to Edit > Preferences, then click Configure Nodes and Add Node. Configure and add each node.**

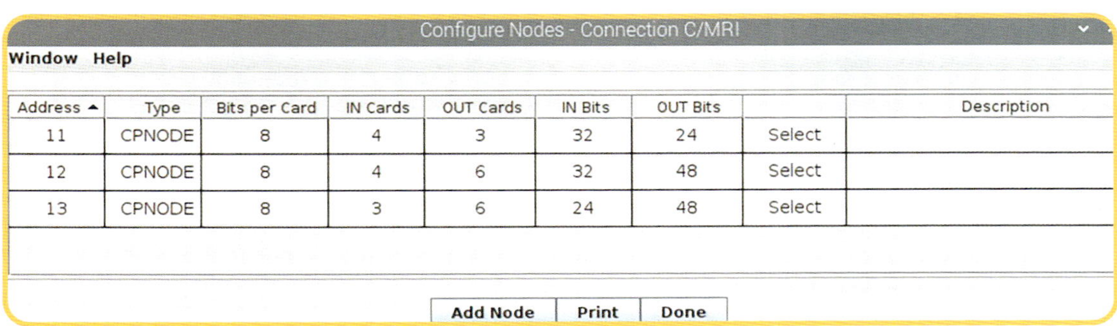

9 **When nodes are entered, you'll see a window showing all nodes currently configured. Node 10 hasn't been added, as that area of the layout is still under construction.**

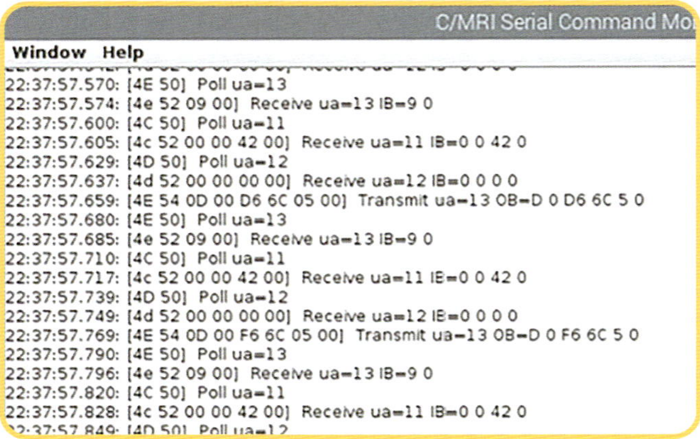

10 **When the system is running, the nodes are polled; their responses will update the sensor tables.**

11 **Below is the schematic for a section of Jim Petro's Rio Grande layout from Grand Junction to Prospect. It shows signal locations as well as block numbers.**

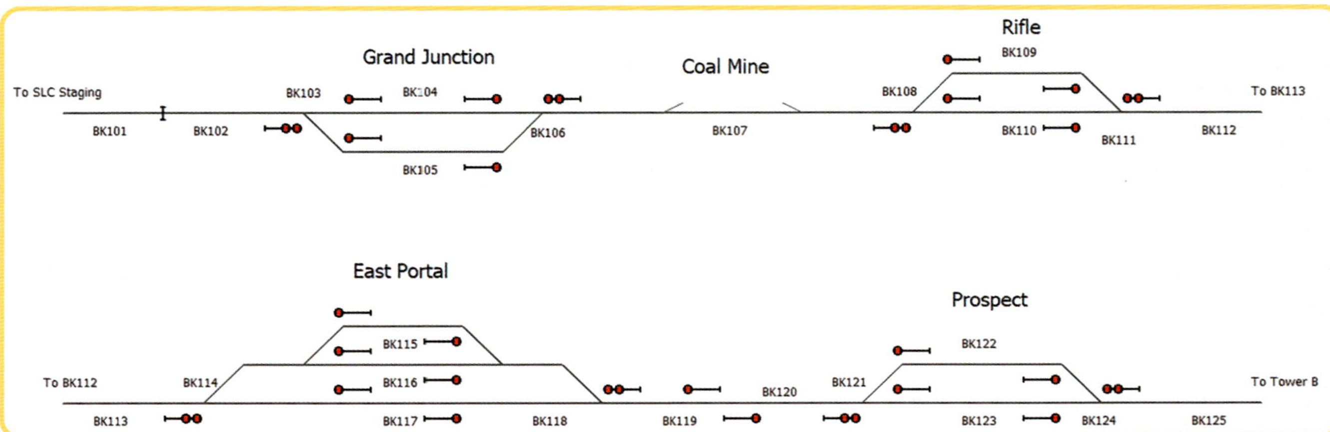

of the Arduino Leonardo that's now out of production. MRCS has since developed replacement cpNode boards using either the Arduino Pro Mini, **13**, or a standard Leonardo. These boards may look slightly different, but their functionality is the same.

The cpNode has 16 pins that can be set up in different input/output configurations. If you need more pins, you can use IOX (Input Output eXtender) boards, **14**. They come in either a 16- or 32-pin format that can be set up as either inputs or outputs.

In CTC systems, the dispatcher controls mainline turnouts. For this you'll need either the RSMC (Remote Stall Motor Controller) or the ITC (Intelligent Turnout Controller). If you want the ability for the dispatcher to grant local control of turnouts to train crews, you'll need the ITC. If local control is not required, the RSMC will work just fine.

12

Jim's layout uses original MRCS cpNodes, which are based on an older (BB Leo) breadboard version of an Arduino Leonardo. The basic setup and functions remain the same for modernized versions.

13

This is the latest MRCS cpNode, based on an Arduino ProMini; a standard Leonardo version is also available. *MRCS*

14 If you need additional pin connections, attach an IOX board to the cpNode. They're available in 16-pin (shown) or 32-pin versions. *MRCS*

These components can be installed on the layout in different ways. A example on Jim Petro's layout, **15**, shows a cpNode hiding behind a freight house in Grand Junction. An under-table mounting is shown in **16**, with the labeling for the signal at East Portal.

Another installation, this one on Dennis Drury's layout, **17,** shows a view of Tortoise switch machines with RSMCs mounted on them, along with a couple of block detectors.

As shown earlier, you need a USB to RS485 as an interface between your computer and the cpNodes. There are many of these on the market; we've mostly used the Gearmo Pro (Gearmo Pro 5-foot USB to RS485/422 Serial Adapter FTDI Chip).

Before going further, I strongly suggest you download all the

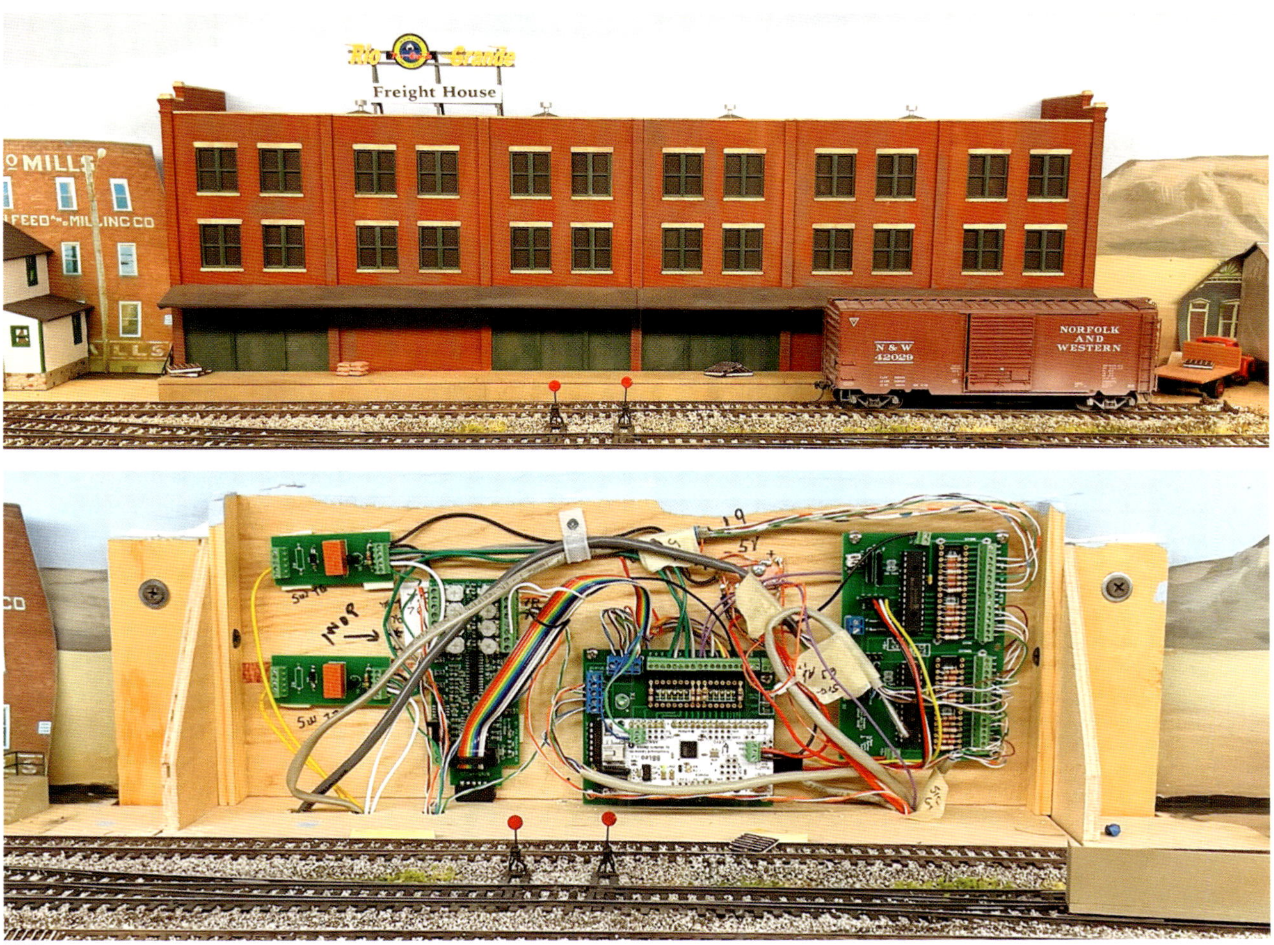

15 A node and related wiring is mounted above the layout and concealed by a freight house structure at Grand Junction on Jim Petro's layout. The location provides handy access to connections for troubleshooting. *Jim Petro*

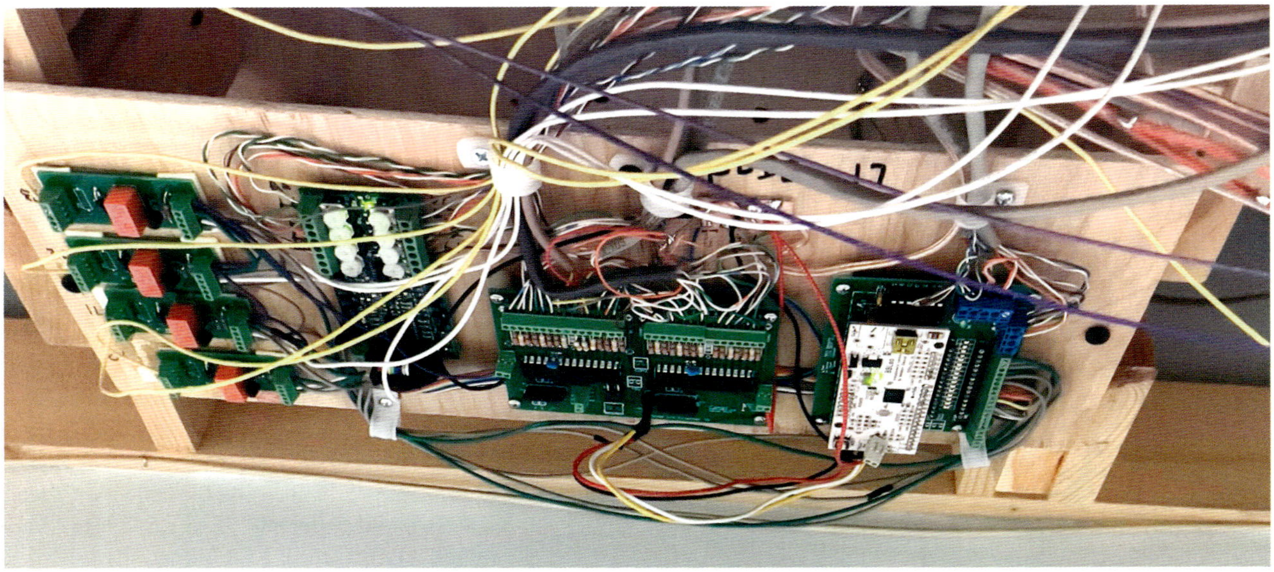

16 **The East Portal node and related hardware, above, are mounted under the layout. The node is at right, the IOX is in the center, and the BOD-8 at left. Above the layout, left, the Yampa Valley Mail is ready to head east to Denver, waiting at signal 54. Labels on the fascia assist operators.**
Jim Petro

17

This is the view under West Klamath on Dennis Drury's layout. The two Tortise switch machines control the turnouts on the crossover. Each Tortoise has an RSMC mounted on it. You can also see two cpOD block detectors at bottom left, with the track feeder wires running through them. You can see the tracks and signals they control in fig. 18.

18 Extra 8351 East is approaching the signals at the West Klamath crossovers on Dennis Drury's layout. The yellow indication tells the engineer to proceed prepared to stop at the next signal. Dispatcher-controlled turnouts and signals are the ultimate goal of installing a CTC system.

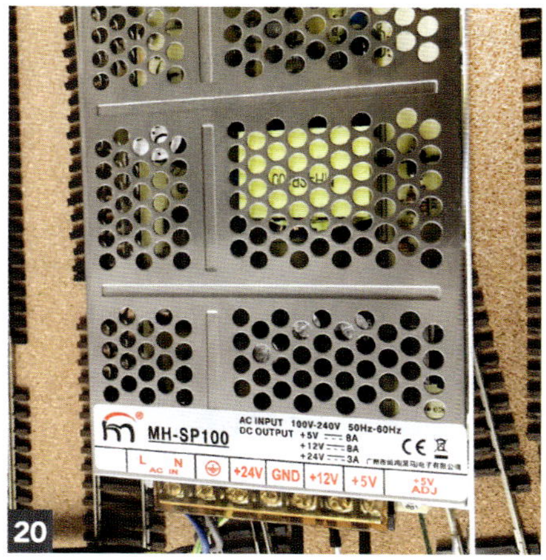

20 You'll need a power supply that provides 5V and 12V DC. These are available from many sources.

cpNode_Kernel_v15

```
/*============================================*/
/*====     NODE CONFIGURATION PARAMETERS     ====*/
/*============================================*/
                                                  //
int nodeID = 20;                                  //
                                                  //
const long CMRINET_SPEED =   9600;                //
                                                  //
boolean Init_CA_Ports_OFF = false;                //
                                                  //
/*============================================*/
/*====     NODE CONFIGURATION PARAMETERS     ====*/
/*============================================*/

//---------------------------------------------------------
//  Uncomment only one of the standard node configurations
//  #ifdef selects the higher order bit definitions
//--------------------------------------------------------
//#define BASE_NODE
#define BASE_NODE_8IN8OUT
//#define BASE_NODE_8OUT8IN    // cpNode System Test Configuration
//#define BASE_NODE_12OUT4IN
//#define BASE_NODE_16IN
//#define BASE_NODE_16OUT
//#define BASE_NODE_RSMC
//#define BASE_NODE_RSMC_LOCK
```

cpNode_Kernel_v15

```
                              // Board Addresses (duplicated for ease of indexing)
const int IOX_devAddr[max_IOX] = {0x20,0x20, 0x21,0x21, 0x22,0x22, 0x23,0x23,
                                  0x24,0x24, 0x25,0x25, 0x26,0x26, 0x27,0x27  },

// I2C port direction bytes 0 = OUTPUT  1 = INPUT  -1 = Not Assigned
//------------------------------------------------------------
                             // Addr  0x20    0x21    0x22    0x23    0x24    0x25    0x26    0x27
                             // Port  A  B    A  B    A  B    A  B    A  B    A  B    A  B    A  B
           IOX_ioMap[max_IOX]   =   {  1, 1,   0, 0,  -1,-1,  -1,-1,  -1,-1,  -1,-1,  -1,-1,  -1,-1 };
```

19 In the Arduino IDE, you'll need to configure the node ID (20), CMRI net speed (9600), and base node configuration (8 in, 8 out), left. You'll need to set up the IOX board as well, bottom. This shows that address 0x20 ports A and B are set up as inputs, while address 0x21 ports A and B are outputs.

documentation for the hardware you'll be using. This can include the cpNode Technical Guide, which includes information on the IOX boards. If you're using the RSMC or ITC boards, make sure you get that documentation as well. Also make sure you have all the documentation for your detectors (note that you can mix and match detector types). Jim and Dennis both use a combination of BOD-8s from RR-CIRKITS and the cpOD from MRCS.

Download and install the Arduino IDE as described in the cpNode technical guide (and Chapter 2). Before configuring the nodes, calculate how many inputs and outputs you'll need. Each block will be one input. Each dispatcher-controlled turnout will be one input and either one or two outputs (one if you're using the RSMC without local control; two if you're using the ITC with the ability to grant local control). Count how many LEDs are in your signals — each LED requires one output.

As an example, look back at **11**. In that section of the layout, there are four cpNodes, one each at Grand Junction, Rifle, East Portal, and Prospect. The node at Grand Junction (node ID 11) will have 8 inputs. These are blocks BK101 through BK106 plus the turnout position inputs from the east and west turnouts. Since there's local control for these, there will be two outputs for each turnout. Adding up the LEDs for the signals gives us 24 LED outputs (3 LEDs in each of 8 signal heads) for a total of 28 outputs for Grand Junction. This will require one cpNode and one IOX32. If we set up the node as a Base_Node_16in, we can then configure the IOX as "all outputs."

Rifle is set up the same way. The inputs will be blocks BK107 through BK112. The east and west turnouts will be two more inputs. The two turnouts will have two outputs each, and there will be 24 LEDs.

East Portal will be a bit different since there are four turnouts plus the intermediate signals between East Portal and Prospect to consider. East Portal will have blocks BK113 through BK119 for a total of seven. The four turnouts will add another four inputs. There will be eight outputs for the turnouts and 36 LED outputs. The added LED outputs are because we'll be connecting the intermediate signals to this node. Because of this we will need the node, one IOX32, and one IOX16.

Finally, Prospect will be configured the same as Rifle and Grand Junction as far as inputs and outputs are concerned. On the nodes and IOX boards there are sockets where you can either put in a jumper if that pin is used for an input or a basic output, or you can install a resistor if that pin is driving an LED.

There are a few things you'll need to configure in the IDE: the node ID, CMRI Net speed, and Base Node configuration, **19**. The speed on all nodes must be the same. It's best to use the lowest speed consistent with proper operation — I've found 9600 is fast enough for all but the largest layouts. If you're using any IOX boards with this node, make sure you uncomment the #define USE_IOX (remove the two slashes before the hashtag) and set up the IOX. The cpNode technical guide goes into greater detail on how everything gets configured.

You'll also need a power supply, **20**, that provides both 5V and 12V DC. These are available from Amazon, Digikey, Mouser and other electronics suppliers.

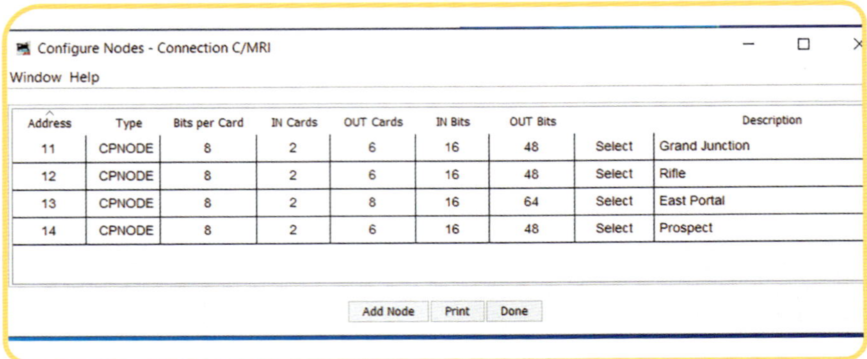
Configure Nodes - Connection C/MRI

Address	Type	Bits per Card	IN Cards	OUT Cards	IN Bits	OUT Bits		Description
11	CPNODE	8	2	6	16	48	Select	Grand Junction
12	CPNODE	8	2	6	16	48	Select	Rifle
13	CPNODE	8	2	8	16	64	Select	East Portal
14	CPNODE	8	2	6	16	48	Select	Prospect

21 **This is the screen showing the four configured nodes: Grand Junction, Rifle, East Portal, and Prospect, with the number of input and outputs for each.**

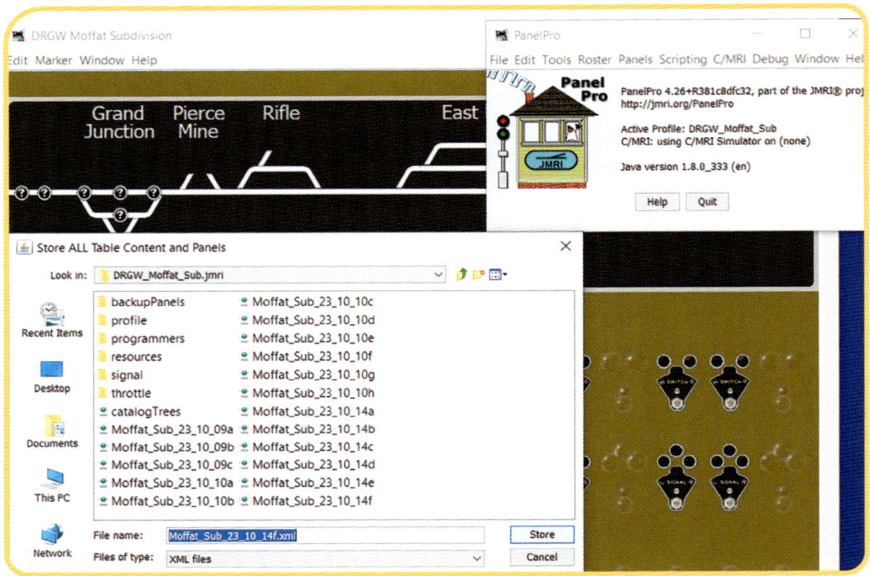

22 **Save your files often. I like to use a name followed by the year/month/day, plus a letter increment for each new version.**

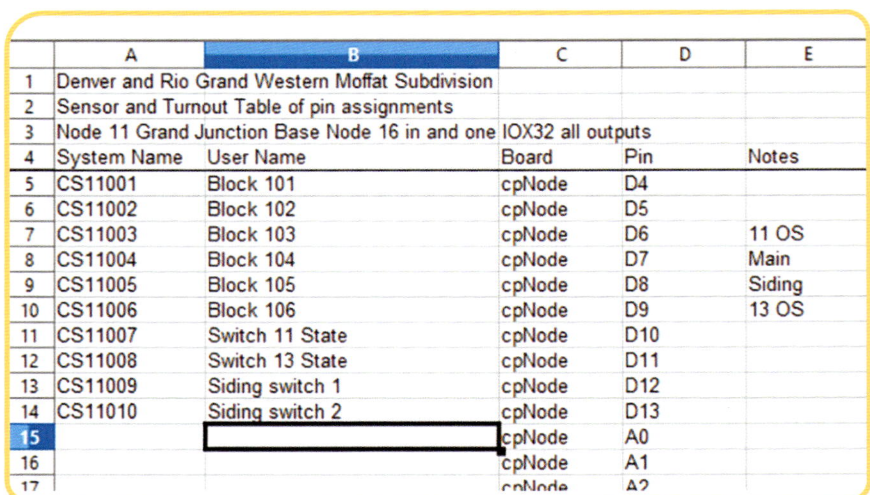

	A	B	C	D	E
1	Denver and Rio Grand Western Moffat Subdivision				
2	Sensor and Turnout Table of pin assignments				
3	Node 11 Grand Junction Base Node 16 in and one IOX32 all outputs				
4	System Name	User Name	Board	Pin	Notes
5	CS11001	Block 101	cpNode	D4	
6	CS11002	Block 102	cpNode	D5	
7	CS11003	Block 103	cpNode	D6	11 OS
8	CS11004	Block 104	cpNode	D7	Main
9	CS11005	Block 105	cpNode	D8	Siding
10	CS11006	Block 106	cpNode	D9	13 OS
11	CS11007	Switch 11 State	cpNode	D10	
12	CS11008	Switch 13 State	cpNode	D11	
13	CS11009	Siding switch 1	cpNode	D12	
14	CS11010	Siding switch 2	cpNode	D13	
15			cpNode	A0	
16			cpNode	A1	

23 **Document details of your work as you go. This is a spreadsheet showing pin assignments with notes and details.**

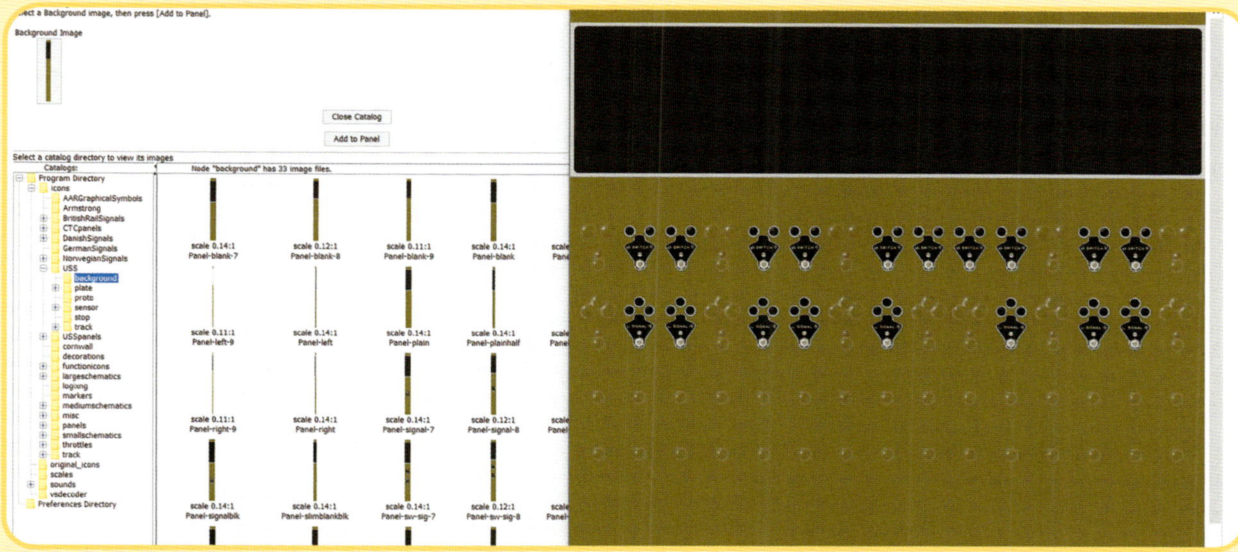

24 **To build a CTC panel, add the appropriate vertical segments from the menu at left side-by-side to create the panel background at right. The track schematic will be added to the black area at the top.**

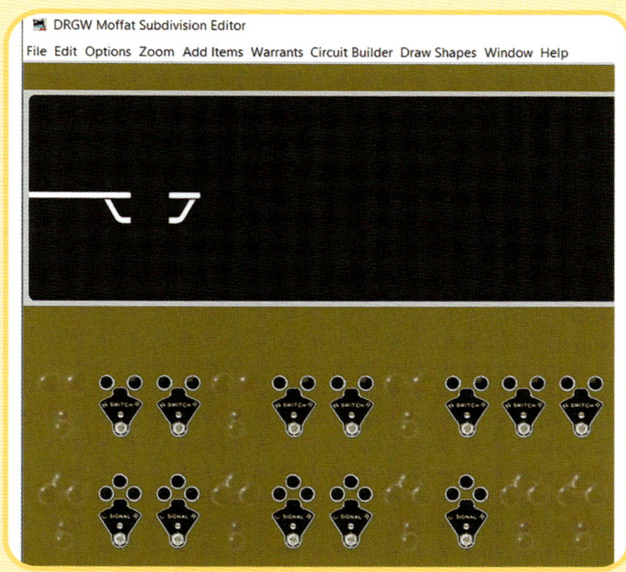

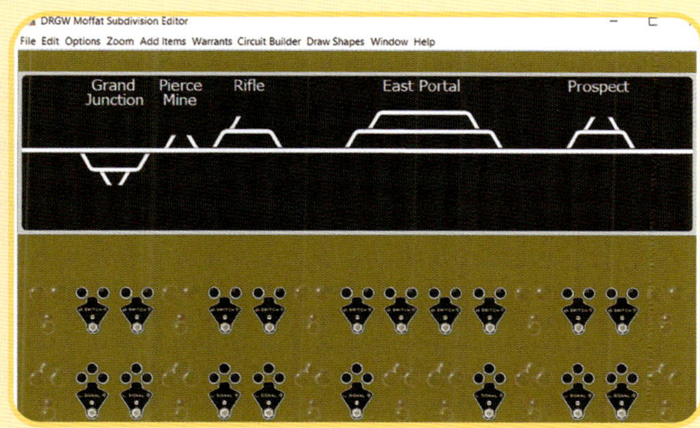

25 **Add the track icons to the panel. There are two ways to move items on the panel: click and drag or right-click on an item and select Set Location, then use the little up and down arrows or use the arrows on your keyboard. Text is added by selecting Text under Item Palette.**

Software

We're now ready to start setting up the software. The version of JMRI we're using is 4.26 (www.jmri.org/releasenotes/jmri4.26.shtml); although there have been upgrades in JMRI since this release, we've found this is the latest version that will run on some older computers. If your computer can use a later version, the steps will remain the same.

Double click the PanelPro icon to start JMRI, and if you haven't already done so, click on "new" to start a new profile and give it a name. The JMRI help window will open — you can close or minimize this window. Set up the connection to the C/MRI system: set the System Manufacturer to C/MRI, the System Connection to C/MRI Simulator, and auto-populate the Connection Prefix and Connection Name. Click "save" and JMRI will ask to restart.

The reason we're starting with the C/MRI Simulator is that I've found it's much easier to program the system without having it connected and the railroad running. After getting everything set with Simulater, we'll then transfer the files into the layout's actual profile.

When PanelPro restarts, make sure all nodes are set up as in **8** and **9**.

As an example, at Rifle the Node Address (UA) was changed to 12, the description updated, then Add Node clicked. This is repeated for the last two nodes, but we had to remember

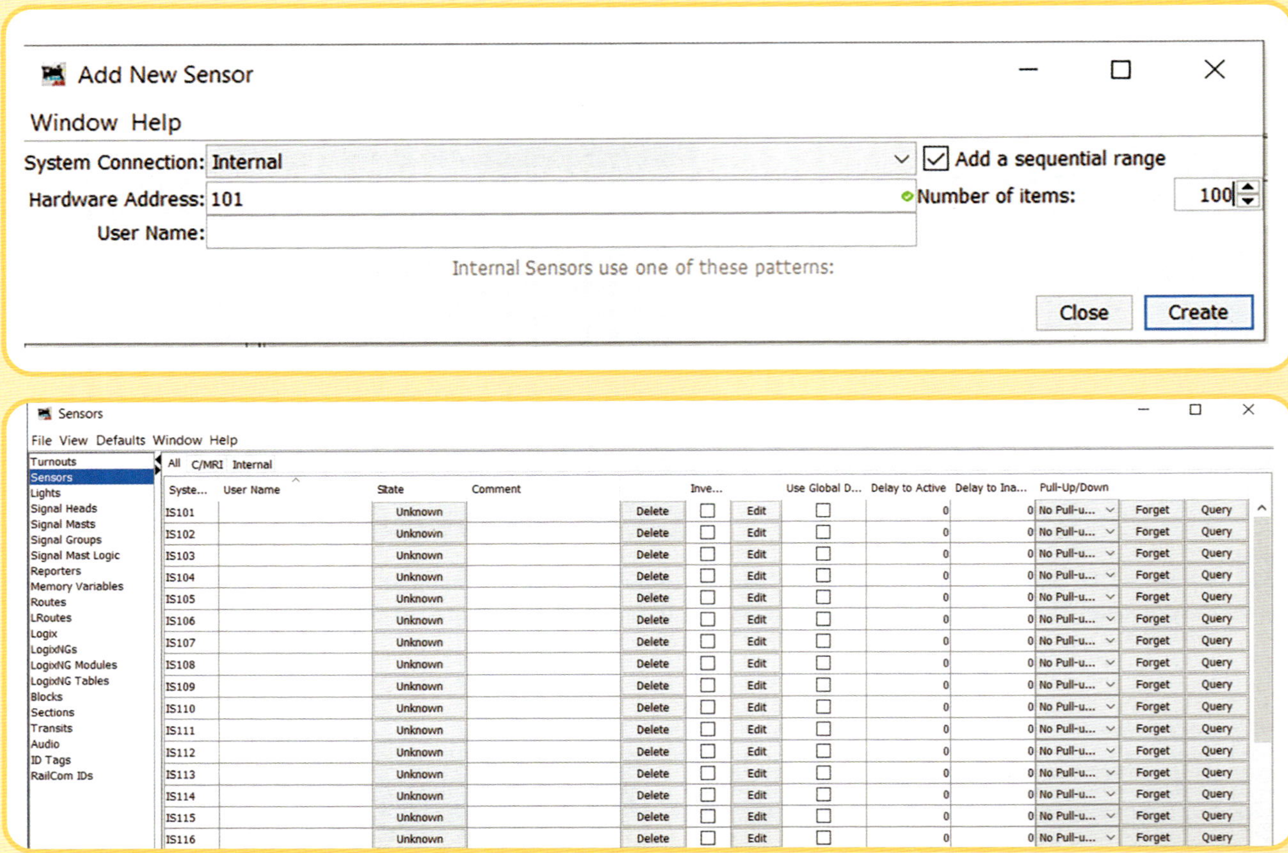

26 **Go to Tools > Tables > Sensors and click Add. Start with Hardware Address 101 and enter 100 as the sequential range. Click Create and the sensor table will populate.**

that East Portal will need 6 output cards. Once all four nodes have been added and you click Done you will get a reminder to save your work, **21**. Remember JMRI is not saving it at this point, it's up to you to save the file in preferences.

There's another idiosyncrasy when using the cpNode system with JMRI. Note that there are more output bits than are available with the IOX boards. This is because the cpNode allocates 16 input bits and 16 output bits for each board. Even though the boards are configured as Base_Node_16in, the outputs are still reserved in JMRI. We can ignore this and know that JMRI will keep everything straight.

I can't stress enough that it's a good idea to frequently save your files (File > Store ALL table contents and panels). I like to use the file naming system shown in **22**: a name followed by the date followed by a letter that increments each time you save. This avoids overwriting a file, and if you make a mistake, you can always go back to a previous version. Also: document *everything* (on paper or electronically) — an example is my spreadsheet for pin assignments, **23**.

CTC panel

Let's start putting the CTC panel together. From the main PanelPro screen, select Panel > New Panel > Panel Editor. Two new screens will open: Panel and Panel Editor. You can then use Select to choose the type of icon to add to Panel. Start by scrolling down to Background. Click on Change Icon, then click on the + sign next to Program Directory to expand the selections. Next click on the + sign next to icons and the + sign next to USS.

Start with the background by choosing "Background," and you'll get a menu of many types of vertical panel components. Building your panel is a matter of combining the various components. Start by adding a left-edge icon by dragging it in place, then click Add to Panel. I used the 9"-high segments, but you can choose the 7"- or 8"-high segments depending on your screen size and resolution. Add blank segments or various switch/signal segments based on your track schematic, **24**.

Once the background is in place, we can start adding the track diagram. This will closely follow the linear diagram in **11** from the previous section, but will use symbols representing how an actual US&S panel would look. Start by changing to Control Panel Editor, which will make it easier to add items. Click on Edit > Open Editor in the Panel window, then File > Change view to Control Panel Editor. We now have another

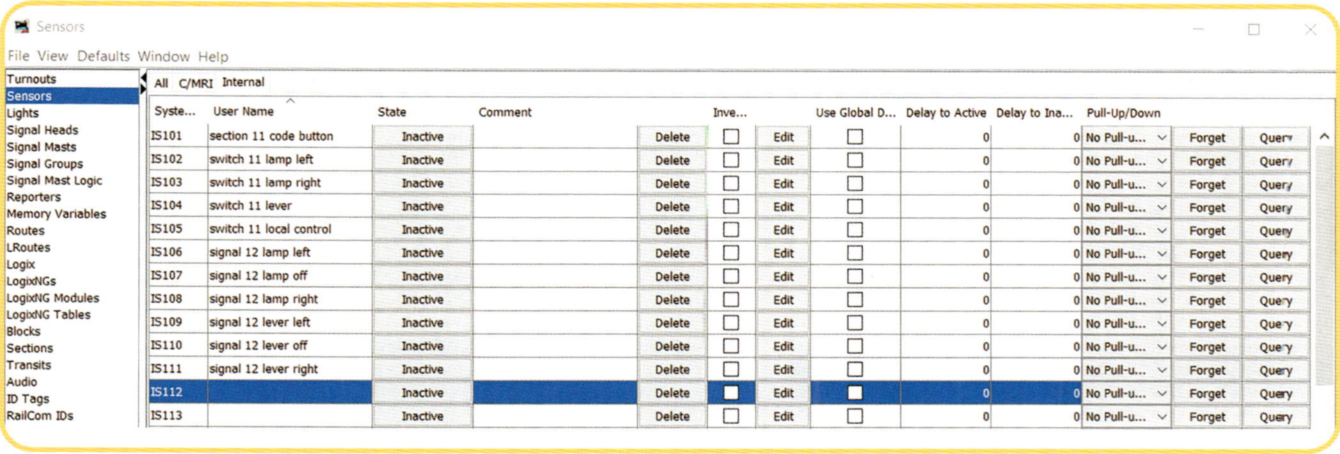

27 **Enter user names for sensors. This view shows the information entered for the West Grand Junction segment.**

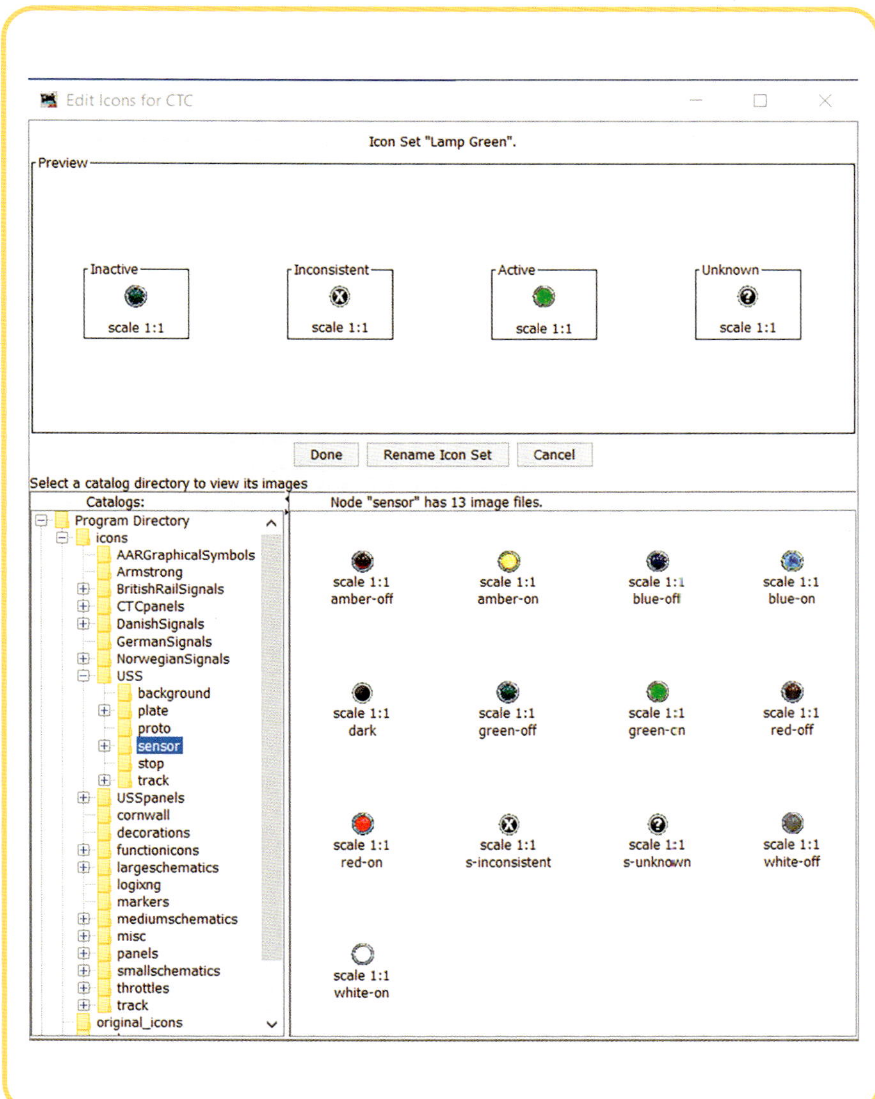

28 **To create a sensor catalog in the panel window, go to Add Items > Item Palette, select the Sensor tab > New Icon Set, and name it. This is the lamp icon set; do the same for switch levers, control toggles, and code buttons.**

panel window open with many more choices on how to add items to the panel. You can also change the name of the panel itself in the Panel Editor window by clicking File > Rename Panel. I named this one "DRGW Moffat Subdivision."

To add track diagram components, click on Add Items > Item Palette. From the selections at the top choose Icon, then Icon Catalog. Once again, we'll need to drop down to the US&S section and select Proto. One of the reasons we switched to the Control Panel Editor is that it's easier to add and move items around on the panel.

Start by dragging the icon labeled "scale 1:1 block" to the panel. You can see this is not very long, so let's make a longer line. You can either drag more icons to the panel or you can right click on the icon and select Duplicate. Either way you can move them to the proper location by either left-clicking and dragging or by right-clicking and selecting Set Location, **25**. A lesson learned is that it's easier to put the switch icons on top of the switch labels lined up to the correct horizontal position. You can then move them using the Select Location command.

Now use more block segments to fill in the gaps. There are also two hand-thrown turnouts leading into the industries in Grand Junction. The dispatcher has no control over them, but you can put them on the panel if you like.

Note that the east and west switch icons at Rifle are backward from what

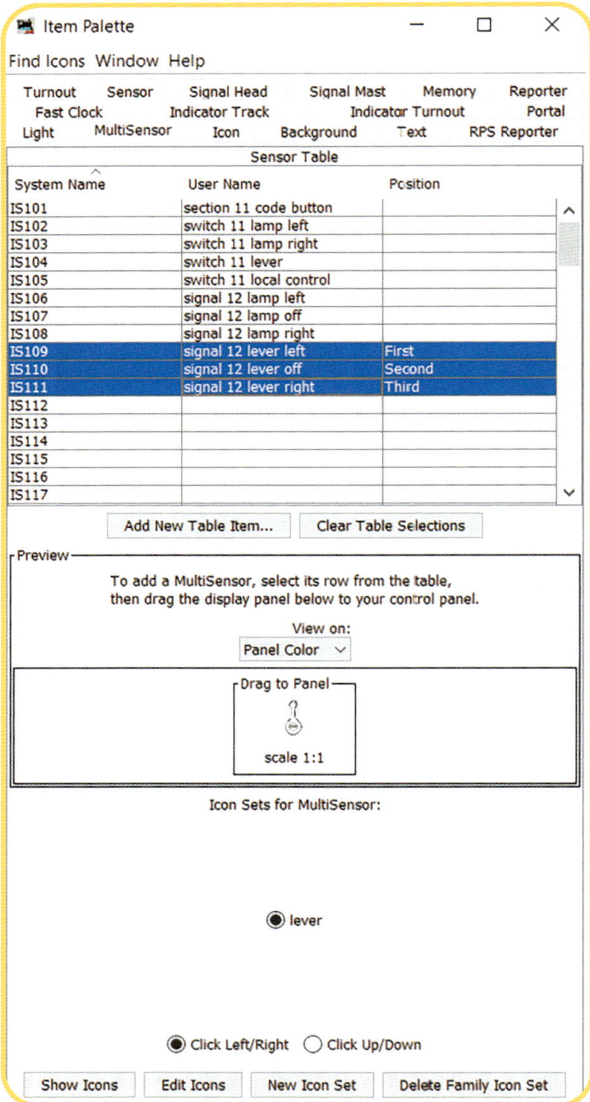

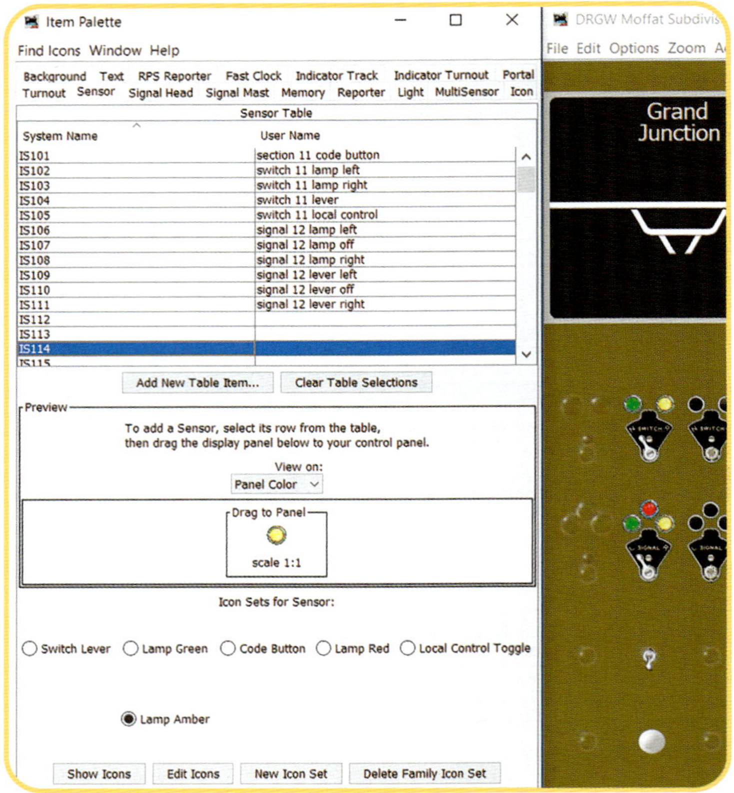

29 For the three-way signal lever you need to select the MultiSensor tab, then select positions for left, center, and right, then drag the icon to the panel.

30 To add items to the panel, select the sensor name, icon set, and drag the icon to the panel. These have been activated to show the lamp colors.

is available in the catalog. To do this, choose the proper left or right turnout, then right-click on it, select Rotate, and change the number to 180.

You can add labels by selecting Text under Item Palette. I set font size to 24, "view on" to dark gray, and "standard color" to white. They're added in the same manner as the track icons.

Lamps, levers, and switches

Now we'll add lamps, levers, pushbuttons, and toggle switches. In JMRI these are implemented with sensors. For this configuration JMRI uses two types of sensors, C/MRI and Internal. C/MRI sensors are inputs from the cpNode system such as block detectors and switch-position inputs. Internal sensors are used to implement the lamps, levers, pushbuttons, and toggle switches.

Prototype US&S CTC panels use odd numbers for switches and even numbers for signals. Block occupancy lamps are amber, switch normal is green, and switch reverse is amber. Signal lamp colors are green for left, red for off, and amber for right. Before we add lamps, we'll need to create some sensors. In the main JMRI window select Tools > Tables > Sensors. There will be tabs at the top where you can select All, C/MRI, or Internal — these tabs can be helpful when looking at either C/MRI or Internal.

To add sensors, click Add and choose Internal. Start with Hardware Address 101 and, since we're going to need quite a few sensors, let's check the "Add a sequential range" box and enter in 100 for the number of items, **26**. For now, leave the User Name blank. Click Create and the sensor table will populate.

A nice feature of JMRI is its group of scripts that can automate repetitive tasks. These can be accessed from the main JMRI screen by selecting Scripting > Run Script. Select the "Setallunknownsensorstoinactive.py" script; when you click Open, all of your sensors will change from Unknown to Inactive. It's a good idea to run this script each time you start JMRI and load your panel file.

Give all sensors user names. Later, when we create the logic to implement

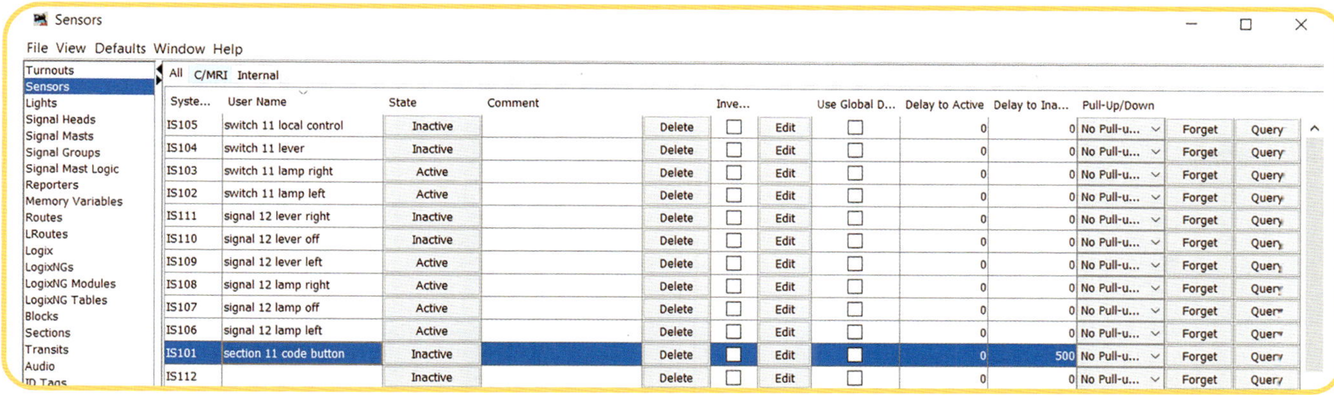

31 To add a delay to the code-button sensors, go to the table and enter the desired delay (half second) in milliseconds (500) as here for the section 11 code button.

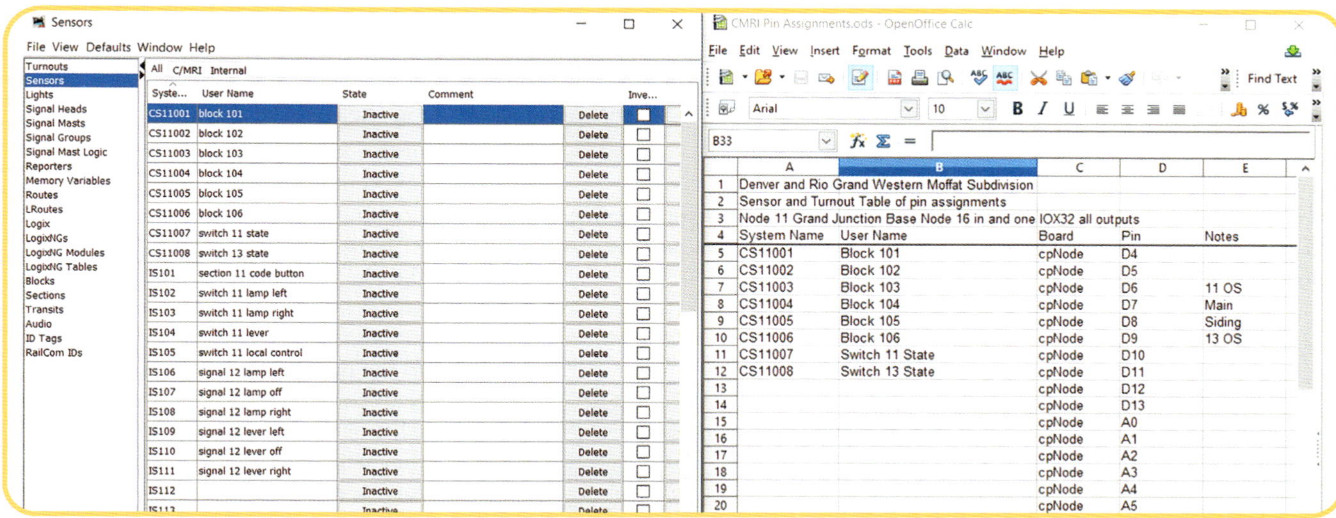

32 We've created new C/MRI sensors for node 11 (see fig. 23) starting with 11001. The first two digits are the node address and the last three are the sequentially numbered addresses.

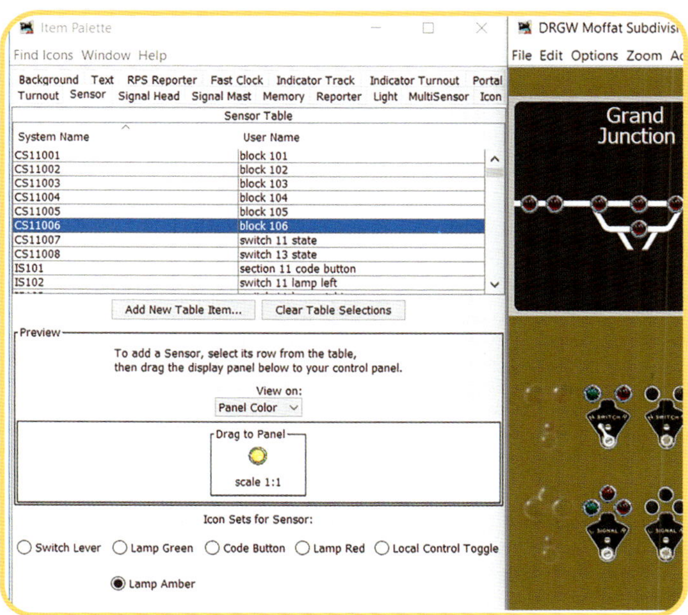

33 The icons for blocks 101 through 106 have been added to the panel. When the detectors in those blocks activate the sensors, the blocks' amber indicator lamps will illuminate.

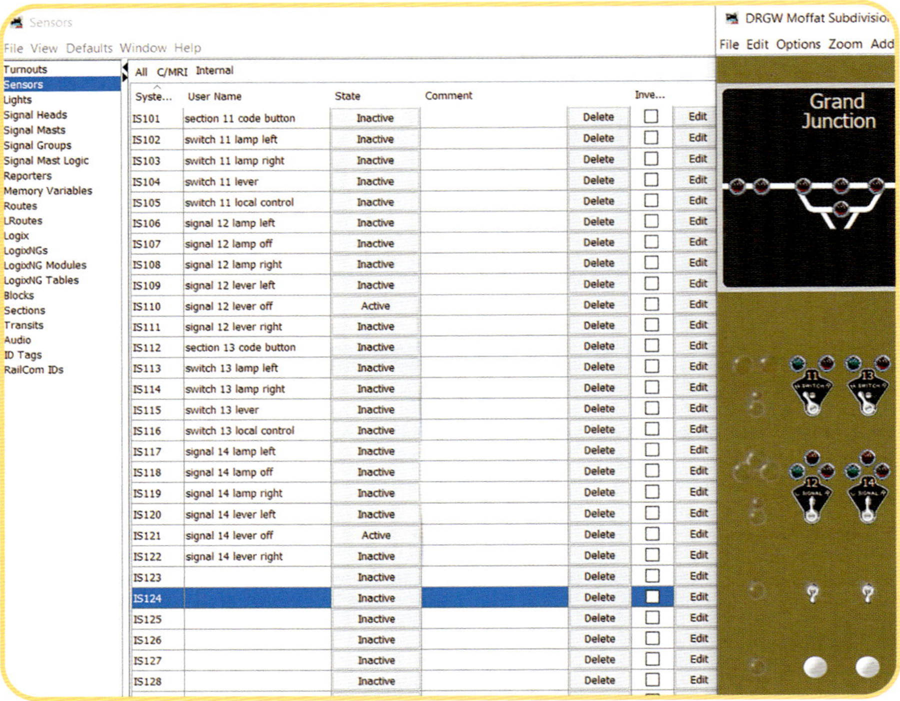

34 **Icons for the sensors created for the east end of Grand Junction have been added to the panel. Switch numbers are odd and signal numbers are even, following prototype practice.**

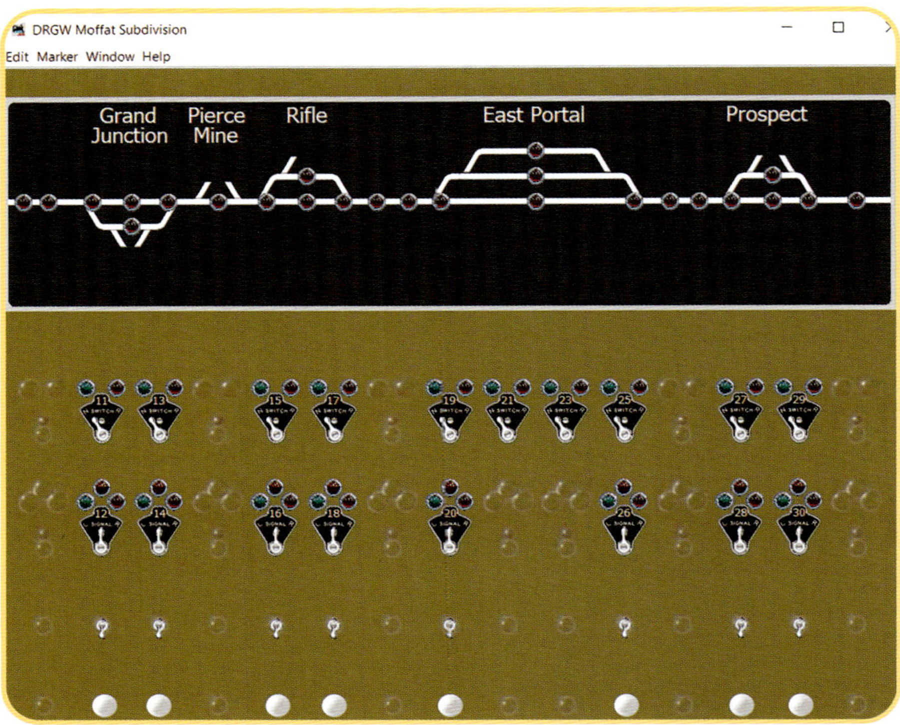

35 **The panel is now complete through Prospect, with all sensors and icons added and locked in place.**

the CTC system, a user name will be much easier to use than a sensor address. Input the user names by clicking in each box and typing it in, **27**. We should also create a sensor catalog. From the panel window, select Add Items > Item Palette. If you don't see the Add Items tab, select Edit > Open Editor.

At the top select the Sensor tab, click on New Icon Set, and give it a name. In the catalog section scroll down to USS and Sensor. Drag the appropriate lamp icons to the red Xs and click Done, **28**. Repeat this process for the switch lever, the local control toggles, and a code button set.

Finally, we'll need the signal control lever. Since this is a three-way lever, we'll need to select the MultiSensor tab. This lever is done a little differently in that you select the positions for the left, center, and right positions, then drag the icon to the panel, **29**.

Now we can start adding items to the panel. You do that by selecting the sensor user name and choosing the proper icon set. You then drag the icon to the panel, then move the icons to their correct locations, **30**. If you keep a list of the Y location for each item, they will align properly as you proceed further down the panel.

The code buttons need to be adjusted. We don't want their sensors to remain continuously active after they're pressed, but we need a brief delay so each button stays active for a short period after it's pressed. Right-click on the code button and select Momentary; go to the sensor table and add a half-second delay, **31**. Verify this by clicking on the code button and watching it change. Save your work; note that when you to quit the program after changing the icon catalog you will be prompted to save that as well.

Now let's add some C/MRI-based sensors. As discussed previously, C/MRI sensors can be inputs from block detectors or switch positions. Remembering the pin assignments from **23**, let's now create some C/MRI sensors. We'll create sensors for node 11 starting with 11001 and going through 11008. The first two

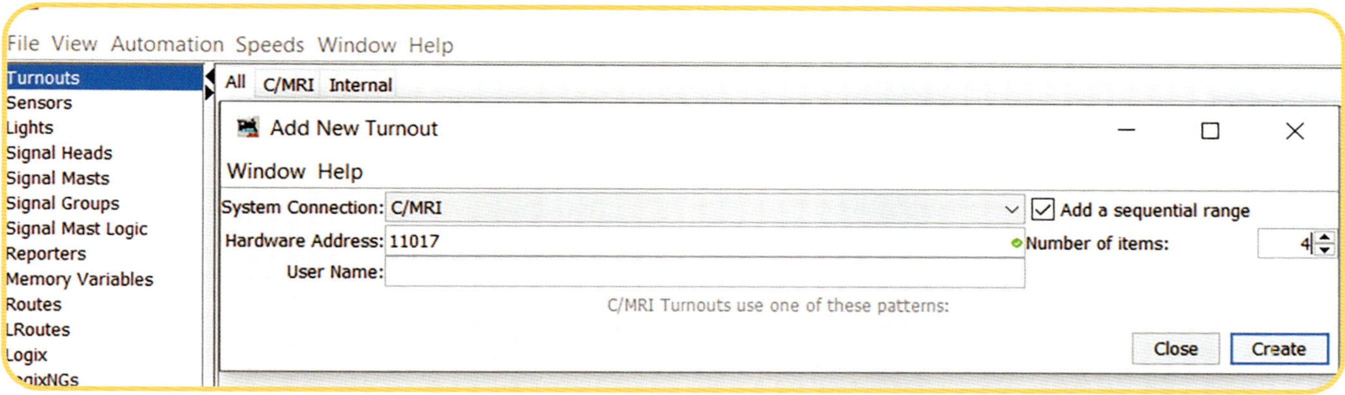

36 **In PanelPro, go to Tools > Tables > Turnouts, then click Add and set up the appropriate information.**

digits are the node address and the last three are the sequentially numbered addresses, **32**. A note on capitalization: I've found it easier to enter data with no capital letters, but how you choose to enter the data is up to you.

In **33** you can see that the icons for blocks 101 through 106 have been added to the panel. When there's a train in those blocks, the corresponding indicator lamps will light up amber. A lesson I've learned is that current detectors will sometimes drop out, which can be caused by dirty track or wheels. To prevent problems, add a 1- to 2-second delay before the block detectors go inactive. Do this the same way as the code button delay earlier.

Remember those two turnouts in Grand Junction branching off the siding to local industries? Even though the dispatcher does not control them, the system needs to know their position. This can be accomplished in two ways. One is to have a wire going from the switch machine (Tortoise, Blue Point, or a slide or toggle switch) to an input on the cpNode. This wire will be set up to pull the input to ground if the turnout is reversed. The other method is to simply add a 10K-ohm resistor so that the resistor is wired across the rails when the turnout is reversed (shown in Chapter 4, page 49). This will activate the block detector to show the block occupied.

Since we have some extra inputs at Grand Junction, I just hooked those turnouts up to the node. There won't be icons on the panel for these sensors, but they'll be used when we start programming the signals.

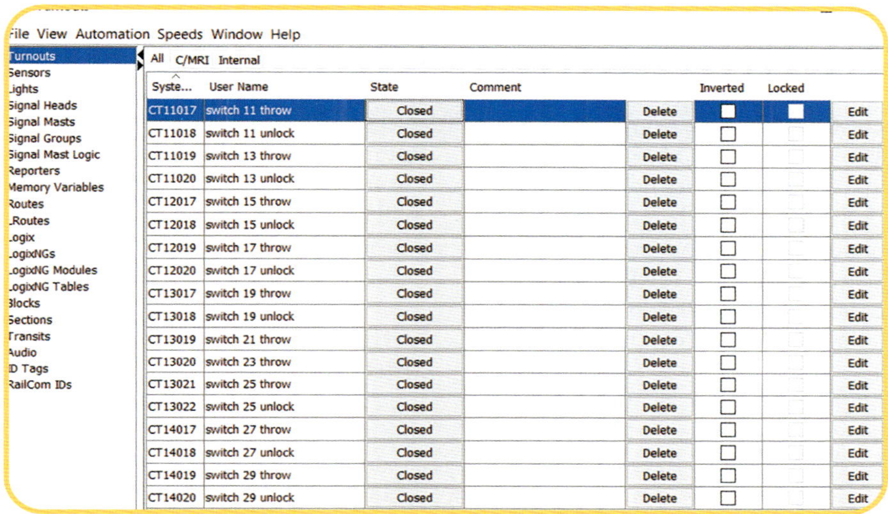

37 **Enter data to the turnout table, and also enter data for all dispatcher-controlled turnouts. Your table should look like this when done.**

Continue adding more icons to the panel with the sensors for the east end of Grand Junction, **34**. We'll also add the switch and signal labels. You can see that the switch numbers are 11 and 13 (odd) while the signal numbers are 12 and 14 (even), in keeping with the US&S standard.

Once you're satisfied with the location of the items on the panel, lock them in place so they can't be moved. This is done by clicking on any icon, then Control-A on the keyboard to select all items, then right-click on any icon and select Lock Position. You can later unlock any icon if needed by selecting it, right-clicking and selecting Lock Position.

Continue the process with other control points. We added the controls and icons from Rifle through East Portal to Prospect, **35**. The segment at East Portal is unique in that it has two switches controlled by one local control toggle and one code button. Since the two switches are close to each other, there's also only one signal lever. This will become clear when we start coding the Logix. Set the sensor delays, lock the icons, and save your work.

Turnout preparation

Let's do a quick review of how a prototype CTC system works. In basic terms, a CTC system is a group of individual interlocking plants connected together. An interlocking is an arrangement of signals and related gear configured to prevent the dispatcher from aligning conflicting movements through a junction, crossing, or siding entrance/exit.

For our model railroad, this will be done using software, but we first

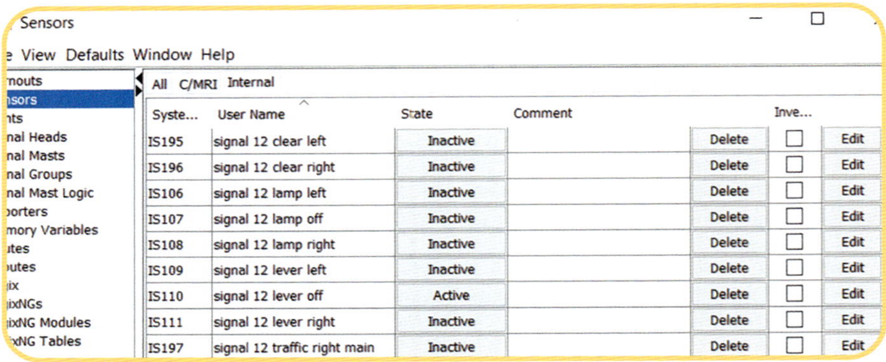

38 Before programming turnouts, the signal clear and traffic sensors must be added. This screen shows those sensors added for signal 12.

need to set up our turnouts. You need to decide the method you'll be using to control your turnouts. The ITC and RSMC boards from MRCS were discussed earlier (ITC allows local control; RSMC does not). To enable local control, we'll be using the ITC boards. Go back and look at **23** for a moment: note that the C/MRI sensors start at address 11001, but turnout addresses start with 11017 and work their way up. This was explained earlier and is an idiosyncrasy of the cpNode system. For now, let's take a look at the first four turnout addresses.

Address CT11017 is for the switch 11 throw and CT11018 is the unlock (these features are covered in the ITC User Guide). The next two turnout addresses are for switch 13. Let's go back into JMRI and set these up. In the main PanelPro window, select Tools > Tables > Turnouts, and a new window will open. We'll use the information in **37** to create four new C/MRI turnouts in the table. Click Add and set up the information as **36** shows. For now, we'll only create four to start with.

When you click Create, you'll see a message asking how many C/MRI bits should be used to control this turnout. Click on Use 1 Bit. Next, you'll get a window asking "Do you want this setting to be used for all turnouts in this range?" Select Yes. Next, you'll be asked to use a steady state or pulsed output; choose steady state, and answer "yes" when you're asked to apply this setting to all turnouts in this range. There's another script that you can use to set all turnouts to closed. Go ahead and run that script now.

Enter the data from the spreadsheet to the turnout table, and while we're at it let's enter the data for all dispatcher-controlled turnouts, **37**. Before we can start programming the turnouts, we'll need to add a few more internal sensors: the signal clear and traffic sensors, **38**.

Setting up the Logix CTC JMRI software

Logix is the tool inside JMRI that allows a user to develop a list of conditions that monitor various parameters. When certain conditions are reached, it describes the task that is then implemented or a command that is sent: for example, "reverse this turnout" or "change this signal LED to red."

The Logix for our CTC system is based on the CTC panel sections in JMRI. Each section will test for the positions of the switch and signal levers, turnout position, block occupancy, signal clear and traffic sensors, and the local control switch sensor. Nothing will change, however, until the code button is pressed.

The conditionals will be divided into several sections. The first will set the switches, the second will set the signal state (Left, Right, and Off, and if necessary, with separate conditionals for the main or diverging tracks), the third will test the block detection or On Station/Sheet (OS) or when the train passes a control point, the fourth will clear the traffic stick sensors, and the last will grant or remove local control. Finally, there will be a set of conditionals that will set the signals to the correct aspects.

The switch conditional will look at the position of the switch lever, the state of the OS detector, and if there are any signal clear sensors active for movements over the switch. Then, once the code button is pressed, it will set the switch to the correct position.

There will be a separate Logix section to set the switch indicators on the panel. When a turnout is closed, the left lamp will be lit and the right lamp will be off. When the turnout is thrown — reversed — the right lamp will be lit and the left lamp will be off. If a crossover is out of correspondence, both lamps will be off.

The signal state clear conditionals will look at the position of the signal lever, the state of the turnout levers (if required), the state of the OS block occupancies, and whether any conflicting traffic sensors or signal clear sensors are active when running on single track. If running on two tracks, you'll need to check the position of

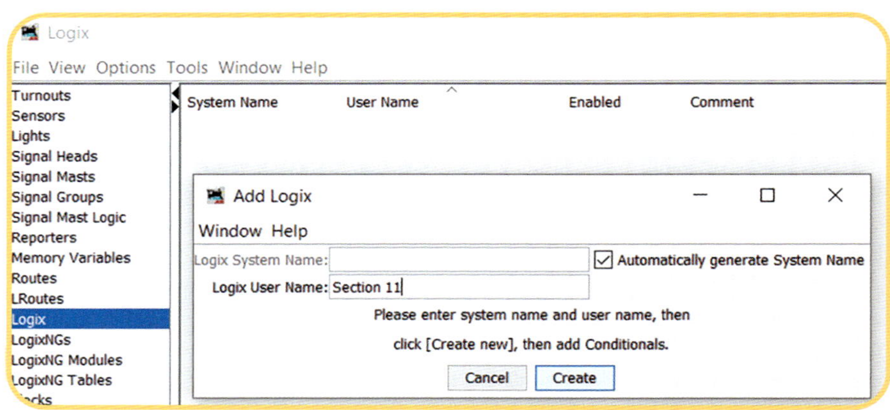

39 Open Logix, enter the user name ("Section 11"), and click Create.

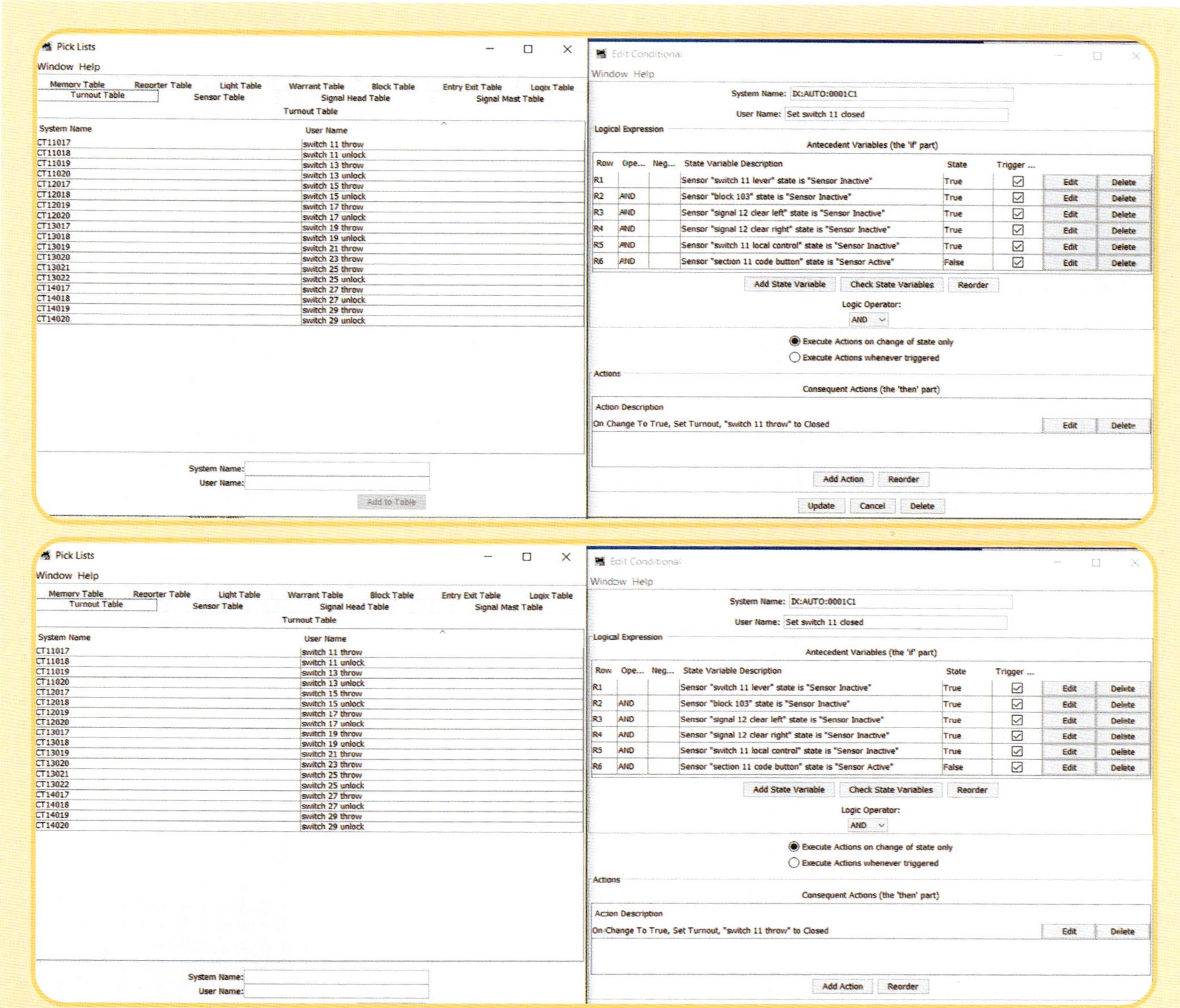

40 **The conditionals (top right) are to set Switch 11 to closed (normal), and at bottom right to set the switch to thrown (reversed). Each line is a statement to check the state of the various sensors, and if the conditions match, the action is taken.**

the turnout. There will be a traffic stick and signal clear for each track that will need to be checked based on the way the switch lever is lined. Then when the code button becomes active, the output will be to turn off any conflicting panel indicators, set the traffic sensor, and activate the panel indicator and signal clear sensors, each with a three-second delay.

The OS section becoming active will turn off the left and right panel indicators, turn on the signal off lamp, and set the signal clear sensors in both directions to inactive.

The east and west traffic sensors will be set to inactive when the block between OSs becomes active when running on single track. If there are two tracks, the traffic sensors for each track will be set to inactive when the destination block between OSs becomes active. The traffic sensor will also be set to inactive if the dispatcher takes down a signal.

The signal conditionals will be "stop," "approach," "clear," "diverging approach" and "diverging clear." There may be several diverging aspects depending on the track arrangements, and not all aspects may be used depending on local circumstances.

The Stop aspect will test for the "signal clear being inactive and CTC On Active," turnout position (if required) and block occupancy in an OR configuration. There is also a need to test for occupancy in a block beyond the OS; if a train enters that block it will set the signal to stop.

Where there is a siding, the logic will look like this: The other aspects will check for the "CTC On sensor inactive" or "signal clear being active," turnout position, block occupancy, and distant signal-head aspect.

Granting local control will check for the local control sensor being

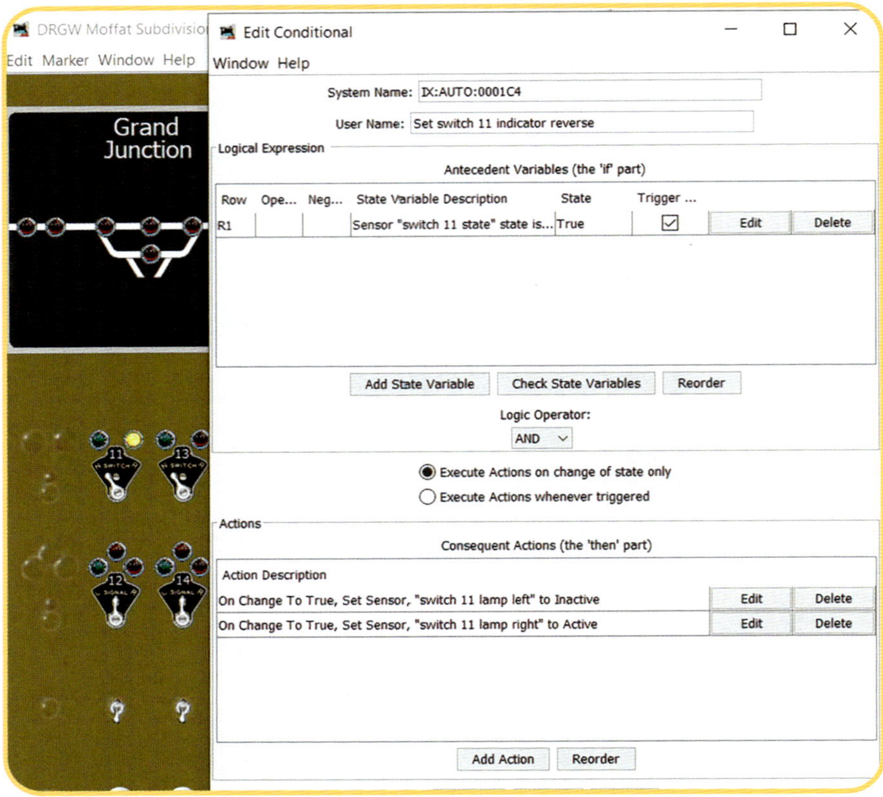

41 **The Feedback pin on the ITC will connect to the pin on the cpNode that is set up for switch state. For Switch 11, that pin is D10 on node 11.**

active, as well as the OS and both signal clear sensors being inactive, as well as the signal lever being in the off position. Once the code button is pressed, the output will be: turn on the signal off panel lamp and set the switch controller to local control. This can be called the Turnout xx Unlock.

Revoking local control will involve turning off the local control switch, verifying the OS is unoccupied, making sure all appropriate signal levers are in the off position, and pushing the code button. The output will turn on the signal off lamp and reset the local control output.

Signals are done on an individual basis and will check for the signal clear sensor and CTC On sensor, turnout position state sensors, block occupancy, and distant signal head status for the route in question. In addition, signals will have their own Logix statements following the interlocking section. The logic for the signals will be: Stop will use "Signal Clear sensor inactive" and "CTC On sensor active" or switch against the route or block occupied.

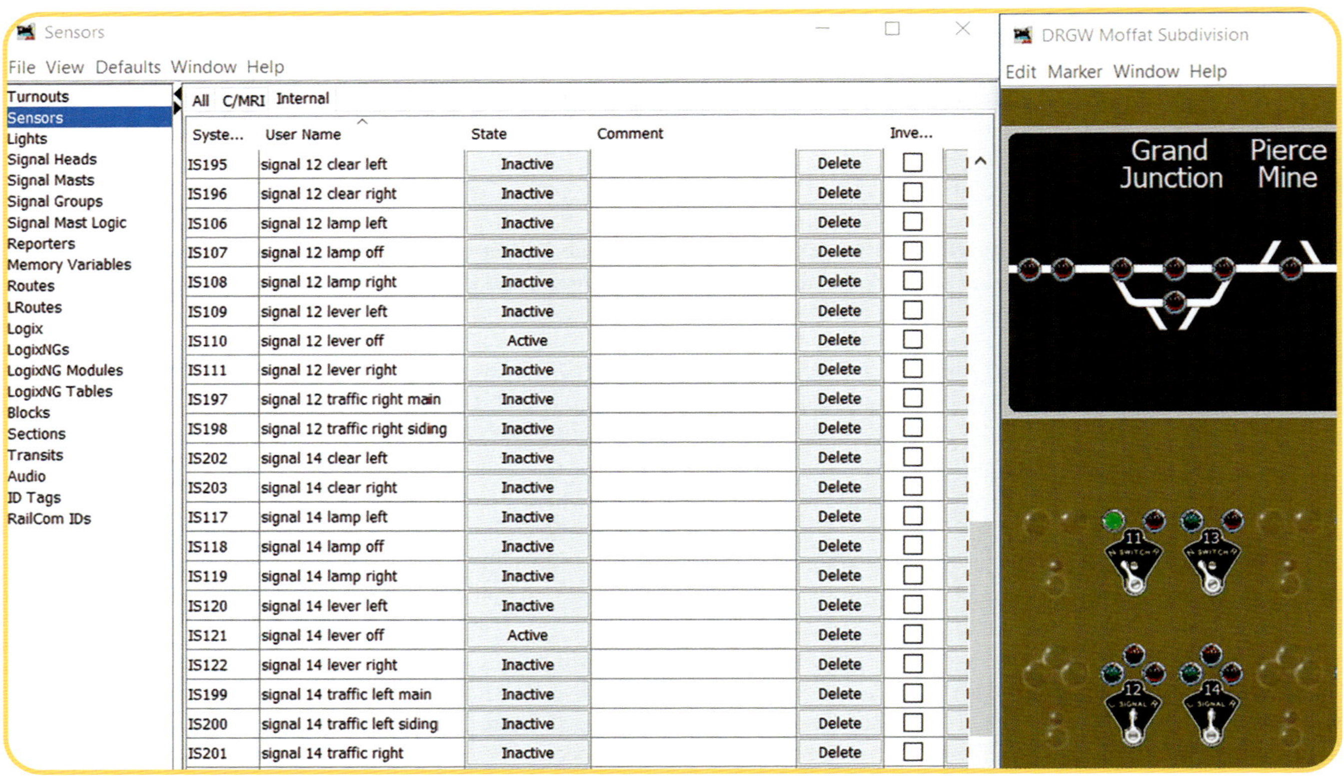

42 **Add additional sensors for Signal 14. These will look at signal lever position, switch lever state, occupancy of OS block and next block, and whether any conflicting traffic sensors or signal clear sensors are active when running on single track.**

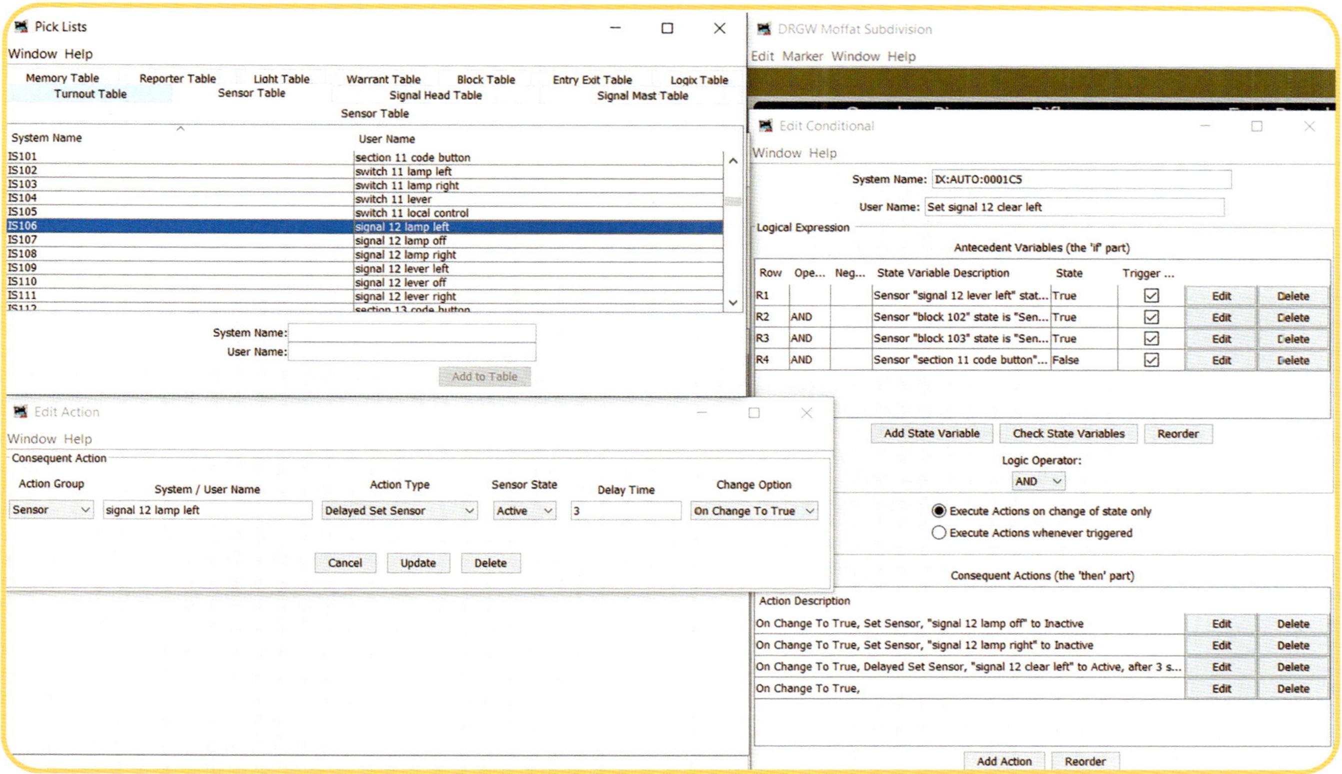

43 This shows how the conditional for Signal 12 clear left is constructed, including how to enter the 3-second delay.

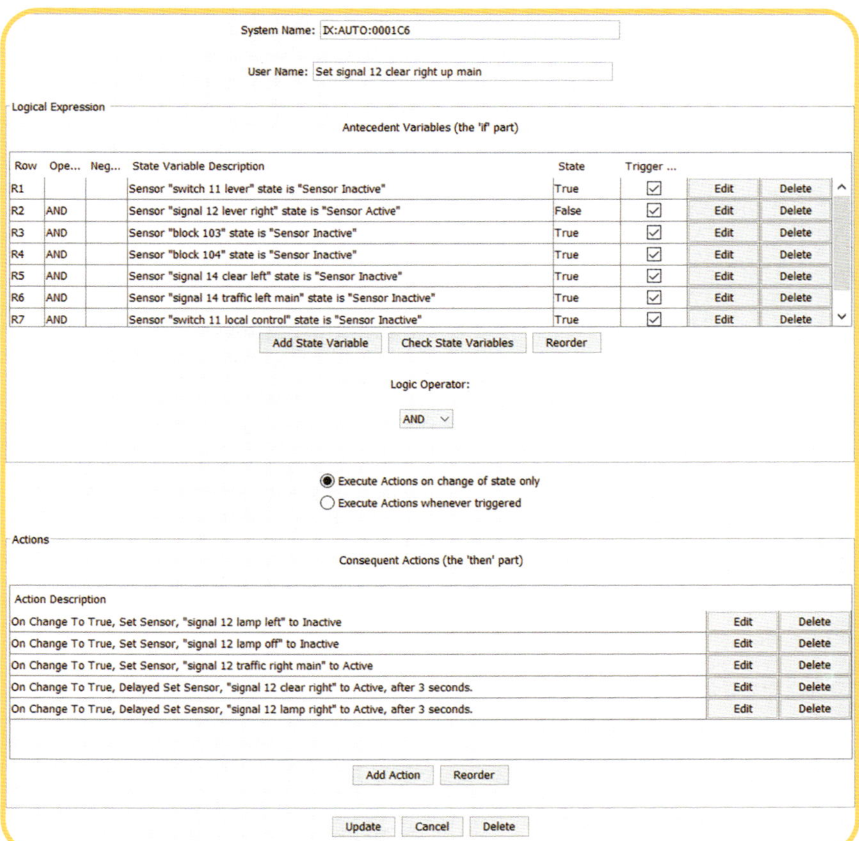

44 This shows how to add conditionals for Signal 12 to clear right. The last variable should be Sensor "section 11 code button" state is "Sensor Active."

Each possible route must be tested. All other signal aspects will use "Signal Clear sensor active" or "CTC On sensor inactive" and switch position and block occupancy and distant signal aspect. There will be a "signal red" output for some signals to set the approach on the block signals. If a signal is either Stop or Restricting, the turnout will be set to closed.

Implementing logic

We can now start applying the Logix to define the conditions that affect the system. As an example, let's set up the controls for switch 11.

If you already have a sensor or turnout table open, simply click on Logix. If not, then in the main PanelPro window click on Tools > Tables > Logix and click Add, **39**. I suggest letting JMRI automatically set the System Name. Enter in the User name, in this case Section 11, and click on Create.

You can see two conditionals that have been created in **40**. One is to set Switch 11 to the closed position and the other is to set the switch to thrown. Each line is a statement to

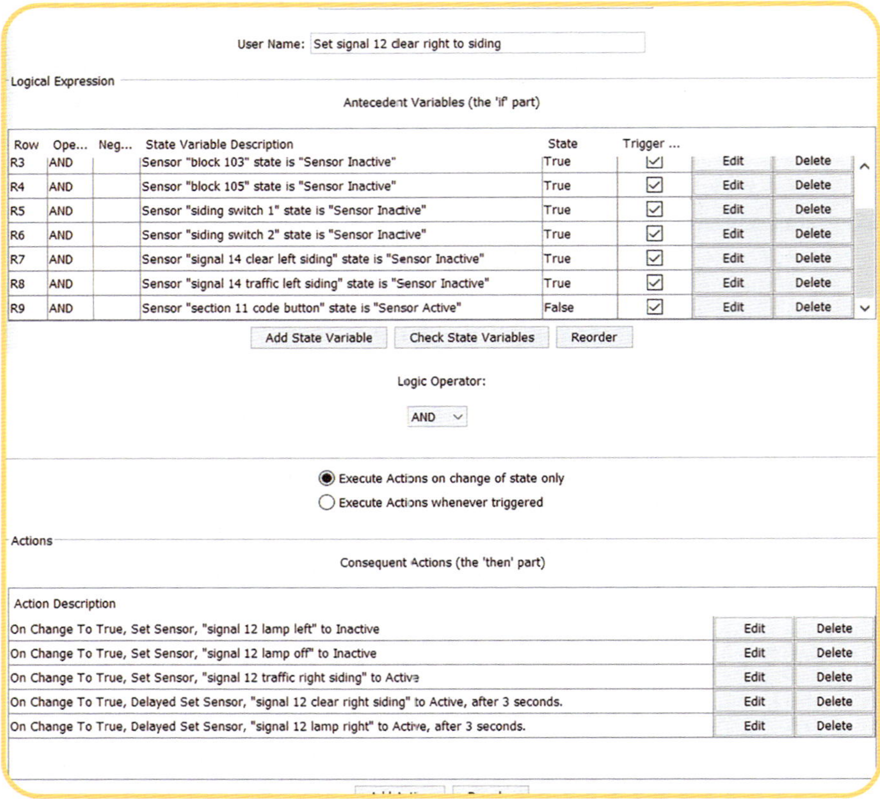

45 **Here are the conditionals for clearing Signal 12 into the siding.**

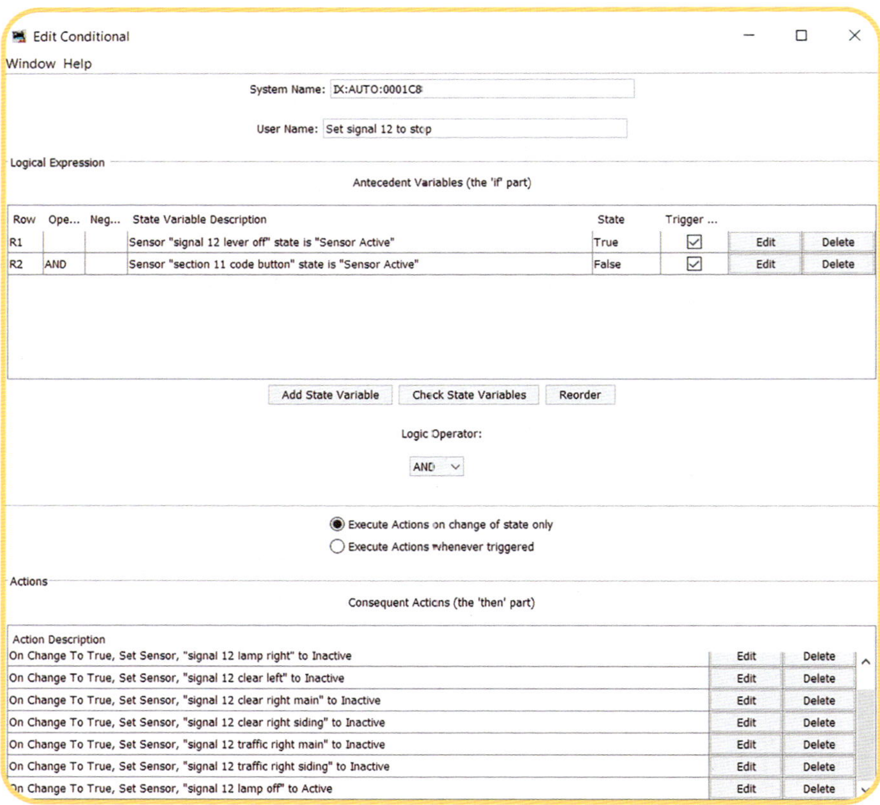

46 **This sequence will turn signals off if the signal lever is set to the center position: The left and right panel indicators will be off, the signal off lamp will be on, and the signal clear sensors in both directions will be inactive.**

check the state of the various sensors and if the conditions match the action taken. We can verify this by looking at the state of the switch 11 throw turnout as we move the switch lever back and forth. Remember you need to press the code button for the action to take place.

The next Logix section will set the switch indicators on the panel. When a turnout is closed (normal), the left lamp will be lit and the right lamp will be off. When the turnout is thrown (reversed), the right lamp will be lit and the left lamp will be off. This will use the Feedback output from the ITC to determine turnout position. The FB pin on the ITC will connect to the pin on the cpNode that is set up for switch state. For Switch 11, that pin is D10 on node 11, **41**.

Note that in simulator mode this will not be active because we're not connected to the hardware, but you can check the logic by clicking on the Active/Inactive button in the sensor table. If you're using a method of turnout control that does not provide positive feedback, you can simply look at the Closed/Thrown status in the turnout table instead of the active feedback.

The next conditionals will be the "signal state clear" conditionals, but before we do that we'll need to create some more internal sensors for Signal 14, **42**. These new conditionals will look at the position of the signal lever, the state of the turnout lever(s) (only needed if there is a choice between proceeding on the main or going into a siding), the state of the OS block and next block occupancies, and whether any conflicting traffic sensors or signal clear sensors are active when running on single track. You'll also need to check for the state of any hand-thrown turnouts.

If running on two tracks, you'll need to check the position of the turnout, and there will be a traffic stick and signal clear for each track that will need to be checked based on the way the switch lever is lined. Then when the code button becomes active, the output will be to turn off any conflicting panel indicators, set the traffic sensor, and activate the panel indicator and signal clear sensors, each with a 3-second delay.

The first conditional we'll create will be for Signal 12 clear left. Since there are no signals to come out of staging there will be no conflicting traffic sensor. Also, since there are two blocks to get into staging, the possibility exists for following movements so we'll only be looking at block 102. Figure **43** shows how this conditional is constructed, including how to enter the 3-second delay. Note that when entering data into the System/User name you can either highlight the user name in the pick list or you can type it in yourself. Looking at the sensor table while clicking the code button allows you to verify the logic is working correctly.

Now let's program signal 12 to clear right up the main line, **44**. Next, we'll create a conditional to set signal 12 to clear into the siding. Remember to check that the two hand-thrown turnouts are lined normal. The conditional for clearing signal 12 into the siding is in **45**.

There is occasionally a need to turn signals off. Setting the signal lever to the center position and pressing the code button will turn off the left and right panel indicators, turn on the signal off lamp, and set the signal clear sensors in both directions to inactive. It will also set any traffic sensors to inactive as required. Note that the dispatcher should ascertain that any train approaching a clear signal is stopped prior to taking it down, **46**.

The OS section becoming active will turn off the left and right signal panel indicators, turn on the signal off lamp, and set the signal clear sensors in both directions to inactive as shown in Block 103, **47**. The signal clear and traffic sensors will also be set to inactive when the block between OS's becomes active. If you look at **48**, you'll notice that Block 105 becoming active or either siding switch becoming active will trigger this event. Up to this point all conditionals have used the default AND function; this is the first time we've used the OR function.

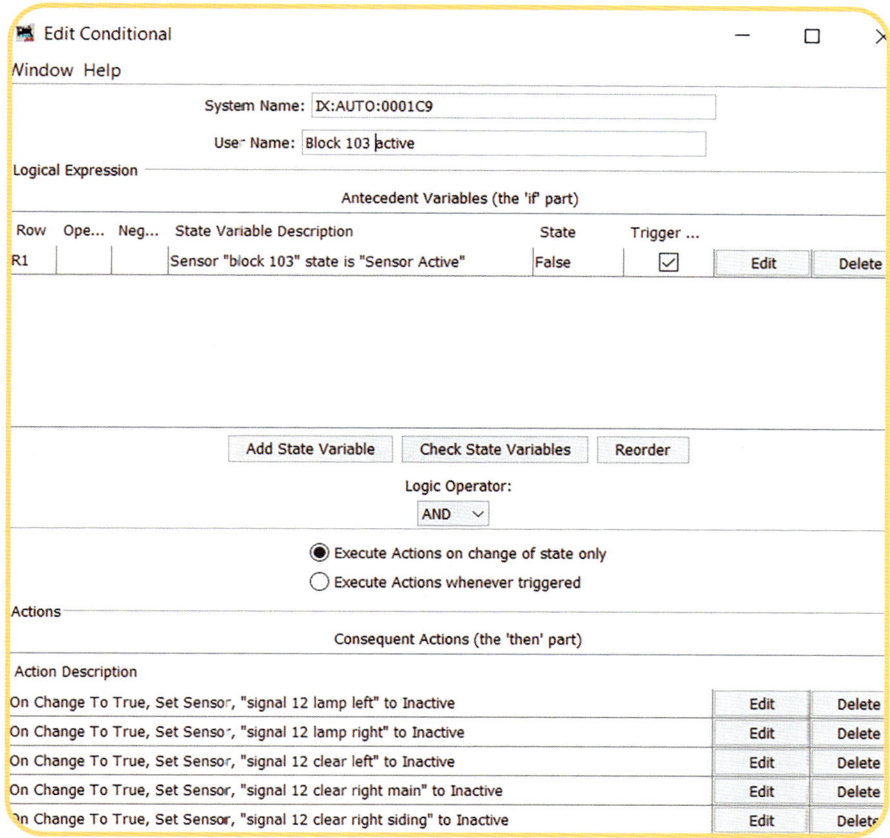

47 **When Block 103 becomes active, this will turn off the left and right signal panel indicators, turn on the Signal Off lamp, and set the Signal Clear sensors in both directions to inactive.**

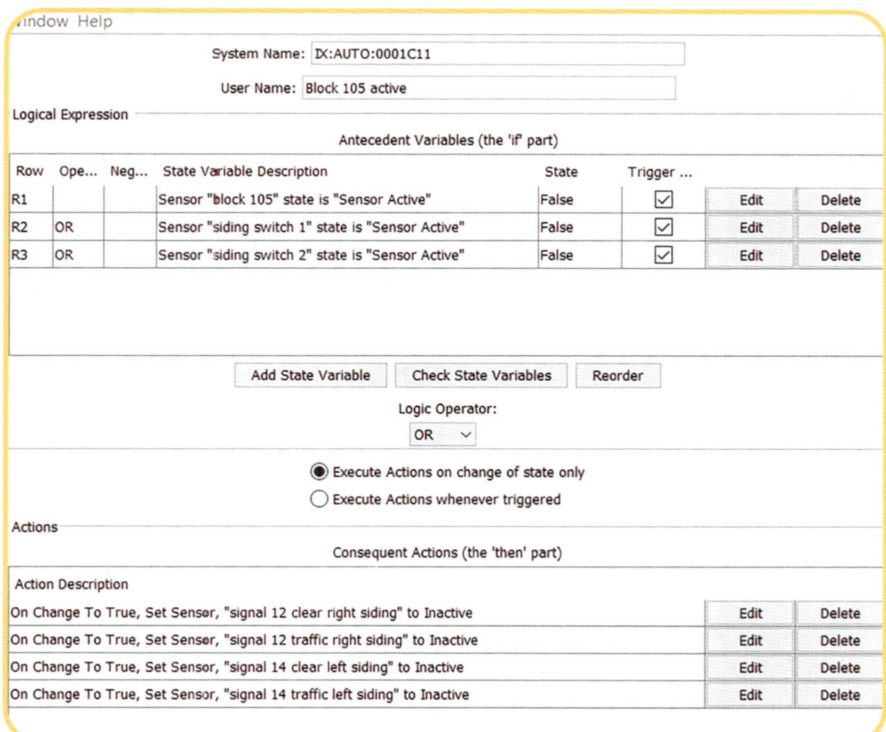

48 **Block 105 becoming active or either siding switch becoming active will trigger the event in 48.**

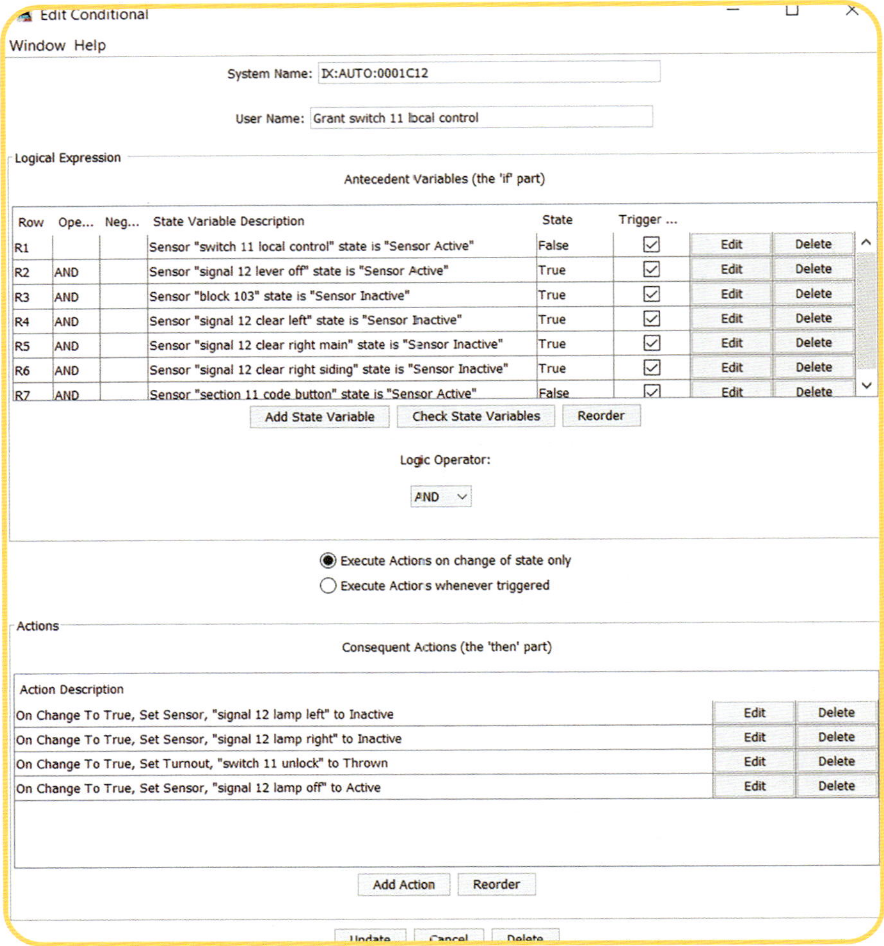

49 **This logic shows how to provide local control for turnouts.**

Local control

Let's look at granting and revoking local control. Local control allows a train crew to have control of a turnout without dispatcher input. Granting local control will check for the local control sensor being active (switch in the up position), as well as the OS and all signal clear sensors being inactive, as well as the signal lever being in the off position. Once the code button is pressed, the output will be to turn on the signal off panel lamp and to set the switch controller to local control (switch xx unlock). Note that when a switch is in local control the CTC signals are set to stop. When local control is granted the train crew knows they can pass a stop signal at restricted speed since they're the only people that can throw the switch. This is set up as in **49**.

Revoking local control involves turning off the local control switch, verifying the OS is unoccupied, making sure all appropriate signal levers are in the off position, and pushing the code button. The output will turn on the signal off lamp and reset the local control output (switch xx unlock).

Signals

Most model railroad signals consist of a mast with one or more heads, with each head housing one to three LEDs (green, yellow, and red). When talking about signals we need to use the correct terminology. The two basic terms are "aspect" and "indication." Aspect is the appearance of a signal — such as red, green, or red-over-yellow — while the name and indication are what information the aspect contains: "stop," "proceed," "proceed on a diverging route prepared to stop at the next signal."

You can go back to **11** (page 70) to see how these signals will be placed for the Rio Grande layout. As an example, section 11 at west Grand Junction has a two-head signal for movements from left to right while there are two single-head signals going in the opposite direction. This is the standard layout for signals in CTC territory.

To control the LEDs, each color will be controlled by one JMRI turnout. Looking at Grand Junction, section 11, the two-headed signal is 12RA and 12RB (RA and RB are the two heads on the mast). The single-head signals are 12LA for mainline movements and 12LB for movements out of the siding. The spreadsheet where the signal LEDs are assigned to turnouts on the IOX board is in **50**; that info goes into the turnout table in JMRI.

Prototype CTC systems keep all signals at "stop" until the dispatcher clears them. Some modelers however, like to have the signals function even if there's no dispatcher present. This can be done with a switch on the panel that sets the signals to an ABS (Automatic Block Signal) mode. It makes the logic a bit more complex, but it can be accomplished. We'll go ahead and set it up here, but if you don't want the ABS mode, it can be taken out. To enable the ABS mode, we'll need to create an internal sensor to allow us to switch back and forth. Let's call it "CTC On" and add a toggle switch to the lower left corner of the control panel (more on that later).

Signal programming is done on an individual basis and will check for the (signal clear sensor and CTC On sensor), turnout position state sensors, block occupancy and distant signal head status for the route in question. In addition, signals will have their own Logix statements. The logic for the signals will be: Stop will use "Signal Clear sensor inactive and CTC On sensor active" or "switch against the route or block occupied." Each possible route must be tested. All other signal aspects will use "Signal Clear sensor active or CTC On sensor inactive" and "switch position and block occupancy and

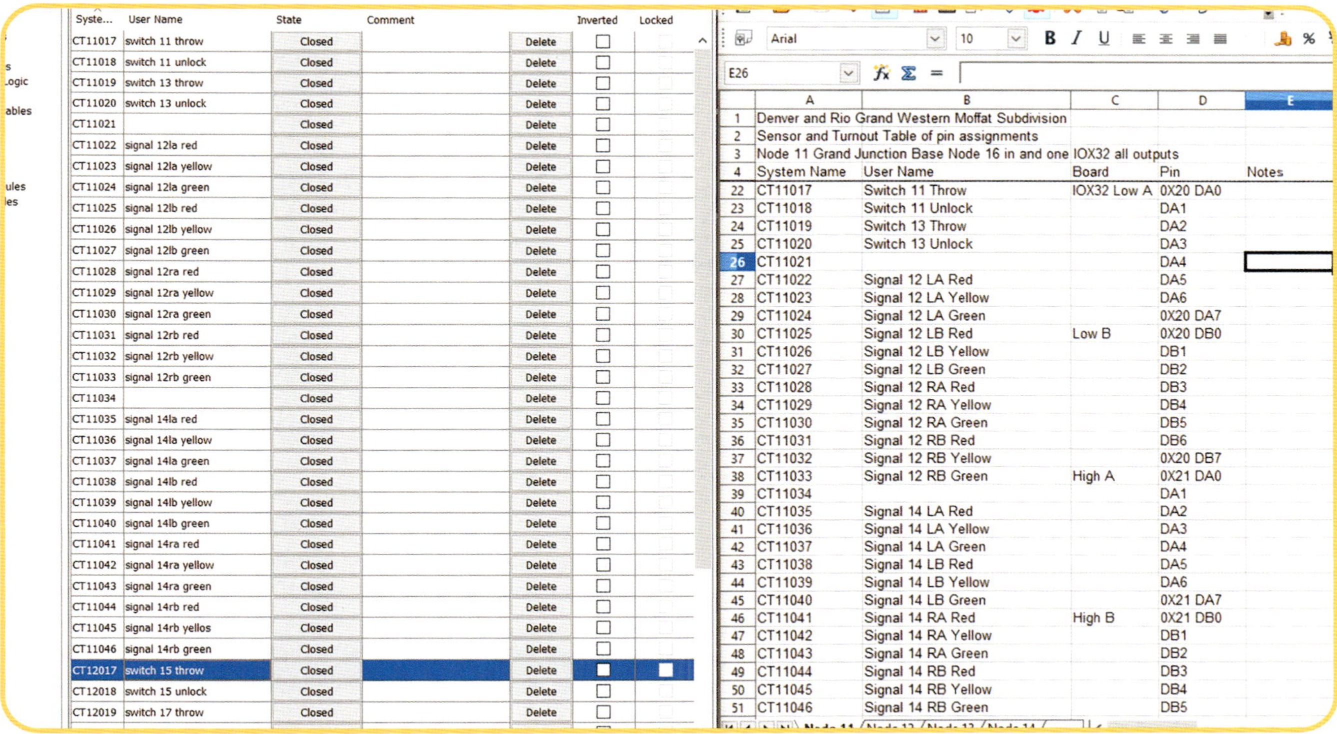

50 I tracked all of the board and pin assignments for each signal/turnout in a spreadsheet (right), then entered all of the information to the turnout table in JMRI.

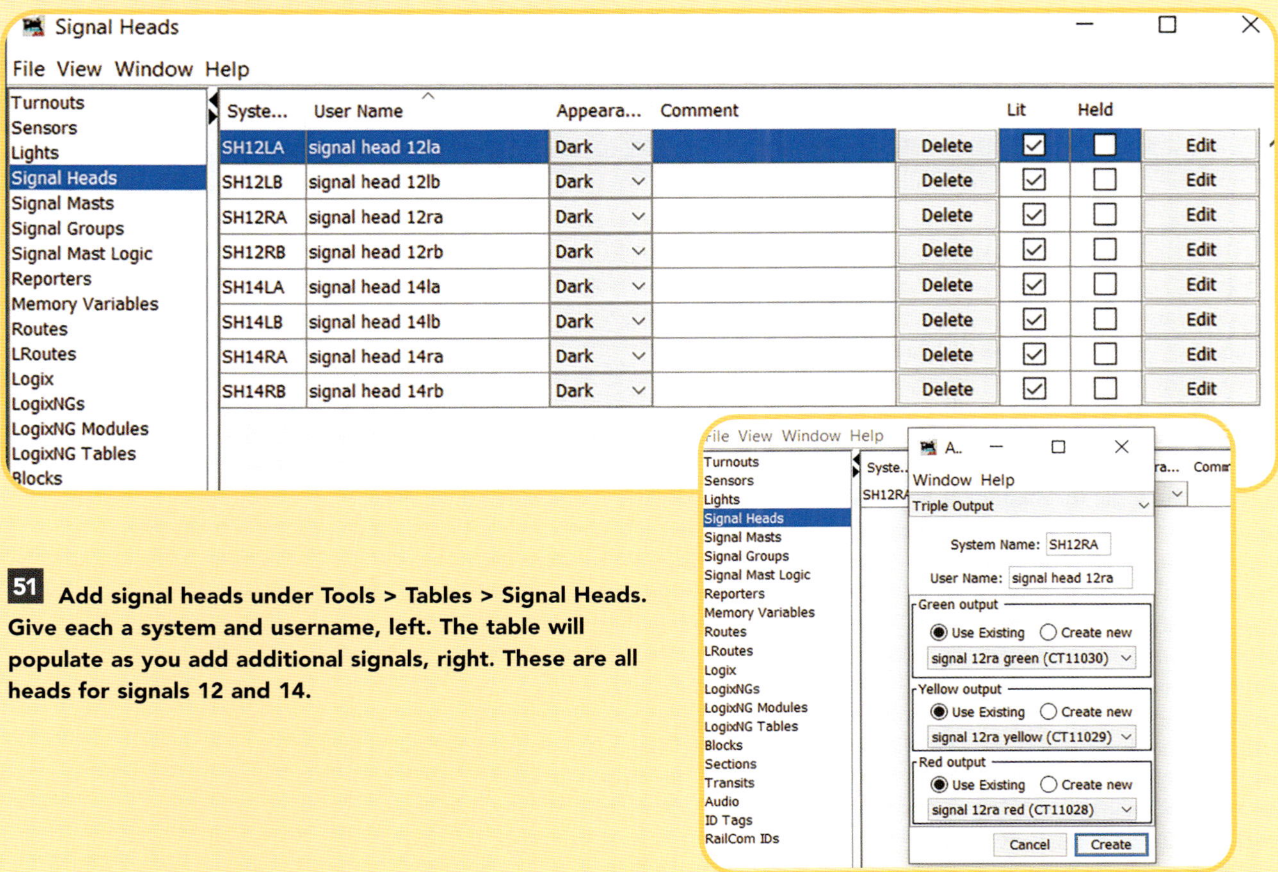

51 Add signal heads under Tools > Tables > Signal Heads. Give each a system and username, left. The table will populate as you add additional signals, right. These are all heads for signals 12 and 14.

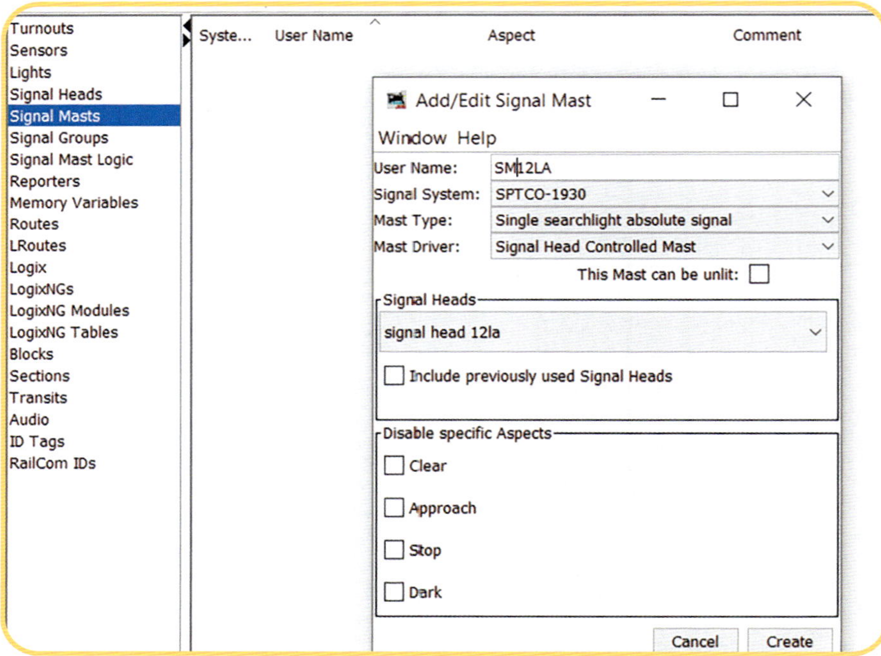

52 **Here's the window for creating the signal masts; this is for Signal 12LA.**

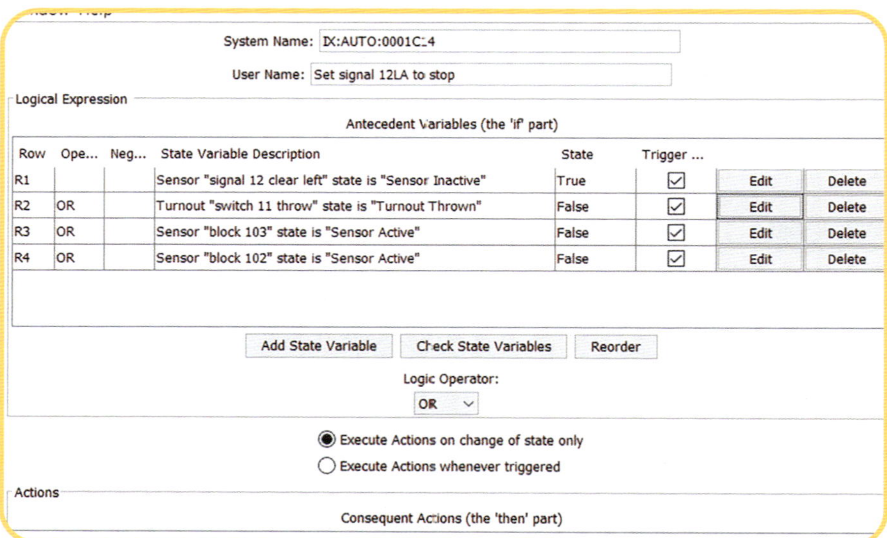

53 **This is the logic for Signal 12LA to set it to stop, without the ABS function.**

distant signal aspect." This might not seem clear right now, but as we get to programming the logic it will start to make sense.

So far, we've entered the LED turnout information for sections 11 and 13. Let's add the signal heads and masts in JMRI. In the Tools > Tables menu, select Signal Heads, click Add, select Triple Output, then give it a system and user name. Use the drop downs to select the proper turnout.

When everything looks good, click Create. Repeat the process until all the heads are completed for signals 12 and 14, **51**.

Next, add the signal masts. When you first look at the number of signal systems available it can seem daunting. If you're modeling a specific prototype, pick one that matches. We'll be using the SPTCO-1930 signal system. This is one of the easiest to use and gives us all the aspects we need. The steps to create signal mast 12LA are shown in **52**. Don't worry that the aspect is unknown — that will change once we start programming them, so let's do that now.

Now we'll program signal 12LA, the mainline signal at West Grand Junction that governs westward movements from the main line. If you're not using the ABS function, the logic is shown in **53**. Notice we're using the OR logic operator for signals at stop. All other signal indications will use the AND operator. If you decide to implement the ABS mode, the logic will look like **54**. This uses what's called Mixed mode operator, and while it looks complex, it's really not. This means that the first two statements must agree, then they are OR'd with the rest.

The logic that sets signal 12LA to approach is in **55**. This also uses Mixed mode logic, where the first two statements are OR'd together, then they need to agree with the rest. If block 101 becomes unoccupied, the signal will be green (clear) — you can program that now. Here's a great example of why we gave the sensors and turnouts unique user names. It's much easier to keep track of them this way rather than remembering sensor numbers. Programming for signal 12LB follows the same logic except for the position of the turnout.

Signal 12R is different in that there are two routes that must be addressed: one following the main and the other into the siding. The conditionals for this signal will be stop up main, stop into siding, approach, clear, diverging approach and diverging clear. The diverging aspects will be for movements into the siding. The logic if you're not using ABS mode is in **56**.

Again, we're using mixed mode logic. If either the signal clear sensor is inactive or the OS block is occupied, then the signal is set to stop. If both of those sensors report back a true condition then the next section of the logic takes over. You can see how the logic is configured when using ABS mode in **57**.

Now let's look at configuring signal 12R for approach, first with no ABS

54 If you're using the ABS function, the logic for Signal 12LA stop looks like this. The CTC on/off toggle can be seen at lower left.

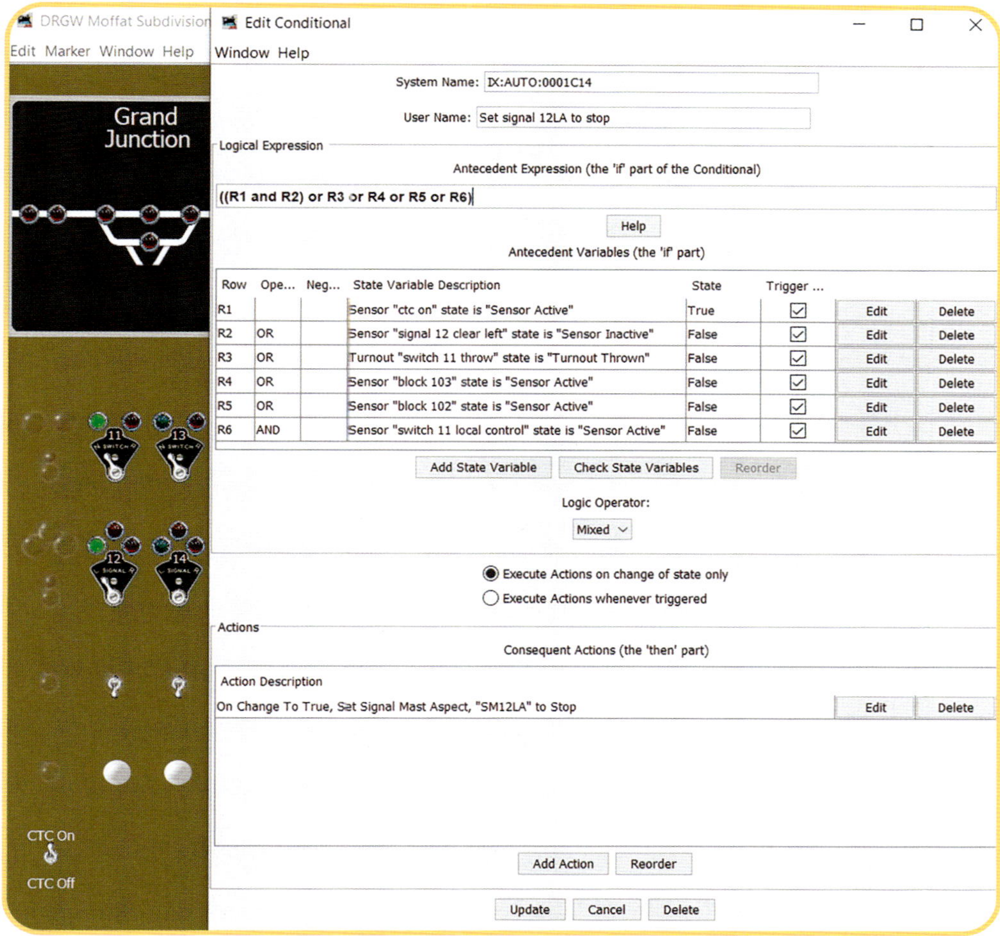

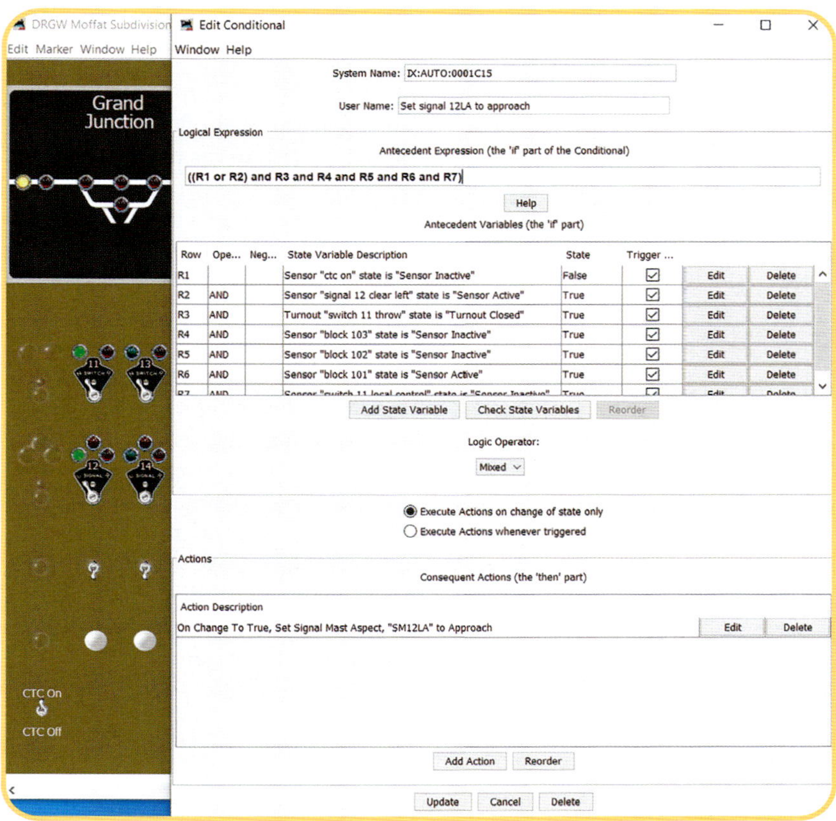

55 This is the logic that sets Signal 12LA to approach.

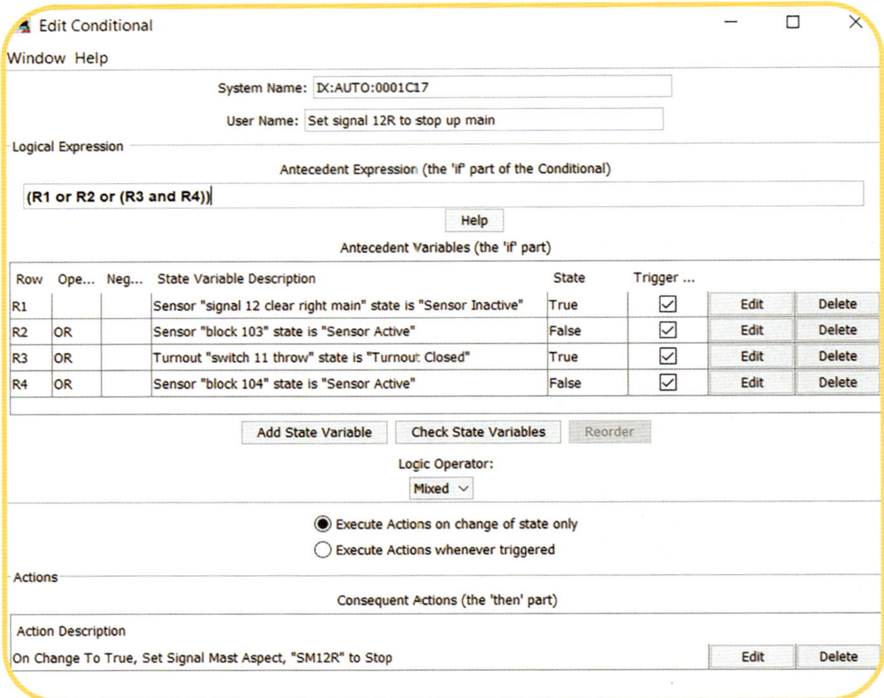

56 **This is the logic for Signal 12R at stop without ABS mode.**

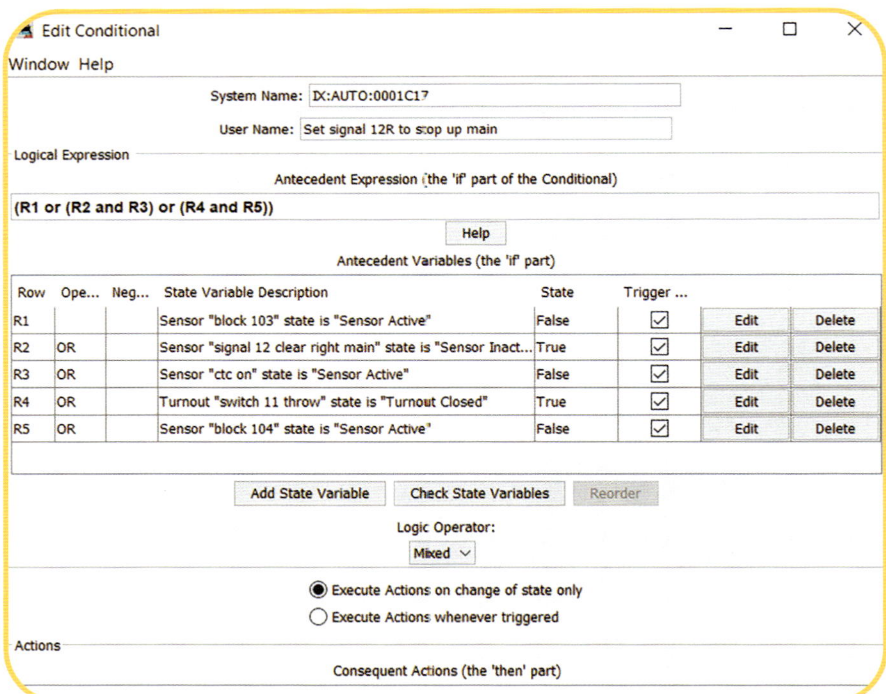

57 **This is the logic for Signal 12R at stop when using ABS mode.**

mode, **58**, then with ABS mode active, **59**. Changing the indication for signal 12R from approach to clear only requires one small update to the logic, **60**. The only change between approach and clear is the addition of the NOT statement added to the last variable. In other words, if signal head 14RA is red, then signal 12R will be set to approach, but if signal head 14RA is not red, then signal 12R can be at clear.

The almost-completed Logix for section 11 is in **61**. The only thing left to add is to add the conditionals for signal 12R stop into siding, diverging approach, and diverging clear. The two diverging aspects will look at signal head 14RB but in all other respects are the same as for the mainline aspects. Once these three conditionals are completed, you'll be done with section 11.

Before moving to section 13, there's one more decision to be made. Look at the prototype panel in **2** (page 67) and you'll see icons on the board that show signal locations. These icons are available in the icon palette, but I've found that most people prefer adding functional icons to their panel. You can find these in the icon palette as well, **62**. Once you select the appropriate signal, simply drag it to the panel (you'll need to rotate the icon). These will repeat the aspects of the signals on the layout.

That's it — we've completed one section of a CTC system. Before trying to set up your own railroad, you might want to attempt to duplicate all the programming we've done here in the simulation to learn how the software works. Use the examples on these pages as your guide.

Once you've done some experimenting with the software and feel confident in how it works, keep repeating what you've learned with succeeding sections. Before you know it, you'll be working on your own fully functional CTC system.

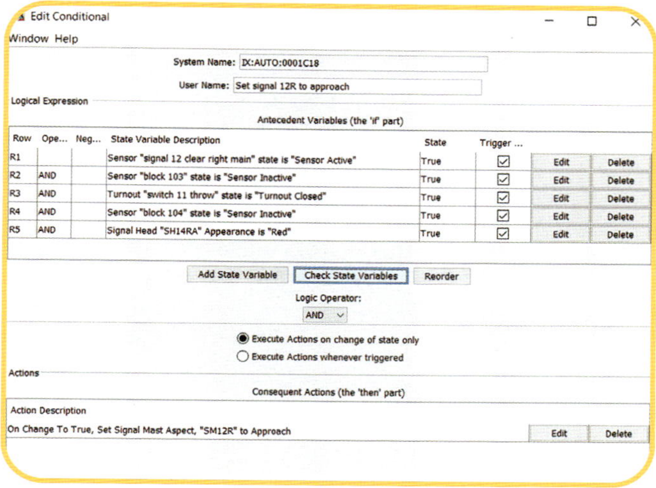

58 Here's the Signal 12R logic for approach without ABS mode.

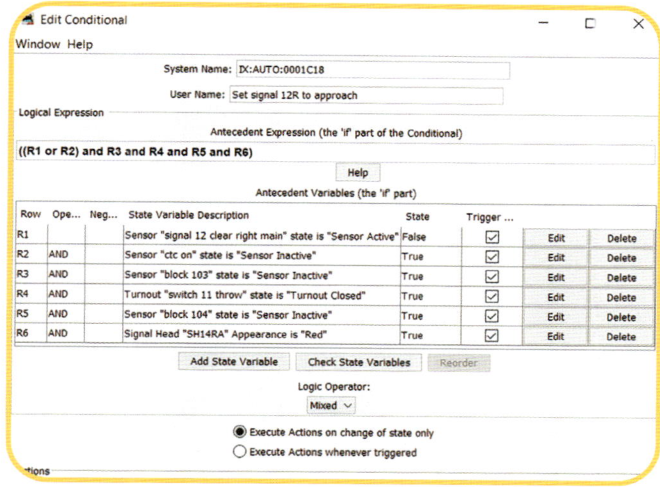

59 This is the Signal 12R approach logic with ABS mode.

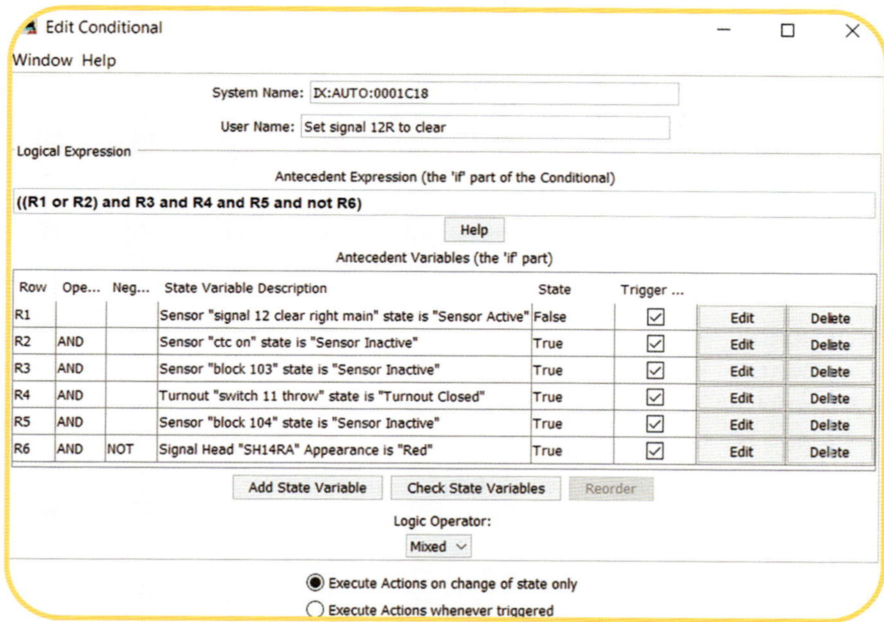

60 The Signal 12R clear logic requires the addition of the NOT statement in the last variable.

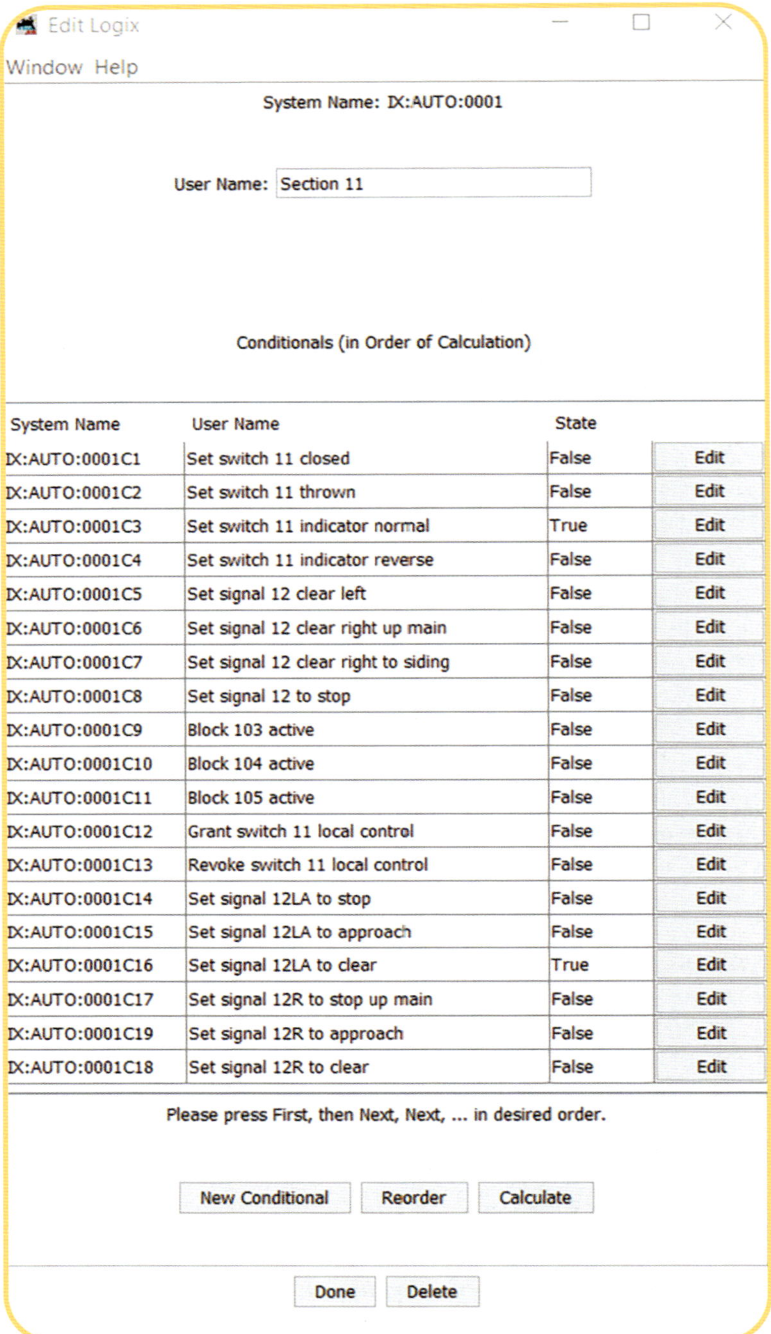

61 This shows the conditionals almost completed for Section 11.

62 You can see the signal icons added over the track diagram on the upper part of the panel; they repeat the signal indications of the signals on the layout. If you choose masts with a lighter color (these are black), you can place them next to the track lines.

CONCLUSION

We hope this book provides ideas, inspiration, and knowledge to model railroaders everywhere regarding how to implement and use the very powerful and versatile Arduino microcontroller. The projects range from relatively easy to more advanced using the Arduino and Raspberry Pi but they are well within the ability of a novice who has patience and willingness to research and practice the skills needed to complete them using this book and all of the online resources.

The best way to gain experience and become comfortable with Arduinos (and JMRI) is to try a basic project or two, then experiment with the code and components.

There are many helpful online groups that are great references. Many have been listed throughout the book in the text; a summary of groups is provided below: .

[1] "Arduini." https://groups.io/g/arduini

[2] "Arduino official website." http://www.arduino.cc/

[3] "Audacity audio file editor." https://www.audacityteam.org/

[4] "Arc Welder." https://circuitcrush.com/arduino/2016/11/05/arduino-model-railroading-arc-welder.html

[5] "IR Sensor code" http://osoyoo.com/2017/07/25/tcrt5000-ir-track-sensor/

[6] "JMRI org." https://www.jmri.org/

[7] "JMRI user group.": https://groups.io/g/jmriusers

[8] "JMRI Arduino setup.": www.youtube.com/watch?v=CDdTcNGVFxY

[9] "JMRI Code." http://jmri.sourceforge.net/

[10] "JMRI and Pi OS." https://mstevetodd.com/rpi

[11] "Layout Sound site." https://groups.io/g/LayoutSound/

[12] "Model Railraod Control Systems." http://www.modelrailroadcontrolsystems.com/

[13] "Model Railroad Hobbyist ABS Code." http://model-railroad-hobbyist.com/node/28644

[14] "Raspberry Pi." https://www.raspberrypi.org/

[15] "Sound files." https://www.soundsnap.com/tags/welding

[16] "SparkFun Electronics." www.sparkfun.com

[17] "Convert Audio Files." https://www.zamzar.com/convert/m4a-to-wav/

ABOUT THE AUTHORS

David Bradt has a BS in mechanical engineering from New Mexico State University and has many years of experience at NASA's Johnson Space Center and in the petrochemical industry. He is a model railroader and enjoys adding realistic Arduino systems and features to his compact HO and N scale layouts. He is also becoming an avid user of 3D printers. David can be contacted at: contact@pdanalytic.com

Paul Bradt has a BS in computer science from the University of Houston Clear Lake. He currently works for a computer game development company as a Live QA Specialist, and has worked as a contractor developing various computer program types. He has experimented with Arduino and Raspberry Pi systems and believes them to be an excellent tool for developing an understanding of how electronic components and hardware interact in integrated systems, and how they are useful as a teaching aid in learning the basics of computer programming. Paul likes to perform sophisticated troubleshooting of computer problems and has found that the online resources associated with Arduino and Raspberry Pi can be a great help for novice users to get projects operating quickly and effectively. He can be contacted at: contact@pdanalytic.com.

Dennis Drury is retired from General Electric. During his career he worked as an electronic and online support engineer. Prior to working for GE, Dennis spent seven years working for the Southern Pacific Railroad in both the signal and engineering departments. He also spent a year in Colombia, South America, helping to install a state-of-the-art CTC signal system on a railroad. Dennis lives with his wife, Ramona, in Dayton, Nev., where he's building an HO scale model railroad in a 400-square-foot room. His layout represents the Southern Pacific and Burlington Northern as it was in 1984. Dennis can be reached via email at cowrr1984@gmail.com.

Other books by the authors: *Arduino Model Railroad Signals, Arduino Model Railroad Animation, Arduino Intermediate Model Railroad Projects,* and *Internet of Things Model Railroad Projects.*